Mel Bay Presents

# Crossing To Scotland

## Celtic Music For The Cello

### By Abby Newton

1 2 3 4 5 6 7 8 9 0

Cover and book design
by David Hornung.

© 2000 BY MEL BAY PUBLICATIONS, INC., PACIFIC, MO 63069

**Visit us on the Web at www.melbay.com – E-mail us at email@melbay.com**

THE MUSIC SHOP
£7.95

# CD Contents

**This book is available either by itself or packaged with a companion audio and/or video recording. If you have purchased the book only, you may wish to purchase the recordings separately. The publisher strongly recommends using a recording along with the text to assure accuracy of interpretation and make learning easier and more enjoyable.**

Traditional music is usually learned by ear, but notation can provide a useful reference for the study of new tunes. When possible, I recommend the combined use of notation and recordings. Reading makes rapid passages and tricky intervals easy to grasp, while hearing reveals subtleties of phrasing and ornamentation that are impossible to notate. Most important, of course, is to turn the notes into music; and to have fun doing it!

A.N.

# Table of Contents

# The Cello, Abby Newton, and Scottish Music

Today the cello is usually considered a classical instrument, but from the late 17th to early 19th centuries it was used in folk ensembles to provide low, driving rhythms for dance tunes and to render haunting Scottish airs. In those days, "folk" and "classical" musics were often performed by the same musicians. Instrumentation was shared too, with violin and cello figuring prominently in both contexts. Many indigenous Scottish tunes were given formal arrangements by the great composers of the period. Haydn, Beethoven, and Mendelssohn all composed settings for traditional Scottish Music. James Oswald, a prominent Scottish composer of the 18th century, integrated his musical activities by composing Italianate settings for folk tunes and also composing tunes in a rustic style that were later assimilated as folk tunes into popular usage.

By the middle of the nineteenth century the division between "high" and "low" music began to be more sharply drawn. The fiddle remained a mainstay in folk music, but the cello was supplanted by other instruments like the piano and (later) the guitar.

Within the folk music revival of the past forty years there has been a small but dedicated movement to restore the unique richness of the cello to traditional music. Abby has been on the forefront of that movement since 1973 when she began two different musical associations that have proven fruitful for her musical career. First, she joined Jay Ungar, Lyn Hardy, and John Cohen in *The Putnam String County Band*. Although classically trained, she adapted her playing to their arrangements of traditional American music and they toured extensively for several years. *The Putnam String County Band* played concerts in a broad range of venues from small coffee houses to large summer festivals. They are still remembered fondly by folk enthusiasts.

She also met Jean Redpath in 1973. Jean was looking for a cellist to accompany her on her first U. S. Release. This began a musical relationship that has spanned sixteen albums and more than two decades.

Abby's deep involvement with the music of Scotland began with and was nurtured by Jean Redpath. It was with Jean that Abby first visited Scotland in 1978. The warmth of the people and the melancholy beauty of the Scottish landscape moved her. On that tour she met Tom Anderson, the legendary teacher and champion of Shetland fiddle music. Tom, Jean, and Abby performed a concert at Blair Castle together that Abby recalls as one of the most inspiring experiences of her musical life.

Since then, Abby has visited Scotland many times and has performed both there and in the U. S. with many prominent Scottish musicians including Aly Bain, Mairi Campbell, and Alasdair Fraser. Alasdair, in particular, enhanced Abby's understanding of Scottish music and was a major force in the creation of *Crossing to Scotland*.

To order the CD or cassette *Crossing to Scotland* please contact Abby Newton at:
P.O. Box 67, Shokan, New York 12481
email: cellonewt@aol.com
website: http://www.abbynewton.com

# About the Tunes

**Catskill Mountain Air/Wagon Wheel Notch** (David Hornung) – David heard me playing Scottish music when we met fifteen years ago and was inspired to write the slow air in this set. Later it was paired with another of his tunes called *Wagon Wheel Notch* after a local landmark; a glacial hollow on the eastern face of High Point Mountain.

**Drunk at Night, Dry in the Morning** (Traditional) – This lively tune is found in the *Gow's Repository of the Dance Music of Scotland (vol. III)*. Niel Gow was one of the most important Scottish fiddlers in the 18th century. In addition to being a renowned performer, he wrote and collected hundreds of tunes. Both his brother Donald and son Nathanial were cellists and sometimes accompanied the great man in performances.

**Loftus Jones** (Turlough O'Carolan) – O'Carolan was a legendary harper who traveled and played throughout Ireland around the turn of the eighteenth century. While there are few verifiable facts about O'Carolan's life, colorful anectdotes are plentiful. These stories present the portrait of a man possessed of rare musical genius and a zest for the human comedy.

O'Carolan composed about two hundred melodies, although none were written down in his lifetime. His compositions fall into three general categories: laments, airs, and planxties. Of the three forms, the planxties are most amenable to expanded arrangements, perhaps because they are influenced by the Italian Chamber music of that period. O'Carolan spent considerable time in cosmopolitan Dublin and encountered the music of Vivaldi, Corelli, and Gemiani who were then very popular. The planxties are represented here by the tunes *O'Carolan's Draught* and *Loftus Jones*. Both are elegant and propulsive and demonstrate Turlough O'Carolan's wit and feeling.

**Tune for Mairead and Anna Ni Mhaonaigh** (Daithi Sproule) – Daithi Sproule, the illustrious Irish singer and guitar player, composed this tune as a birthday tribute to his nieces Mairead and Anna. When I heard it on one of Liz Carroll's recordings, I felt that its warmth and lyricism would be well served by the sound of the cello.

**Sister Jean** (Traditional) – This is an ancient tune from the Shetland Islands with an unusual and haunting melody.

**Tarboltan Lodge** (Traditional) - Also known as *Hatton Burn*, this reel appears in the *Skye Collection*.

**Crossing to Ireland** (Traditional) - This appears as a slow air in the key of A flat minor in the *Simon Fraser Collection*. While visiting Cape Breton as few years ago, I heard it played as a waltz and was charmed by its lilt.

**The Earl of Dalhousie's Happy Return to Scotland** (Traditional) - I learned this march from a recording by Natalie MacMaster. It commemorates the emotions on his return to his beloved country and is truly one of the happiest tunes in the Scottish repertoire.

**Da Full Rigged Ship and Da New Rigged Ship** (Traditional) - Tom Anderson taught me these tunes one cold spring evening while sitting by the peat fire in his home at Lerwick, Shetland. The uneven rocking rhythm of *Da Full Rigged Ship* suggests the motion of an old sailing vessel out on a bumpy sea. *Da New Rigged Ship* seems to show off its new sails in this playful reel.

**Independence Trail** (Alasdair Fraser) - This tune floated around in my head for months after first hearing Alasdair play it at a recording session. Its bounce and optimism are contagious.

**Heroes of Longhope** (Ronnie Aimes) - I had the pleasure of studying Scottish Highland music with Angus Grant a few years back and this was one of the tunes that went straight to my heart. Aimes wrote it to celebrate the heroic men who lost their lives trying to rescue fellow fishermen after their boat capsized during a storm in the North Alantic.

**O'Carolan's Draught** (Turlough O'Carolan) - I think of this piece as a country cousin to the *Bach Cello Suites* written around the same time.

**Cropie's Strathspey** (P. Milne) / **Spootiskerry** (Ian Burns) / **Sleep Sound in Da Morning** (Traditional) / **Lasses Trust in Providence** (Traditional) - The first tune in this set can be found in *The Fiddle Music of Scotland* by James Hunter. The last three are all from the Shetland Islands.

**Gin Ye Kiss My Wife, I'll Tell the Minister** (Traditional) - This is an ancient tune that I learned from *The Caledonian Companion* by Alastair Hardie. It was originally a highland dance tune that has evolved into a slow air over the centuries.

# Catskill Mountain Air

# Wagon Wheel Notch

© David Hornung

9

# Drunk at Night, Dry in the Morning

Traditional

# Loftus Jones

O'Carolan

12

13

# Tune for Mairead and Anna Ni Mhaonaigh

© Daithi Sproule

14

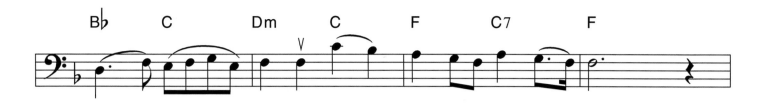

# Sister Jean

Traditional

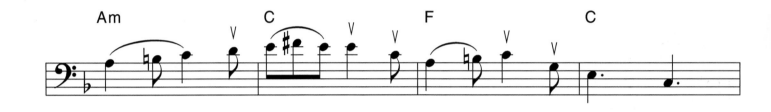

# Tarboltan Lodge

Traditional

# Crossing to Ireland

Traditional

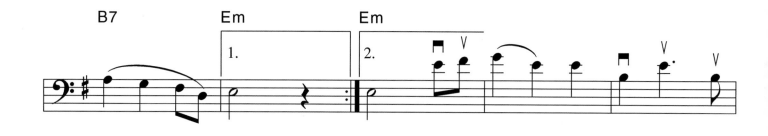

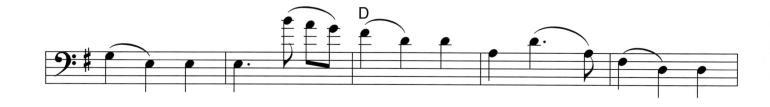

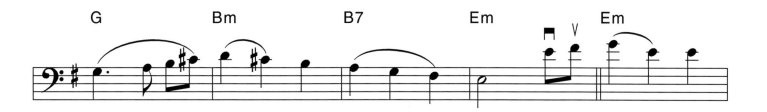

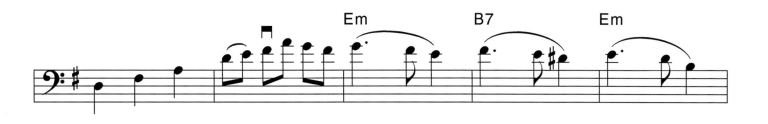

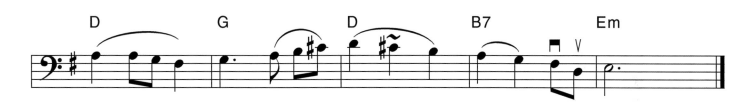

# The Earl of Dalhousie's Happy Return to Scotland

Traditional

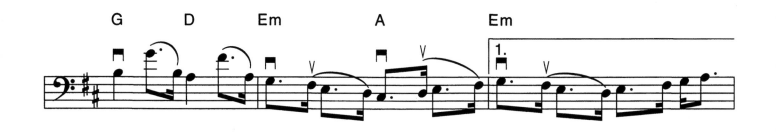

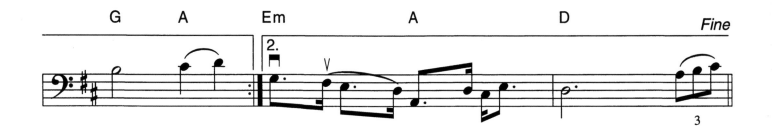

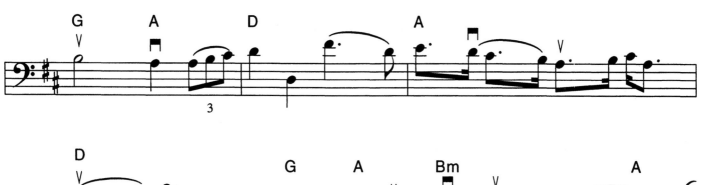

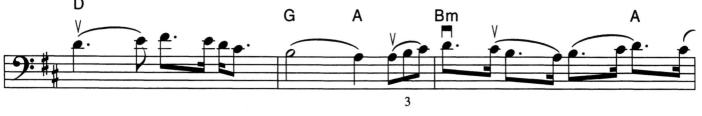

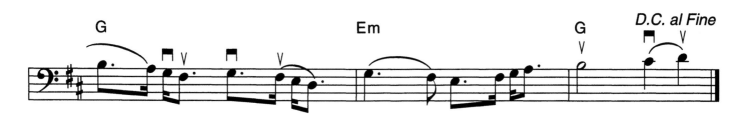

# Da Full Rigged Ship

Traditional

# Cropie's Strathspey

P. Milne

# Spootiskerry

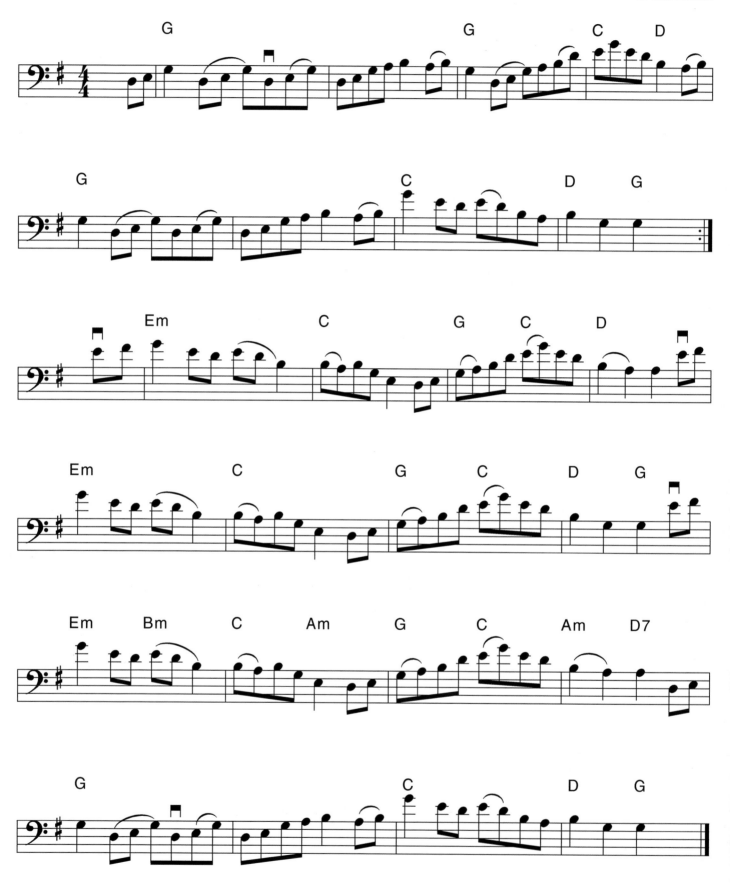

28

# Sleep Sound in Da Morning

Traditional

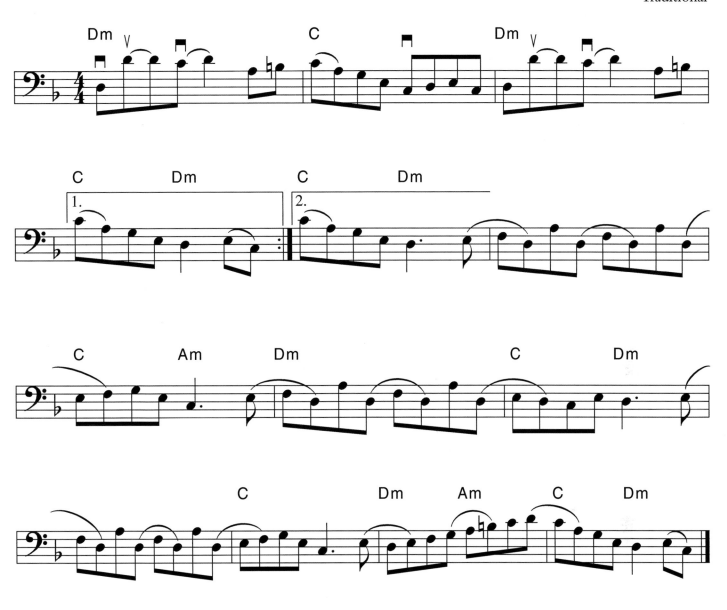

# Lasses Trust in Providence

Traditional

# Gin Ye Kiss My Wife, I'll Tell the Minister

Traditional

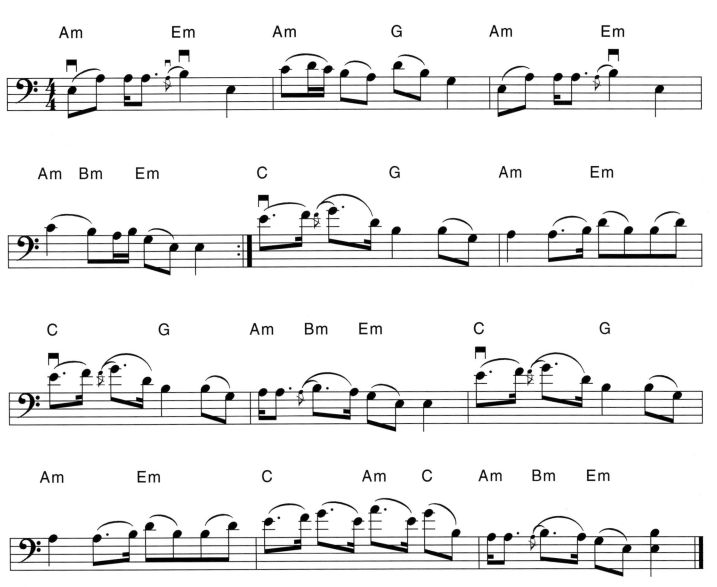

# Reviews of the CD *Crossing to Scotland*

*"This is the most absolutely elegant album I've heard in a long time...The cello has always been the instrument I'd want to be shipwrecked on a desert island with; now I know who I'd want to have there to play it."*

The Atlantic Celtic Quarterly

*"...the connections between Irish music and classical Baroque have been increasingly recognized. Nowhere better than in this fine collection which shows a quality of tone and intonation, plus innate musicianship and good taste to attract any listener."*

Irish Music Magazine

*"Newton plays with sensitivity and soul, resisting always the temptation to turn traditional tunes into classical-music museum pieces. This album is as well conceived as it is well-crafted."*

Sing Out! Magazine

*"An exquisite blend of skill and feeling."*

Victory Review

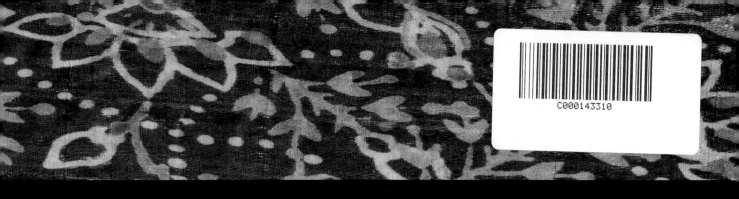

# the doors

# dance on fire

ROSS CLARKE

FOR THE LATE BILL GRAHAM

THANK YOU FOR THE MUSIC

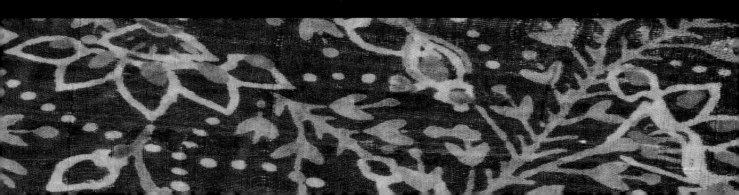

# the doors

# dance on fire

ROSS CLARKE

CASTLE COMMUNICATIONS

CASTLE COMMUNICATIONS PLC
A29 Barwell Business Park,
Letherhead Road,
Chessington, Surrey KT9 2NY England.

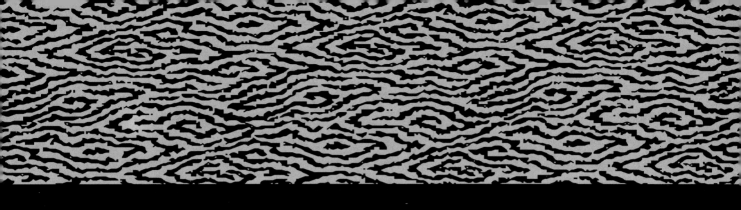

# CONTENTS

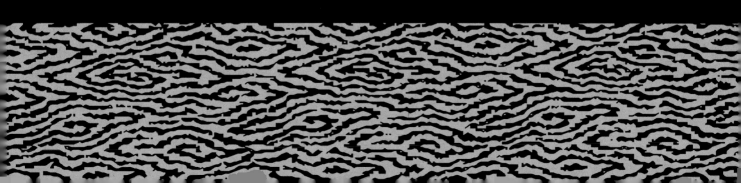

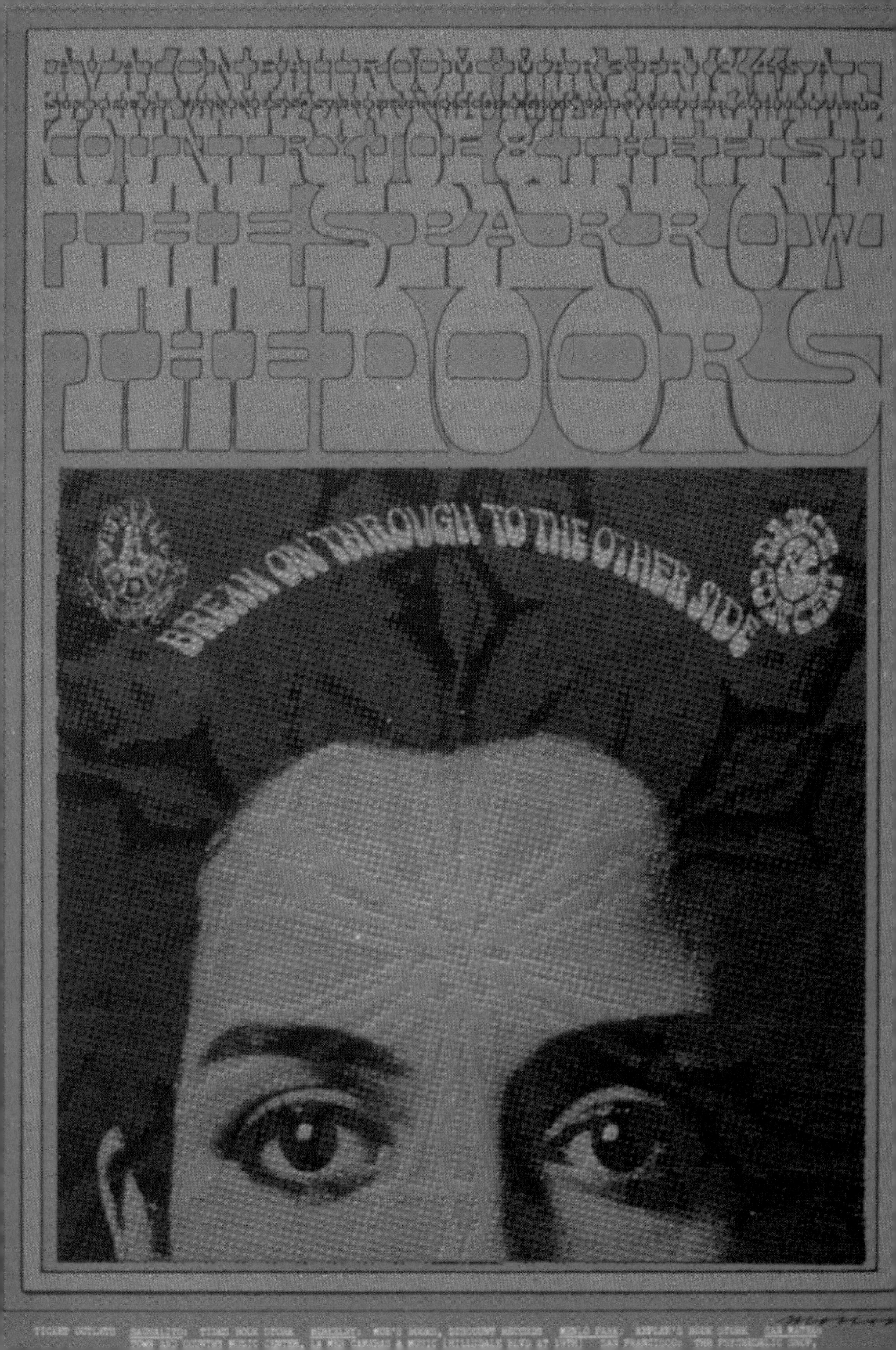
COUNTRY JOE & THE FISH
THE SPARROW
THE DOORS
BREAK ON THROUGH TO THE OTHER SIDE
TICKET OUTLETS SAUSALITO: TIDES BOOK STORE BERKELEY: MOE'S BOOKS, DISCOUNT RECORDS MENLO PARK: KEPLER'S BOOK STORE SAN MATEO:
SAN FRANCISCO: THE PSYCHEDELIC SHOP,

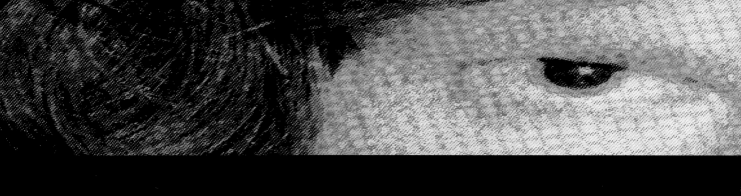

# INTRODUCTION

For five short years The Doors were the most influential rock band in America. Led by the enigmatic Jim Morrison, they produced music which, although laden with violence, sex and death, was bouncy, funky and timelessly commercial. So much power did Morrison have over his audience that he could incite them to riot at will. He was cool, sexy, complex and turned in the most energetic performances ever seen at that time. He was also a young man who possessed a personality which thrived on excess and it was this excessive lifestyle that turned him from a beautifully lithe, aggressive rebel to a bloated, shabby alcoholic and, probably, finally destroyed him. He died in Paris in mysterious circumstances in July 1971.

In the twenty years since he died, Jim Morrison has gradually been rehabilitated into one of the most widely revered heroes of the Sixties and the contemporary rock audience find in him something that cannot be found in the musicians of its own generation - defiance won with courage. It is that courage that today's audience recognises and loves about him and they refuse to let him die.

Jim Morrison stated in The Doors' early days:

"I see myself as a huge fiery comet, a shooting star. Everyone stops, points up and gasps 'Oh, look at that!' Then - whoosh, and I'm gone...and they'll never see anything like it ever again...and they won't be able to forget me - ever."

He was right

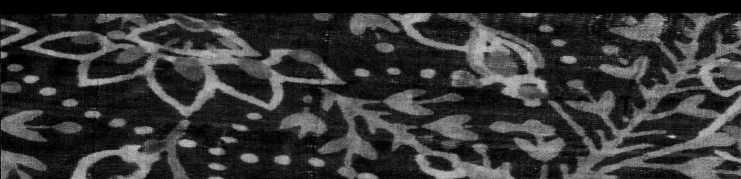

9

# BEFORE THE
# DOORS OPEN

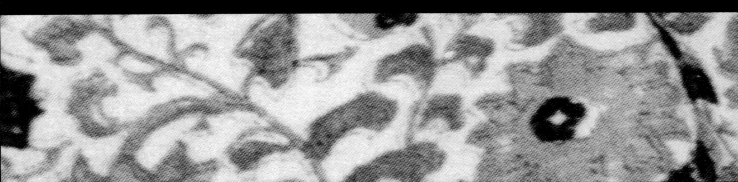

James Douglas Morrison was born on December 8th, 1943 in Melbourne, Florida near Cape Canaveral. His father, George Stephen Morrison, was a career man in the US Navy and had just returned from mine-laying duties in the Pacific. After Jim's birth, his father returned to the war to take part in the recapturing of islands from the Japanese by flying Hellcats from an aircraft carrier. For the next three years, Jim spent his life with his mother, Clara, living with Steve Morrison's parents in Clearwater on The Gulf of Mexico. Jim's paternal grandparents were originally from Georgia and insisted that good old Southern behaviour was drummed into the young boy from a very early age.

In 1946, a year after the war ended, Steve returned and was posted to Washington DC for six months. Clara, relieved to be away from Steve's stuffy parents, accompanied him along with Jim. From Washington he was posted to Albuquerque in New Mexico, where the family spent a year whilst Steve held a position as an instructor in an atomic weapons program. Whilst in Albuquerque, Clara gave birth to her second child, Anna, providing a sister for Jim.

Whilst travelling by car with his parents and grandparents on the sixty-mile stretch of road from Santa Fe to Albuquerque Jim witnessed an event which he would describe as "the most important in my life". They happened upon a road traffic accident involving a truckload of Indians. Many were badly injured. Jim recalled later: "I must have been about four of five and I don't remember if I'd ever been to a movie, and suddenly there were all these redskins, and they're lying all over the road, bleeding to death. I was just a kid, so I had to stay in the car while my father and grandfather went back to check it out...I didn't see nothing - all I saw was funny red paint and people lying around, but I knew something was happening, because I could dig the vibrations of the people

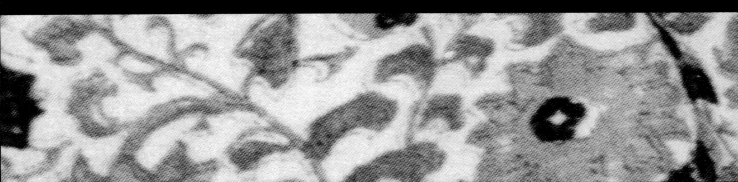

12

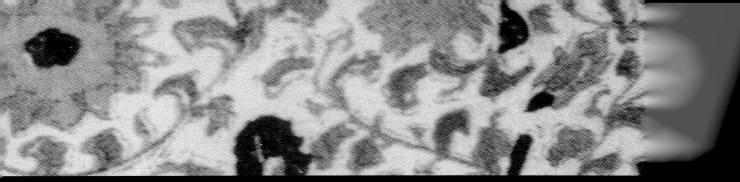

around me, 'cause they're my parents and all, and all of a sudden I realised that they didn't know what was happening any more than I did.  That was the first time I tasted fear...and I do think, at that moment, the souls or the ghosts of those dead

Indians - maybe one or two of 'em - were just running around, freaking out, and just landed in my soul, and I was just like a sponge, ready to sit and absorb it...it's not a ghost story, it's something that really means something to me."

In later life, Jim always claimed that he was possessed by the spirit of an ancient Indian medicine man - a shaman.  Whether this experience laid the seeds for the idea that a shaman was

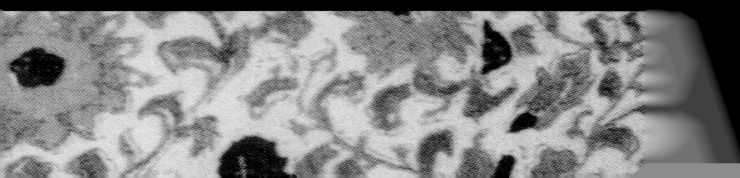

BILL GRAHAM PRESENTS IN SAN FRANCISCO

# THE DOORS
## LONNIE MACK
## ELVIN BISHOP Group

### FRIDAY · JULY · 25TH 8 P.M.
### COW PALACE

©BILL GRAHAM 1967 #67 · R.TUTEN..

TICKETS $6.50 5.50 4.50 3.50

Advance tickets available in San Francisco: Downtown Center Box Office, City Lights Bookstore, Town Squire. Outside in Oakland, Sherman & Clay, Berkeley: Discount Records, Shakespeare & Co. San Rafael: Record King, Sausalito: The Tides Bookstore, Menlo Park: Discount Records, San Mateo: Town & Country Records, Redwood City: Redwood House of Music, San Jose: Discount Records.

the driving force behind him can only be speculated upon, but witnessing this scene of carnage obviously made quite an impression on the boy. Jim never forgot the tragedy and the accident haunted him for a long time after the event, although his father, in desperation, finally told him that it never happened, that it had been a dream.

In February 1948 the family moved to Los Altos in northern California and Steve took up a post of Special Weapons Officer aboard another aircraft carrier. Clara had another son, Andrew, a brother for Jim and Anne. This was to be a relatively stable period in Jim's early life and the family remained there for two years. Jim started school and was reported to have been an intelligent child but one who was shy and withdrawn.

When Jim was seven he was uprooted again and The Morrisons moved back to Washington DC for a year. In 1952, Steve was sent to Korea and the rest of the family settled in Claremont, California for two years. When Steve returned, the family moved back to Albuquerque for a further two years and then transferred to Alameda in northern California - a small island in San Francisco Bay which was home to the largest US Navy air station in the world. It was here that Jim started high school, attending Alameda High. Again, it was noted that he was an intelligent boy who had a penchant for attention-seeking schoolboy pranks and was an avid reader.

Eighteen months later, Jim's father was again posted to Washington and the family moved to Alexandria in Virginia. They rented a large, elegant house in the stylish, upper class Braddock Heights neighbourhood and Jim was enroled at the George Washington High School where he would remain for three years. Jim's grades were extraordinarily high, much to the surprise of his teachers and fellow pupils. He never appeared to study particularly hard and his attitude was defiant. His behaviour veered from shockingly bad to crossing the boundaries of good taste. He hated authority and challenged it continually. His parents were finding him increasingly more difficult to cope with - they were continually clashing over the length of his hair and his taste in clothes- but he was growing closer to his younger brother, Andy, of whom he had always been jealous and had previously tormented. It was at this time that he first formed a relationship with a

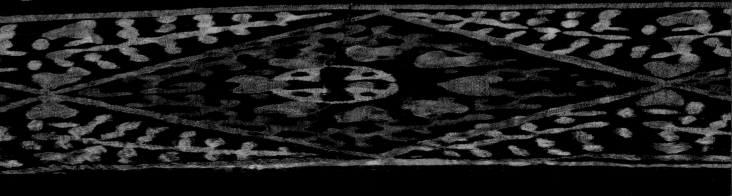

girlfriend, a pretty girl called Tandy Martin, who he teased
mercilessly.  Tandy said later that Jim's bullying and tricks
were the only way that he felt he could keep her interested in
him.

He also began keeping a diary and developed an interest
in poetry and literature.  In his daily journals, he would
meticulously jot down random observations, opinions
and thoughts as well as lines of his own poetry.  A great deal of
this early work provided inspiration and ideas for many of the
Doors' first songs  His English teacher later told biographer
Jerry Hopkins: "Jim read as much and probably more than any
student in class.  But everything he read was so offbeat I had
another teacher who was going to the Library of Congress
check to see if the books Jim was reporting on actually existed.
I suspected he was making them up, as they were English
books on sixteenth and seventeenth-century demonology.  I'd
never heard of them.  But they existed, and I'm convinced from
the paper he wrote that he'd read them, and the Library of
Congress would've been the only source."

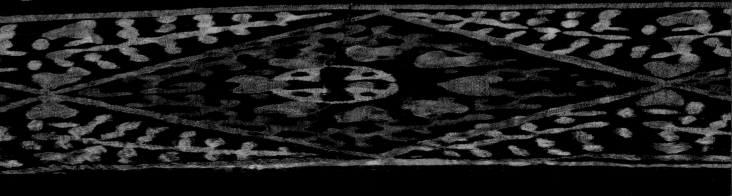
18

Jim's other interests included painting - he had aspirations of
becoming an artist - and the blues.  He would sneak out at
night to the sleazy bars near Fort Belvoir to listen to black
blues players.  At this time he claimed to hate rock and roll
and played blues records incessantly in his basement room.
His love for the blues was only exceeded by his love of poetry.
He idolised Blake, Rimbaud, Kerouac and Baudelaire and read
their work voraciously.

He later told Rolling Stone: "I kept a lot of notebooks through
highschool and college and then when I left school, for some
dumb reason - maybe it was wise - I threw them all away.
There's nothing I can think of I'd rather have in my possession
right now than those two to three lost notebooks.  I was
thinking of being hypnotised or taking sodium pentothal to try
to remember, because I wrote in those books night after night.
By maybe if I'd never thrown them away, I'd never have written
anything original - because they were mainly accumulations of
things that I'd read or heard, like quotes from books.  I think if
I'd never got rid of them I'd never been free."

Jim had not given much thought to what he would do after he
graduated from George Washington High.  His parents,
however, had and insisted that he attend St. Petersburg Junior

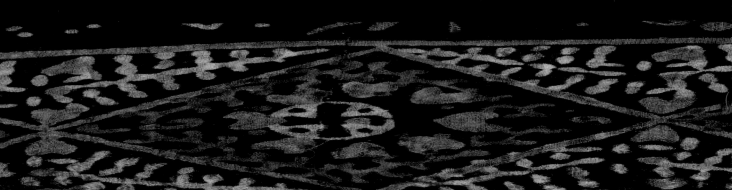

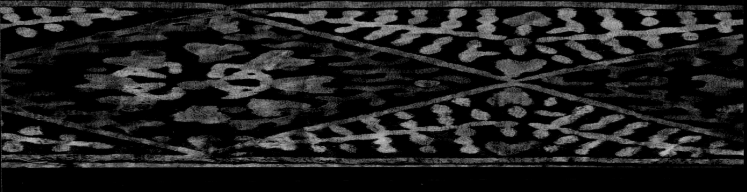

College in Florida. They had also arranged for him to stay with his grandparents in Clearwater whilst he did so. Initially Jim had reservations and told them so, but gradually he began to see the move as freedom from the restrictions imposed by his parents. Finally, he agreed and moved to Florida whilst the Morrison family moved on, once again, to San Diego in California.

Although the move did, indeed, prove to provide more freedom for Jim, his grandparents were continually upset and confused by his attitude and behaviour. He refused to shave, cut his hair or take any pride in his appearance and insisted on leaving dozens of empty wine bottles in his room, mocking their fundamentalist morals. They were at a loss to know how to deal with him, especially as Jim often refused to talk to them for days on end. His school work, however, did not appear to suffer and, after a year at St. Petersburg, he transferred to Florida State University in Tallahassee. He arranged to share a house a mile from the university campus with five other students, much to his grandparents relief.

Free from the restraints of any kind of parental authority, Jim began to live his life exactly as he pleased. He had become a huge fan of Elvis Presley and insisted on playing his records at full volume at all hours of the night and day. He refused to contribute in any way to the running of the rented house, leaving everything to his roommates. He did, however, contribute quite considerably to the depletion of the food and beer stock in the house and would constantly borrow his co-tenants' clothes without permission. He teased them, he lied to them, he 'tested' them to the very limits of breaking point. After just three months, they conceded defeat and asked him to leave. The very next morning he had packed his belongings and gone.

Jim found himself a small, shabby trailer near the campus, costing $50 per month in rent, a sum that he could easily afford as his grandparents sent him twice this amount on a monthly basis. He moved in immediately and it soon felt as near to a home as Jim had ever had, littered with his beloved books. It was a perfect base from which he could attend class or make regular sorties into bars and poker parlours. He could drink, play loud music - anything he pleased. There was nobody but himself to annoy.

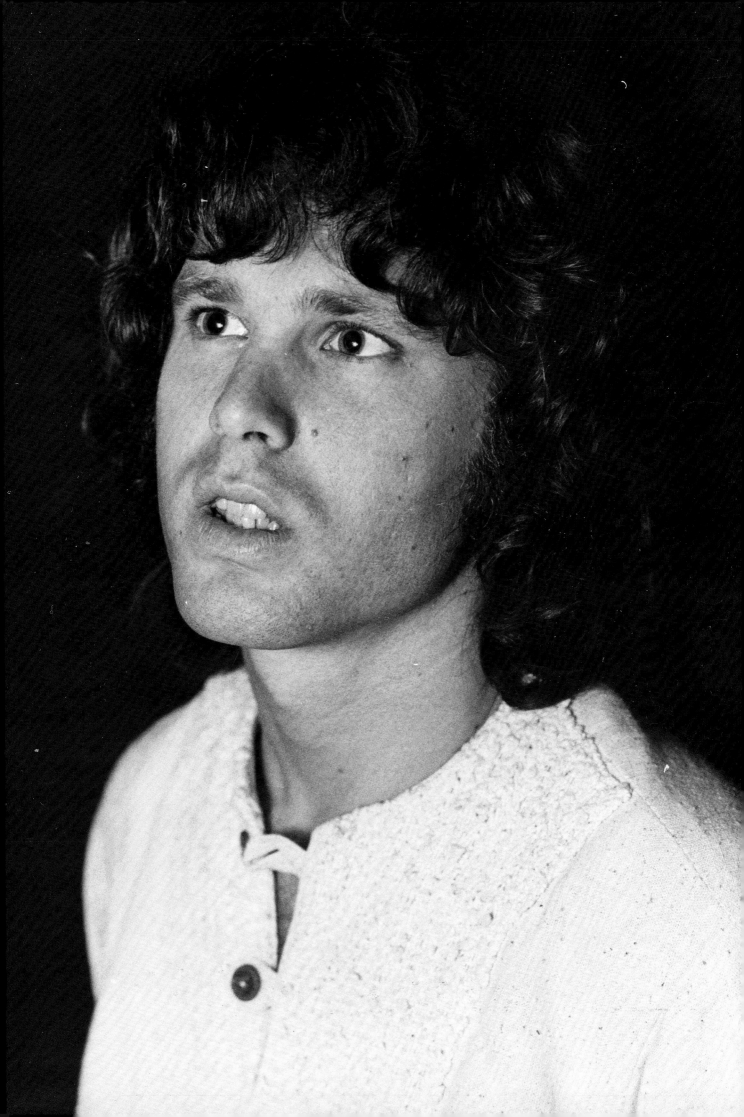

Jim returned to the family home in California during the spring vacation and announced to his dumb-struck parents that he was considering transferring to UCLA (the University of California in Los Angeles) to study film. They were less than impressed with the idea for a number of reasons. Firstly, they considered the university far too liberal and secondly, knowing Jim's off-beat tendencies, they were concerned that this wild side of him would get out of control in trendy Los Angeles - the city of sex and drugs. They emphatically forbade the move and escorted him to the next Florida-bound plane.

Despite his parents' opposition to his plan, Jim had made up his mind that UCLA was most definitely the place he wanted to be. He begrudgingly returned to FSU but immediately began to arrange to take classes which would give him a foundation for the course in cinematography. They included an introduction to the theatre, theatre history, the principals of scene design and the essentials of acting He also formally applied for his grades to be transferred to the UCLA register.

During Jim's last term at FSU, he had taken up with a group of hard-drinking older students who knew how to seriously party. On one occasion, Jim was involved in a drunken fracas on the way to a football game, resulting in him being arrested and charged with petty larceny, disturbing the peace, resisting arrest and public drunkenness. It was only the timely intervention of his history professor, Ralph Turner, who spoke on his behalf that saved him from a far harsher sentence than the fine of $50 that he received as punishment. His dazzling academic performance prevented him from being disciplined by the university and his parents never got to hear of the incident. He finished the term without further mishaps.

Jim spent Christmas with his family. His parents, whilst not being able to condone his transfer to UCLA, had stopped condemning it too much and he spent early 1964 in Los Angeles registering at the university and enroling in the theatre arts department. His parents had refused to help him with his tuition fees, so he used the money which had accumulated in a trust fund that his father had set up for him when he was a boy. This accomplished, he then set about finding himself a place to live. He finally found a small apartment situated close to the campus. Jim had arrived.

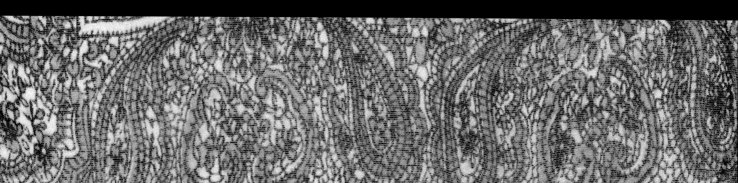

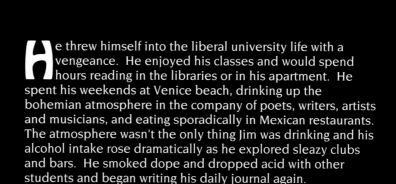

He threw himself into the liberal university life with a vengeance. He enjoyed his classes and would spend hours reading in the libraries or in his apartment. He spent his weekends at Venice beach, drinking up the bohemian atmosphere in the company of poets, writers, artists and musicians, and eating sporadically in Mexican restaurants. The atmosphere wasn't the only thing Jim was drinking and his alcohol intake rose dramatically as he explored sleazy clubs and bars. He smoked dope and dropped acid with other students and began writing his daily journal again.

His appearance began to change dramatically. On his arrival at UCLA, he was chubby with short hair. Always prone to chubbiness, he had been ordered to cut his long dark hair due to a visit in January 1964 to the carrier of which Steve Morrison was now Captain - the Bon Homme Richard. Although Jim's hair had been trimmed for the occasion, it wasn't short enough to please his father who ordered him to the ship's barber only minutes after he boarded. However, after a while his fitful eating habits and his habitual LSD taking had produced a darkly handsome, slim young man with a perfectly sculptured face, mesmerising eyes and hair which curled thickly past his shoulders. He had taken to wearing tight jeans and white T-shirts and had a knack for looking seductively sexy.

Although most of his peers at the university remember him as shy and withdrawn, Jim still managed to leave his mark. His circle of friends included some of the most wild and radical in the film school and he grew increasingly close to four of them: Dennis Jakob, John DaBella, Phil Oleno and Felix Venable. Even by the university's liberal standards, these five were overtly radical, belligerent and rebellious as well as being very intellectual.

Older than Jim at twenty-five, it was with Dennis that Jim endlessly discussed the German philosopher Nietzche's work. He was particularly impressed by Dionysus. During one of these debates, Jim quoted William Blake's immortal line: "If the doors of perception were cleansed, everything would appear to man as it truly is, infinite," which Aldous Huxley later used in the title of his book 'The Doors Of Perception'. Immediately fascinated by the thought, Jim suggested that he and John should form a duo and call themselves The Doors: Open and Closed. The idea never got past the drunken conversation stage.

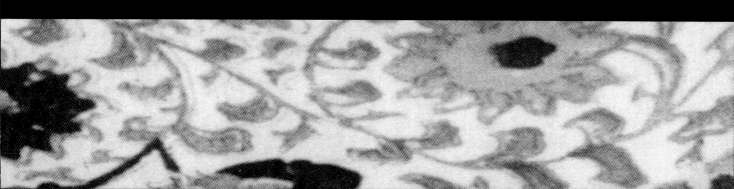

John DaBella introduced Jim to shamanism and the subject enthralled him. Michael Harner wrote in 'The Way Of The Shaman': "Through his heroic efforts, the shaman helps his patients transcend their normal ordinary definition of reality, including their definition of themselves. The shaman shows those in his audience they are not emotionally and spiritually alone in their struggle against illness and death. The shaman shares his special powers and convinces these people, on a deep level of his consciousness, that another human is willing to offer up his own self to help them. Students in the West particularly have demonstrated again and again they can be easily become initiated into the fundamentals of this ritual. The ancient way is so powerful and taps so deeply into the human mind that one's usual cultural belief and systems and assumptions about reality are essentially irrelevant."

'Big' Phil Oleno claimed to have read the entire works of Carl Jung, discussions about which were a firm favourite with Jim who was developing his own interest in psychology.

Felix Venable was, at thirty-four, the oldest student in the film school and a great influence on the young Jim. He was rebellious, rowdy and enigmatic. His fondness for booze and drugs was legendary and it didn't take long before Jim fell under his, some say evil, influence, drinking huge quantities of alcohol and taking as many hallucinogenics as he could get his hands on. Jim found Felix engaging and somewhat of a kindred spirit. Other friends recalled that he seemed to change suddenly after his forming this association with Felix. He became, they said, out of control, aggressive and usually too stoned on drugs or booze to reach. He seemed more interested in pulling outrageous stunts, daring feats of bravado and generally showing off than he was in what was really going on around him.

To be fair, mind-altering drugs such as LSD and marijuana were not, at that time, illegal and were not thought of as harmful. However, Jim's passion for these substances soon became more than youthful dabbling, it became an addiction, compensating for his natural shyness and lack of self confidence. With drugs and booze he was outgoing, witty, intelligent, different and daring - a member of an elite clique. He could also be childishly unpleasant and cruel to both friends and strangers. Drugs and alcohol - probably more so alcohol - brought out the dark side of Jim Morrison, producing

irrational mood swings of alternating depression and elation and he loved the sensation. He began to experiment with a cocktail of different drugs, once even stealing a doctor's case and taking every drug in it!

Felix, like Jim, was on a direct course to self-destruction. He mysteriously vanished from UCLA one day and was found dead some years later from alcohol and drug abuse.

In his journals, Jim wrote down glimpses of his psyche and noted his experiences and soon he had literally hundreds of notebooks full of drug-induced observations, notes and poetic lines. Sex, death and violence seemed to take priority. Four years later, some of them would be published by Simon and Schuster as 'The Lords: Notes On Vision' and the majority of the remainder would later surface as lyrics in Doors songs.

At the end of 1964, Captain Steve Morrison left his post on the

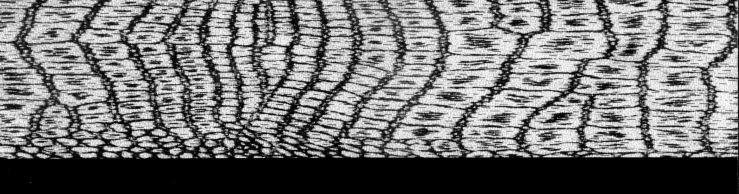

Bon Homme Richard and left for London, where he was to
serve under the Commander-In-Chief of the US Naval Forces
in Europe. Before doing so, he travelled to the West Coast to
spend some time with his family. Jim joined them for
Christmas and this was, allegedly, the last time he saw his
parents. He would later claim that they were dead, for reasons
best known to himself.

**W**hen Jim returned to university he seemed hell bent on
continually pushing back the bounds of reality as well
as doing as doing as little work as possible. His tutors
were baffled by his behaviour but many of them saw in him
real talent and were prepared to put up with his destructive
attitude. When Jim finally got round to making his first film,
however, those same tutors were confounded and confused
with the result.

He used John DaBella as his cameraman and put together a
rather abstract montage which was supposed to portray an
essay on the film making process. The film opened to a black
screen accompanied by strange sounds - erotic noises and
children's religious chanting - which was rapidly followed by a
scene of John DaBella's German girlfriend, semi-naked and
dancing on top of a television set revealing marching Nazi
soldiers. The scene changed again to Jim's bedroom where
the camera panned his wall which were covered with Playboy
nudes. Also in the room were a number of men, apparently
waiting for blue movies to begin on the same television, who
began to make finger shadows against the screen. The film
ended by the television being switched off and the picture
fading.

The subtleties of the film were lost on the majority of the
students and all of the tutors present at the screening. Many
faculty members called him degenerate and even his
staunchest supporters amongst the lecturing staff were
dumbfounded. The erotic and violent images seemed to have
no relevance and proved offensive to the audience, many of
whom saw his efforts as a waste of good celluloid.

Jim was terribly hurt by the criticism levelled against him and
his film, of which he was rather proud. Soon after the
screening, he announced that he would be leaving UCLA, a
move which did happen but not until after a chance meeting,
which was to change the course of his life forever.

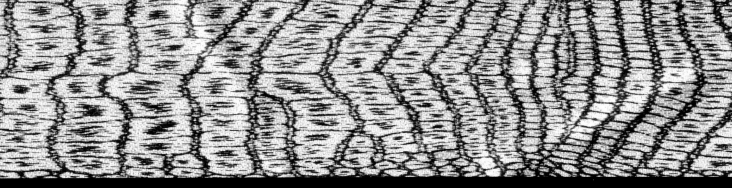

Ray Manczarek (he would shorten it later to Manzarek making it easier to pronounce) was a friend of John DaBella. He had achieved a bachelor's degree in economics at De Paul University and had transferred to UCLA to study law. After only two weeks, he decided that law was a less than rivetting subject and switched to the film school, studying cinematography. His studies were abruptly halted in December 1961 due to a failed romantic attachment and he

joined the US Army in a fit of pique. After the emotional turmoil of the lost love affair had receded, Ray sensed the error of his ways and spent the next year trying to get an early discharge. He finally achieved this by telling an army psychiatrist that he was developing seriously homosexual tendencies. In the early Sixties, this was tantamount to treason and he was discharged soon after, enabling him to continue his course at UCLA - coincidentally, the same course on which Jim Morrison had embarked.

Ray had always had an interest in music, showing real talent from an early age. In the press release issued by Elektra to accompany The Doors' debut album, he stated: "I grew up in Chicago and left when I was twenty-one for Los Angeles. My parents gave me piano lessons when I was around nine or ten. I hated it for the first four years - until I learned how to do it - then it became fun, which was about the same time I first heard Negro music. I was about twelve or thirteen, playing baseball in a playground; someone had a radio tuned into a Negro station. From then on I was hooked. I used to listen to Al Benson and Big Bill Hill - they were disc jockeys in Chicago. From then on all the music I listened to was on the radio. My piano playing changed; I became influenced by jazz. I learned how to play that stride piano with my left hand, and I knew that was it: stuff with a beat - jazz, blues - rock.

"At school I was primarily interested in film. It seemed to combine my interests in drama, visual art, music, and the profit motive. Before I left Chicago I was interested in theatre. These days, I think we want our theatre, our entertainment to be larger than life. I think the total environmental thing will come in. Probably Cinerama will develop further."

Jim knew Ray from class and had secretly admired his decision to feature himself and his girlfriend, Dorothy Fujikawa, nude in a shower and his subsequent refusal to edit the scene from one of his films. Jim had also gone along with a bunch of friends to hear Ray and his band. Called Rick and the Ravens, the band

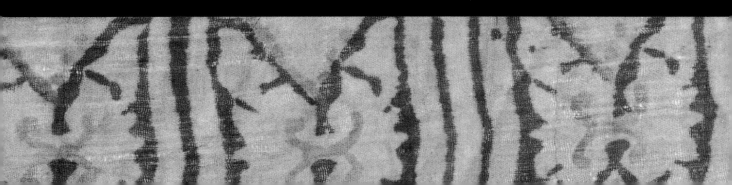

comprised of Ray, his two brothers Rick and Jim and three
others and they played regularly at the Turkey Joint West in
Santa Monica, just yards from the beach. Ray provided the
vocals under the pseudonym Screaming Ray Daniels and most
weekend nights they would steam into numbers such as

'Money', 'Louie Louie', 'Hoochie Coochie Man' and 'I Know
What You Need'. The gig was always frequented by a large
university crowd and often twenty or more would join the band
onstage, jumping around and singing along with the songs. On
one occasion Jim had joined Ray, providing hand claps and
tambourine to tumultuous applause from his friends from the
film school.

Soon after, Ray asked Jim to help him out of a tight spot. Rick
and the Ravens were booked to support Sonny and Cher at a
graduation dance and, on the eve of the hop, one of the band
members walked out. Contractually, Ray was obliged to

provide six musicians onstage or they wouldn't be paid. Although he didn't play an instrument, Jim agreed, and appeared at the side of the stage with an electric guitar strapped around his neck. The guitar was neither switched on nor plugged in and Jim mimed his way through the set, pocketing his fee at the end of the night. He said later that it was the easiest money that he had ever made.

'Olivia's' - the restaurant that "Soul Kitchen" was written about.
Photo: Rainer Moddemann

As graduation day grew closer, Jim pondered his future. He told his friends at UCLA that he planned to move to New York to make movies but, instead, he remained in Los Angeles to look for a job. However, his search to further his

career was short-lived. A few weeks after leaving UCLA, he suddenly discovered that he had lost his student deferment and had been classed AI at his army physical. This meant he was liable to be drafted at any time. In a desperate attempt to dodge the draft, he re-enroled for several courses at UCLA and took off, fast, for Venice moving in with Dennis Jakob and hanging out with Felix Venable.

Venice was an ideal location for Jim and he spent the summer on the beach surrounded by the artistic, hippy community which populated the area. Drugs were plentiful and Jim expanded his mind with acid and mellowed out with booze and grass. The addition of the warm sunshine made it seem like paradise on earth to him.

He soon found himself a home, on a rooftop above an abandoned warehouse beside a canal. Only a blanket kept him warm and he used candles for light. His intake of drugs increased still further and his writing became prolific, echoing his thoughts of loneliness, love and fear. It was during this period of abject poverty that many of the songs which would form the Doors' first two albums were written - the same songs that would change the lives of generations of fans.
Jim revealed later: "The birth of rock and roll coincided with

my adolescence, my coming into awareness. It was a real turn-on, although at the time I could never rationally fantasize about ever doing it myself. I guess all that time I was unconsciously accumulating inclination and nerve. My subconscious had prepared the whole thing. I didn't think about it. It was just thought about. I heard a whole concert situation, with a band and singing and an audience, a large audience. Those first five or six songs I wrote, I was just taking notes at a fantastic rock concert that was going on inside my head. And once I had written the songs, I had to sing them.

"Actually, I think the music came to my mind first and then I made up the words to hang on to the melody, some kind of sound. I could hear it, and since I had no way of writing it down musically, the only way I could remember it was to try and get words to put to it. And a lot of times I would end up with just the words and couldn't remember the melody."

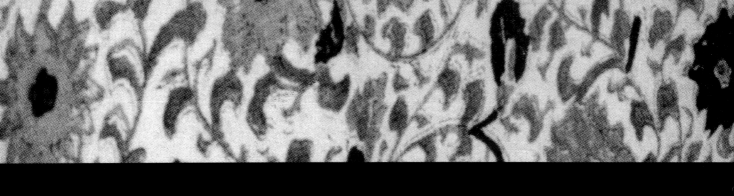

The handsome, mystic shaman that came down from the roof did not resemble the Jim Morrison of earlier times. He had become even thinner, his hair was long and his dark eyes reflected a strong belief in himself. A confidence which was not apparent before glowed from deep within him as he realised that music could become a vehicle for a new religion - with himself as the high priest.

Jim discussed the concept with Dennis Jakob, even going so far as to suggest a name for the band. He liked the name The Doors, the idea of which he had taken from the Blake line. Dennis was impressed but couldn't see how the idea could progress further due to the fact that Jim claimed he couldn't sing and Dennis was no musician. However, a chance meeting on the beach at Venice enabled Jim to turn his dreams into reality.

In August 1965, Jim encountered Ray Manczarek who was living in Venice, on the oceanfront south of Santa Monica, with his girlfriend Dorothy. Ray recalled the meeting when being interviewed by Digby Diehl from Eye magazine in 1967.

"I had been friendly with Jim at UCLA, and we talked about rock 'n' roll even then. After we graduated, he said he was going to New York. Then, two months later, in July, I met him on the beach in Venice. He said he had been writing some songs, so we sat on the beach and I asked him to sing some of them. He did, and the first thing he tried was 'Moonlight Drive'. When he sang those first lines - 'Let's swim to the moon / Let's climb through the tide / Penetrate the evening / That the city sleeps to hide' - I said: 'That's it.' I'd never heard lyrics to a rock song like that before. We talked a while before we decided to get a group together and make a million dollars." Ray added in 1981 that as Jim was singing the LSD-soaked lyrics, he could already hear the chord changes and the beat in his head.

When Jim told him he wanted to call the band The Doors, Ray was impressed, particularly with its reference to the Blake line 'If the doors of perception were cleansed, man could see things as they truly are; infinite.' Ray was also doing a fair amount of psychedelic drugs himself at this time and the idea of using a name associated with Aldous Huxley's book 'The Doors of Perception' - which was effectively an account of his experiences with the drug mescaline - appealed to him enormously.

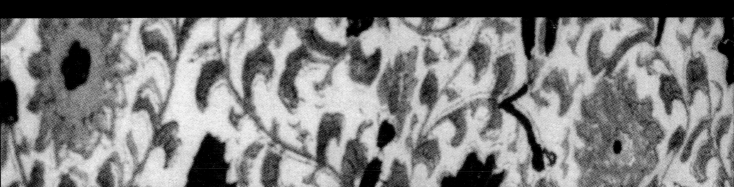

THE PASADENA J.C. PRESENTS IN CONCERT

THE LOVE DOORS

WEST COAST POP ART EXPERIMENTAL BAND

CANNED HEAT

MAGNIFICENT LIGHT SHOW

TICKETS FROM 2.50

PASADENA CIVIC AUDITORIUM

FRI. JUNE 2nd. 1967 8 P.M.

©1967 WEISSER

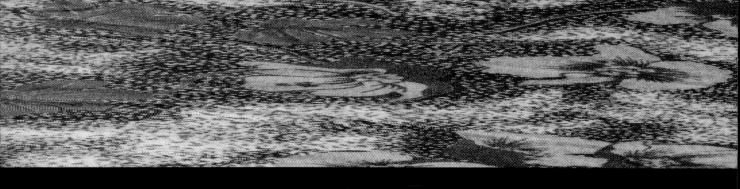

**P**oignantly, the last paragraph in Huxley's book reads: "But the man who comes back through the Door in the Wall will never be quite the same man who went out. He will be wiser but less cocksure, happier but less satisfied, humbler in acknowledging his ignorance yet better equipped to understand the relationship of words to things, of systemic reasoning to the unfathomable Mystery which it tries, forever vainly to comprehend." Ray and Jim were both about to embark on a journey which would take them face to face with The Door. Ray would be content to look at it but Jim had to take it further. Soon, he would touch the handle of The Door and immediately establish himself as something much more than a pretty lead singer - he would become a spokesman for a whole generation and a self-styled rock 'n' roll rebel. When he took the step through The Door he would become a legend.

Although Jim and Ray were opposites - Ray believed the answer to The Great Question Of Life was to be found by studying and practising  transcendental meditation whilst Jim was convinced that the road to higher knowledge lay within shamanism and a large intake of mind-altering drugs - but Ray was astute enough to realise how big an impact Jim's lyrics would have if he was able to provide the right melodies. He was also developing a deep affection for Jim and, as a result, he asked Jim to move in with Dorothy and himself. Dorothy was at work all day, allowing Ray and Jim to devote their time getting the songs into shape. Jim accepted the invitation and they went to work.

First up was work on Jim's vocal ability.  Although his voice was weak, he undoubtedly could sing and Ray thought that his weakness was just a matter of confidence. He also knew that if just a little of Jim's enigmatic personality could be projected to an audience along with his voice, the band would be in business. Consequently, Ray worked on Jim's voice for weeks whilst also trying to create the music to accompany the lyrics, spending  hours at his piano. Jim was very self-conscious, initially finding the whole concept of standing up and singing his lyrics mortifyingly embarrassing. However, after weeks of Ray's encouragement and influence, he began to relax enough to discover his voice although he was never to find performing in front of an audience a particularly easy task.

After two weeks, Ray felt they were sufficiently rehearsed to introduce Jim to the rest of Rick & the Ravens. They went up

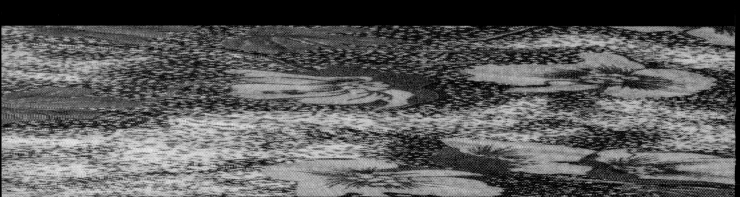

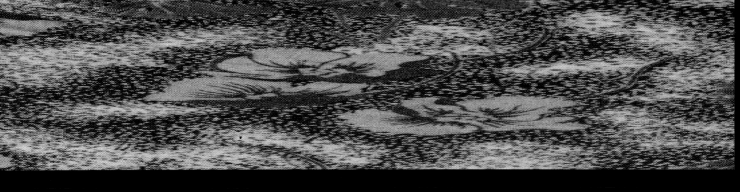

to Ray's parent's house in Manhattan Beach and Ray announced to his brothers that Jim was to be their new vocalist. Rick and Jim Manczarek didn't share Ray's enthusiasm or vision, failing to see any potential in either Jim or his lyrics. They did, however, agree to try to work with him although the arrangement was to be short-lived affair. However, for a time they kept their scepticism to themselves.

Rick & the Ravens now consisted of the three Manczarek brothers, Jim (harmonica), Rick (guitar) and Ray (keyboards) along with Jim handling the vocals. They lacked both a drummer and bass player, having previously picked up whoever was available when they landed a gig. Ray was quick to realise that, if they were serious about forming a commercial band, they were going to need a permanent rhythm section. It was at this time that Ray met John Densmore at the Maharishi Mahesh Yogi's Third Street meditation centre. Ray had been discussing his plan of getting a rock 'n' roll band together whilst at the centre, when John Densmore was pointed out as being a drummer. Ray explained the situation to John and asked if he would be interested in filling the vacant drum stool - an invitation which John jumped at.

35

John was twenty-years old and still living with his parents. The son of an architect, he was born and raised in Santa Monica, California and had begun playing drums at the age of twelve. He had originally wanted to learn to play the clarinet, but his teacher felt that this would damage his teeth and suggested he learned to play drums instead. He soon realised that he had aptitude and began to take private lessons. Before long, he was playing in dance bands, marching bands and playing timpani in the orchestra of University High School in West Los Angeles. This gave him a good grounding as he was having to switch styles daily. When he started college at Santa Monica City, he developed a healthy interest in jazz, regularly going to see Art Blakey, Elvin Jones and Coltrane and taught himself intricate jazz rhythms and fills by listening tirelessly to records. To enable him to play in bars and clubs and so earn himself some money he drove down to Tijuana and obtained a false ID.

He was majoring in music at college and, although he loved it , he began to have serious misgivings about his ability to support himself through music. Because of this, he switched to a business course and failed miserably. He switched again,

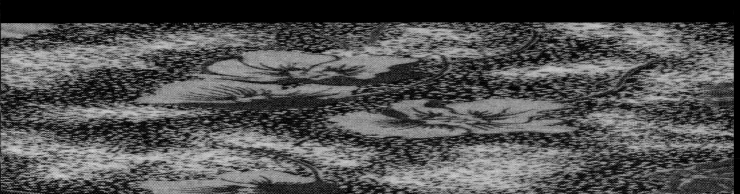

this time to sociology and then to anthropology which he took at San Fernando Valley State. He finally ended up at UCLA where he dropped out just one year before gaining his B.A., preferring instead to drum in a band called Psychedelic Rangers whose one recorded song 'Paranoia Blues' was never released.

Although John had a loose arrangement with a couple of bands at the time, he was always on the lookout for something more secure, so he agreed to Ray's proposition to try out with the band. John Densmore wrote about his first meeting in his own biography 'Riders On The Storm': "He (Ray) invited me down to his parents' place in Manhattan Beach to play. I entered by the beach house just in time to hear his parents make several unkind remarks about their son living with a Japanese girl. I exited quickly and went out to the garage/rehearsal room. Out came Ray with his beach thongs on and a daisy in his shirt. This time he seemed warm and friendly. Good-natured. I liked his frameless glasses, which to me looked groovy. intellectual-like. He introduced me to his two brothers, Rick, the guitarist, and Jim the harmonica player. The band was called Rick and the Ravens.

"They seemed like your basic hippy types to me, with Jim wearing those corny granny glasses. No originality. They were playing a few riffs I recognised from 'Money', 'Louie Louie' and 'Hoochie Coochie Man'. Rick was an adequate rhythm guitarist, but something was lacking. I thought they needed a good lead guitar player. Ray played some nice blues licks, coming from his Chicago roots. Growing up back there, he listened to the all-blues radio station, all day and all night.

"Lurking in the corner of the garage, meanwhile, was this guy wearing standard collegiate brown cords, a brown T-shirt and bare feet. Ray introduced him as 'Jim, the singer.' They had met at UCLA film school. Ray was moonlighting whilst pursuing his master's degree in film, after a BS in economics, and Jim was finishing up a four-year degree in film. He was in an accelerated two-and-a-half-year program. Smart guy. They had played together once when Ray was stuck with a union obligation for a sixth member of the band, and he convinced Jim to stand off to the side of the stage with a guitar that wasn't plugged in. They were backing Sonny and Cher. It was Jim's first paying gig and he didn't sing a note of music.

"The twenty-one year old Morrison was shy. He said hello to me and went back to the corner. I suspected he felt uncomfortable around musicians, since he didn't play an instrument. While Morrison moped around the garage looking for a beer, Ray grinned like a proud older brother as he handed me a crumpled piece of paper."

On the piece of paper were some of Jim's lyrics from what was to become the single 'Break On Through' and John immediately started to put some rhythm to the bass line that Ray had already devised. They were joined by Jim Manczarek on harmonica and Rick who was playing very soft rhythm guitar. After some time, Jim timidly began singing the first verse and the first thing that struck John was the vocalist's incredible good looks twinned with his alarming self-consciousness. He sung facing the wall, unable to look any of

the other musicians in the eye and although John found Jim
curious, the rehearsal ended on a high note and he agreed to
attend more of the same to see where it would lead.

It led, a fortnight later, to a session in World Pacific Studios
where the band recorded six demos. For some time, Rick and
the Ravens had been the under a recording contract with Aura
Records. The relationship had not proved particularly fruitful
for either party. Aura had released one single that had
promptly sunk without trace and didn't feel positive enough
about the band to commit to more expense by releasing a
second. To compensate, the record label offered the band
some free studio time and Ray felt that now was the time to
use it. Within three hours, often only using one or two takes,
they had recorded six tracks including: 'Moonlight Drive',
'Hello, I Love You', 'Summer's Almost Gone', 'My Eyes Have
Seen You', 'End Of The Night' and 'Go Insane' The band at this
time consisted of the three Manczarek brothers, Jim, John and
an anonymous girl bass player and the session was
engineered by the owner of the studio and close friend of
Ray's, Dick Bock. The band left the studio with an acetate of
the six very roughly recorded songs.

The next stage was to try and secure a recording contract
with the aid of the acetate and, to this end, they played
the material to all the major record labels on the West
Coast. The various A&R men were unanimous in their opinion
that the tracks were dreadful. No one seemed prepared to
look beyond the recording of the songs to the potential
beyond. The biggest signings on the West Coast in 1965 were
bands like the fun-loving Beach Boys and The Mamas and
Papas who were busy spreading the word of peace and love.
To the record company moguls, The Doors' dark message was
not acceptable and they were rejected by every label they
visited, a situation which is experienced by most truly great
bands.
Ray recalled in Musician magazine: "We would go from record
company to record company to record company, saying we're a
band called The Doors, and they'd go, 'The what? The Doors?
How do you spell that?' And then we'd play the demo for
them - we got rejected by everyone in town. Even got thrown
out of a few offices. Everyone, but everyone, said 'No! You
can't - that's terrible - I hate it - no, no.' I especially remember
one guy at Liberty. I played him 'A Little Game' and said 'You
might like this one.' He listened, then said 'You can't, you

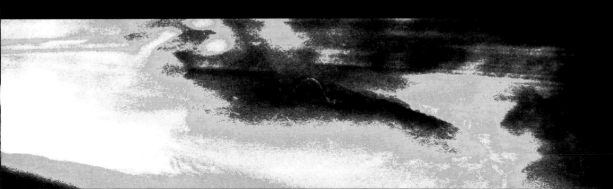

can't do that kind of stuff!'  Because it said things like 'go insane.'"

Along with the rejection came the sudden realisation by Jim and Rick Manczarek that the dream they had of being part of a successful rock 'n' roll band was not going to be plain sailing.  They decided to hedge their bets and quit the band to go back to school.  Although Ray was upset by this move, John felt that it was probably for the best hoping that they might be replaced by a more competent guitarist.  Jim seemed not to notice that they had gone.

Although the majority of record labels in Los Angeles had passed on The Doors, there was one man who was, if not convinced, intrigued by their music and curious to know more about them.  His name was Billy James and he had previously been based in New York and responsible for Bob Dylan's publicity at Columbia Records.   After his move in 1963 to the West Coast, he remained with Columbia but was given the job of finding and developing new talent.

 He was visited by Jim, Ray, John and Dorothy one afternoon and they played him the acetate.  He was immediately impressed with Jim's lyrics and the raw, simplistic feel to the music.  He was also impressed by the band themselves as they sat in his office, confidently explaining what they wanted and where they wanted to go.  However, Billy was not altogether sure that he had the ability to bring the best out of the band due to the fact that he was relatively inexperienced in the studio.  He felt that if he could get another Columbia producer interested in them they would be in business.  He was also shrewd enough to realise that this would not be an easy task so he offered them a five and a half year contract, the option of which would be picked up after an initial six month period.  During this time, Columbia would produce a minimum of four sides and release a minimum of two.
Encouraged by this, Ray and John were determined to try to knock some shape into the band.  Jim preferred to leave the musical decisions to Ray.  After Rick Manczarek's departure, it was apparent that they would need another guitarist and also a bass player.  So the search began.  It was at John's suggestion that they auditioned another former member of the Psychedelic Rangers - Robby Krieger.

Robert Alan Krieger was born on January 8th, 1946 in Los Angeles and, at nineteen, was the youngest of the four.  The son of an affluent aeronautical engineer, he possessed a quick

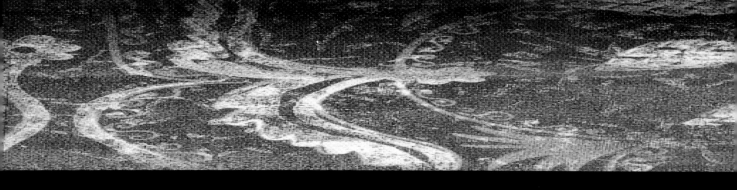

mind and a passion for music. His youthful love of classical music soon gave way to an infatuation with various rock 'n' rollers of the time: Elvis Presley, Fats Domino and The Platters. His career in music, however, didn't begin until he started to flunk out of University High in Los Angeles, preferring instead to spend his time surfing. His parents became aware of his errant ways and immediately sent him to Meleno Park, a private school near San Francisco. At Meleno, the only legitimate alternative to three hours' studying every night was to practise a musical instrument and Robbie took up the guitar without hesitation - copying the Mexican classical style of 'Dos Flamencos'.

After graduating from Meleno, he enroled at the University of California at Santa Barbara and his musical interests began to expand rapidly. Inspired by Bob Dylan, he played gigs singing folk songs with his guitar and a neck-mounted harmonica. He was also in a jug band called The Back Bay Chamberpot Terriers. He started listening to a plethora of styles, including jazz and blues and developed a love of Indian sitar and sarod music.

It wasn't until he saw Chuck Berry live that he decided that his future lay in music. He remembers: "I saw Chuck Berry at the Santa Monica Civic Auditorium. That was the greatest Chuck Berry show I've ever seen because he was still young and not jaded or mad or something. He was really great that night and that did it for me. He had this red, rockin' guitar, you know. The next day I went out and traded my classical in on a Gibson SG. My first electric was the SG, the same one I had in The Doors. I played that one until it got ripped off, and then got another. If I hadn't gone electric, I probably wouldn't have got into rock 'n' roll. I wanted to learn jazz really. I got to know some people who did rock 'n' roll with jazz and I thought I would make money playing music." The money that he would eventually earn with The Doors, however, was beyond his wildest dreams.

Slight, with green eyes which had a vagueness about them and frizzy, prematurely receding light brown hair, Robby had met Ray at the Meditation Centre and was immediately interested when John called him up and explained that they needed a guitarist. He had heard a lot about The Doors from John, who had spoken often of their wild and crazy lead singer, Jim Morrison. John suggested that he and Jim should call over to

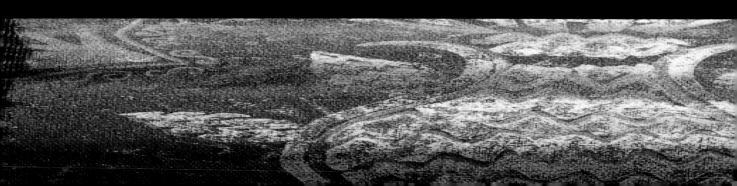

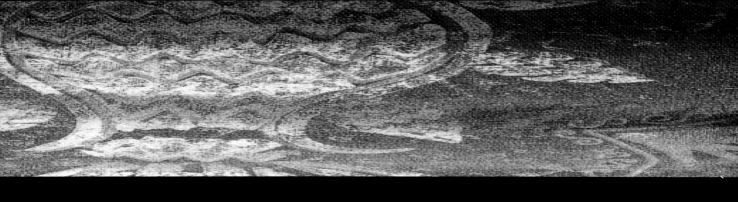

Robby's house in the Palisades to decide whether he felt that he could work with the highly unconventional vocalist. John's fears that Robby would find Jim too intense were unfounded, however, as the pair hit it off right away. Robby agreed to join the band in rehearsal which were now being held in a garage behind the Greyhound bus station in Santa Monica.

Ray commented later: "Robby came down with his guitar and bottleneck. When he put that big glass bottle on his finger and went 'boiiinnnggg', I said 'What a sound! Incredible! That's it, that's The Doors sound.' The first song we played was 'Moonlight Drive', because it didn't have too many chord changes and, after playing that, I said 'This is it, this is the best musical experience I've ever had.' Of course, we were a little high at the time, but it was just...right, it was right from the beginning. The combination, the chemistry was right, the way John, Robby and I, with our placid, meditation kind of thing, balanced off Jim's Dionysian tendencies. It was a natural - it couldn't miss. I thought, this is it, we're gonna make it. We're gonna make great music and the people are going to love it."

The search for a bass player, however, proved more difficult and eventually Ray found a Fender Rhodes keyboard bass eliminating the need for one. Ray revealed in Modern Keyboard: "I always felt we had to have somebody on the bottom, because I could never get it out of the Vox Continental that I was playing. We never found a bass guitarist we wanted to work with. The bass players invariably played too much. No bass player would want to play the way we wanted, which was very sparse and hypnotic. Then one day we were auditioning at some place - we didn't get the gig of course because we were too weird - but the house band there had an instrument called a Fender Rhodes piano bass sitting on top of the Vox Continental organ just like I had. I switched on the amplifier, played the thing and realised it was a keyboard bass. When I saw that I said: 'This is it. We have found our bass player."

The nucleus of the band was now complete and they met every day in an attempt to form The Doors' sound. Occasionally, they played at a wedding or bar mitzvah, where Ray would usually provide the vocals to the covers of 'Louie Louie' and 'Gloria'. Jim hadn't overcome his shyness of performing and on the rare occasions he did sing, he would do so with his back to the audience or with his eyes tightly closed.

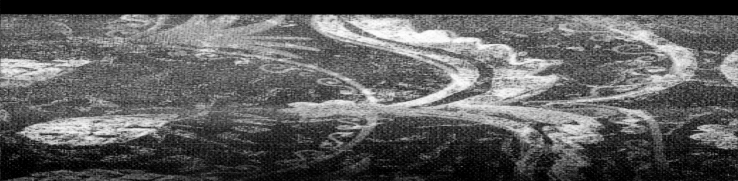

Their daily rehearsals began to pay off and the band became tight, providing a blank canvas on which Jim's lyrics could be orchestrated. They would have the basic structure of a song and then all four would improvise, hacking out the final version together. Jim had a natural instinct for

melody but no knowledge of chords, so it was up to the others to tell him which notes he was actually singing. Jim said later: "In the beginning we were creating our music, ourselves, every night...starting with a few outlines, maybe a few words for a song. Sometimes we worked out in Venice, looking at the surf. We were together a lot and it was good times for all of us. Acid, sun, friends, the ocean and poetry and music."

At around this time, Jim met and grew close to nineteen year-old Pamela Courson. She had the looks of a delicate, porcelain figure, pencil-slim with long, fine red hair that swept past her shoulders. Her complexion was pale with a sprinkling

45

of freckles and her eyes were unusually large, giving her a fawnlike, vulnerable appearance.

Born on December 22, 1946 in Weed, California, Pamela's father had been a navy flyer, like Jim's, but was now principal of a high school in Orange County. She had dropped out of art school just before meeting Jim and quickly became captivated by him. He taught her about philosophy and she encouraged his poetry. This was the beginning of a relationship which, although sometimes stormy, would be the most permanent one of Jim's life.

In January 1966, The Doors began auditioning for clubs on Sunset Strip in earnest. There was no word from Columbia and they were short of cash. They were rejected time and time again but were eventually offered a job as the house band at the London Fog, a small beer bar just a few doors from the Whisky. John explained: "How we got into The London Fog was, we went down to the audition with about fifty of our friends to pack the place out - because it wasn't very big, and they all applauded us frantically. Jesse James, the owner, thought 'My God!' and hired us. Next night, the place was kinda empty.'

The deal they struck with the unlikely named Mr. James was appalling. They earnt ten dollars each night from Thursday to Sunday and for this they played five sets a night, from 9 pm to 2.00am with a fifteen-minute break between each set. The clientele consisted mainly of hookers, sailors, the occasional tourist and little else and, although, the band found the atmosphere depressing, it gave them an excellent opportunity to arrange and experiment with their original material. It also gave the reticent Jim some much-needed practice in stage-craft techniques. At the start of the residency, Jim was still insisting on singing with his back to the audience, such as it was, but he soon built up his confidence and began to direct his energy toward the crowd, enjoying his growing ability to manipulate them with his actions. Ray recalled: "We had the chance to develop songs like 'Light My Fire', 'When The Music's Over' and 'The End'. 'The End' was originally a very short piece but because of all the time we had to fill onstage, we started extending songs, taking them in to areas that we didn't know they would go into...and playing stoned every night. It was the great summer of acid and we really got into a lot of improvisation, and I think the fact that no-one was at that club really helped us to develop what The Doors became."

Within a month, the band had twenty-five original songs in
their repertoire but there was still no action from Columbia.
Their spirits were lifted briefly when a staff producer, Larry
Marks, appeared at the Fog one night and introduced himself,
but they never heard from him again. Although Billy James
was still enthusiastic, he couldn't persuade any of Columbia's
producers to take the band into the studio and none of the
other A&R staff thought the band commercially viable. As a
result, James was sent a memo informing him that the
company would not be picking up the option. They were to be
'dropped' from the label. James had not mentioned this to the
band as he was keen that the they should stay on the label for
the full six months, when they would be paid $1,000 as
compensation for being dropped, however, the band
themselves pre-empted the situation.

John decided to pay James a visit to try to find out why the
record company were stalling and, whilst in his office at
Columbia, he spotted the memo on the A&R man's desk.
John's heart sank and he made his excuses and left. That night
at the Fog, he told the others what he had seen. They were
devastated and went on to perform a particularly uninspired
set. Later that night they held a meeting to consider the
implications of the bad news that John had disclosed. They
came to the conclusion that although it was undoubtedly
depressing, it was probably for the best if, as it appeared, the
record company didn't understand what they were trying to
do. The next day they called James and asked to be officially
released from their contract. Despite his encouragement that
they should remain under contract until the end of the six
months thus collecting their $1000 - which they were in
desperate need of - they refused. A couple of days later they
were legally free and Columbia had officially lost The Doors.

The band were understandably depressed but decided not to
let the lack of foresight of others sway them from their course.
Each individual handled the situation in his own way and Jim's
disappointment manifested itself onstage. He was becoming
fascinated with his own power over his audience and began to
experiment with it. His onstage behaviour gradually became
more reckless and crazed which served to scare people in the
audience. Some were attracted to his rebellious antics but
many were repelled by it. He would smoke dope all day, then
begin drinking in the early evening sobering himself with

speed at regular intervals. He would then drop some acid before a set and took great delight in producing little bottles of amyl nitrate which he would systematically wave under the noses of the rest of the band as well as his own during their performance. Without this chemical crutch, Jim was still very nervous of performing, believing he lacked real talent and that he was guilty of being a complete sham. In his drug-induced state, however, these self-critical feelings drifted away and a darker side of his mind would take control. He could make people fear him or love him and he set out to test this ability to the utmost limit.

Journalist Richard Blackburn saw Jim performing one night at the London Fog: "The club was a narrow, smoky, dirty bar frequented by a clientele that ranged from bikers to gays. Jim used to get up and pop amyl nitrates right onstage and then collapse over the piano, cutting off his own improvised lyrics. I often saw him outside, crazed on acid, bumping into telephone poles."

Soon after the blow of being dropped by their record label, they were also dropped from the London Fog. A fight broke out in the bar one night between some drunks and Joey, the bouncer, and this incident was used as an excuse to get rid of the band. This final rejection would probably have finished The Doors had it not been for the timely interjection of Ronnie Haran, the pretty talent booker for the most important rock club in Los Angeles, the legendary Whisky.

Jim had visited Ronnie on several occasions at the Whisky in an attempt to persuade her to book The Doors. Minutes after they were fired from the Fog, she finally arrived to watch them play and liked what she saw. John Densmore later wrote: "Ronnie had an ear for talent and an eye for a lover. To her, the back-up band was adequate but the lead singer was everything a rock star should be. Raw talent. An Adonis with a microphone. She had to have him."

Haran was so impressed with Jim that she managed to convince Elmer Valentine, the part-owner of the club, to hire The Doors as their new house band without an audition and by so doing gave them their first important break. The band went from $10 a night to the union scale of $135 a week each and Ronnie went to work on Jim's image, dressing him in T-shirts and turtle necks. She also suggested that he stopped wearing underwear onstage, for reasons best left to the imagination.

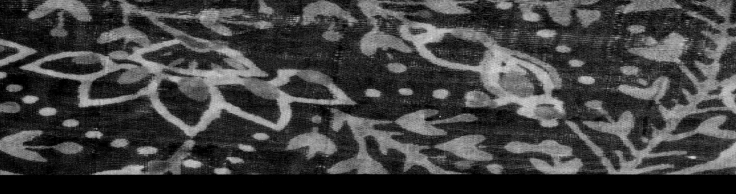

Between May and July of 1966, The Doors supported bands such as The Rascals, The Paul Butterfield Blues Band, The Animals, The Beau Brummels, Buffalo Springfield, The Byrds, Love, Frank Zappa and the Mothers Of Invention, Them and Captain Beefheart.

*The Whisky-a-go-go in 1990.*
Photo: Rainer Moddemann.

Although they were rapidly earning a reputation on the street as the hottest band in town, Pete Johnson of the Los Angeles Times was not convinced: "The Doors are a hungry-looking quartet with an interesting original sound but with what is possibly the worst stage appearance of any rock 'n' roll group in captivity. Their lead singer emotes with his eyes closed, the electric pianist hunches over his instrument as if reading mysteries from the keyboard, the guitarist drifts about the stage randomly, and the drummer seems lost in a seperate world." Instead of being hurt by the review, the band felt it summed up their stage presence perfectly and were pleased that people were taking notice of them at last.

Their time at the Whisky gave them more experience playing live and, more particularly, they began to learn from the more experienced bands they were supporting. Jim worked hard to perfect the dark, threatening, yet sexual, image he was creating. He swung between vulgarity and violence, often horrifying the audience with his antics. He also continued to

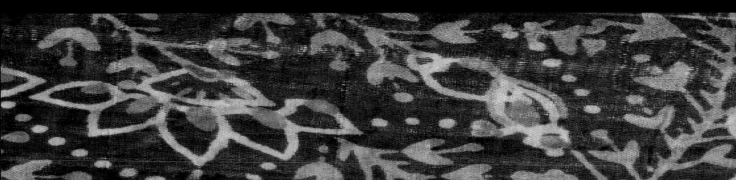

improvise onstage with his lyrics and, due to this, the band were able to perfect two numbers which would prove to be future masterpieces - 'The End' and 'When The Music's Over'. The sound produced by the band just kept getting better and better, despite Jim's increased intake of acid which had reached epic proportions by any standard.

Every week, new stories about the band's stoned adventures were hot gossip amongst the movers and groovers and soon the groupies began to check out the blatantly sexual Morrison for themselves. Every woman who saw the dramatic, crazy vocalist seemed to fall under his spell and would watch his performance as if hypnotised, hanging on to his every word. Call it charisma, call it star quality - whatever it was, Jim certainly had plenty of it.

**M**orrison said later: "I just remember that some of the best musical trips we took were in clubs. There's nothing more fun than to play music to an audience. You can improvise at rehearsals, but it's a kind of a dead atmosphere. There's no audience feedback. There's no tension, really, because in a club with a small audience you're free to do anything. You still feel an obligation to be good, so you can't get completely loose; there are people watching. So there is this beautiful tension. There's freedom and at the same time an obligation to play well. I can put in a full day's work, go home and take a show, change clothes, then play two or three sets at the Whisky, man, and I love it. The way an athlete loves to run, to keep in shape."

The band had developed a large and loyal following and were making a powerful impression on all who saw their performance. There were two men that were not impressed, however, and they were the long-suffering owners of the club Elmer Valentine and Phil Tanzini. They were repeatedly infuriated by the band's attitude and would fire them at least once a week, either because they insisted on playing at full volume in order to blow the headliners off the stage or because Jim always arrived drunk or stoned or both. Sometimes he failed to make an appearance at all, enraging them further. On each occasion they were reinstated thanks to some manipulation on Ronnie's behalf. She would call up one of The Doors' considerable female following who would pass word on to all her girlfriends and then they would all bombard the Whisky with telephone calls enquiring when the band

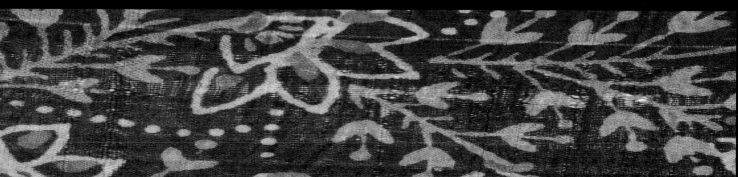

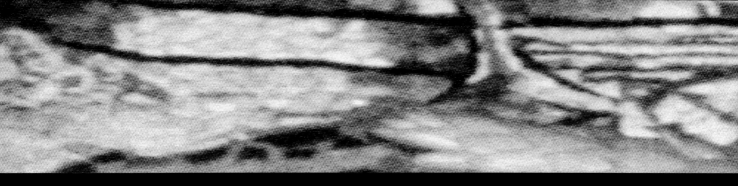

would be next appearing.  The ruse never failed.  Elmer was always eager to provide the public with what they wanted and never once doubted the integrity of the calls.

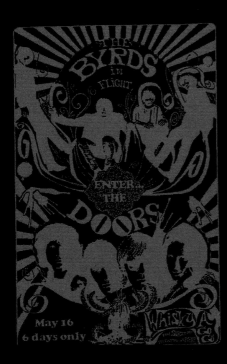

Ronnie had effectively taken over the management role of The Doors and set about contacting the various record companies in order to secure the band she called "America's Rolling Stones" a recording contract.  This was not a particularly taxing task as the majority of the labels were not oblivious to the fact that there was a buzz about the band on the street and wanted to check them out for themselves. They were pulled in to the club by reviews such as the one Bill Kerby wrote in the UCLA Daily Bruin: "And there he was; a gaunt, hollow Ariel from hell, stumbling in slow motion through the drums.  Robbie turned to look with mild disgust but Jim Morrison was oblivious. Drifting, still you could have lit matches off the look he gave the audience.  There was a mild tremor of excited disbelief as he dreamed that he went to his microphone, slack.  Just for a flash, his beautiful child's face said it was all a lie.  All the terror, all the drugs, all the evil.  Gone!  The unhuman sound he made into the microphone turned the carping groupies to stone; alternately caressing, screaming, terraced flights of poetry and music, beyond visceral.   For an hour on that Friday night, a modern American pop group got right out on the edge and stayed there.  And because they are great and because the edge is where artists produce the best, there occurred a major black miracle."

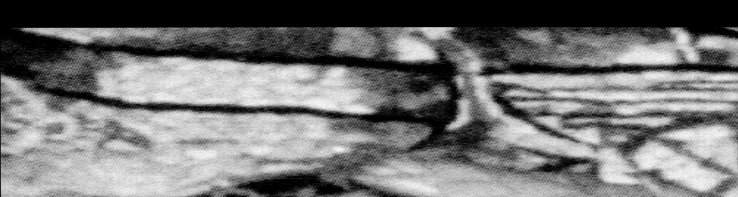

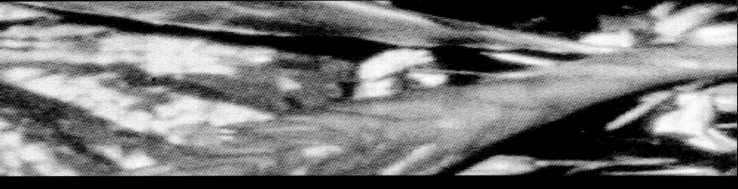

For the majority of the label representatives who saw The Doors play live, they were far too left-field. Even if they saw the band's potential, they were nervous about signing something so different are were at a loss to know how to market them effectively. It was, they felt, too big a risk. One man, however, felt differently but not until he had seen them four times.

55

Thirty-six year-old Jac Holzman was the president of Elektra Records. A small company, they primarily specialised in folk, having signed Judy Collins. They were, however, anxious to break into the rock market and, to this effect, had recently signed both Love and Paul Butterfield. At Ronnie's insistence Jac flew from his base in New York to see The Doors play at the Whisky and was unmoved by their performance. What did intrigue him, however, was the reaction of the audience who were packing the club and giving

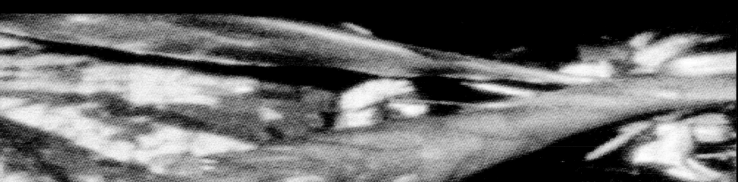

the band a tumultuous reception, a factor which seemed to have been overlooked by the other labels.

At the personal recommendation of Arthur Lee of Love, Holzman decided to give the band another chance and saw them again the following night. This time, although he was still not knocked out by the band, something about them fascinated him. On the third night he began get a clear picture in his own mind of how they could be developed and by the fourth night he decided that although signing them would be a gamble, it was one he was prepared to take. However, the label was too small to make mistakes and Holzman decided to seek the advice of Elektra's senior staff producer, Paul Rothchild before offering the band a deal.

Paul Rothchild had previously produced albums for both The Butterfield Blues Band and Love and lived on the East Coast. He received a call from Holzman one night and was on a flight to Los Angeles the following day to check the band out for himself. The first time he saw the band he thought they were awful and began to seriously doubt Holzman's talent spotting ability. He said later: "I caught a horrible show. At the same time they were awful, I could tell they were very different from anything I'd heard before. I had nothing to relate them to. This intrigued me, so I decided to stay for the second set. The second set was brilliant. I had religion. In that second set I heard 'The End', 'Light My Fire', 'Twentieth Century Fox', 'Break On Through' and a few others, and I was convinced."

With Rothchild confirming his own feelings, Jac Holzman offered The Doors a recording contract. The deal was for three years (with an option after the first) and three albums. He offered an advance against future royalties of $5000 and a 5% royalty rate.

The band were relieved by Holzman's proposition but they were not totally convinced that Elektra was the right label for them. Although it had seen a certain amount of success, it was a small operation and the band worried that it might not be big enough to break them nationally. They thanked Holzman for his offer and requested time to think about it which was a risky move due to the lack of other firm offers. However, the band regarded contracts with caution after their disastrous experience with Columbia. They decided they needed some advice and called their old ally at Columbia, Billy James. This

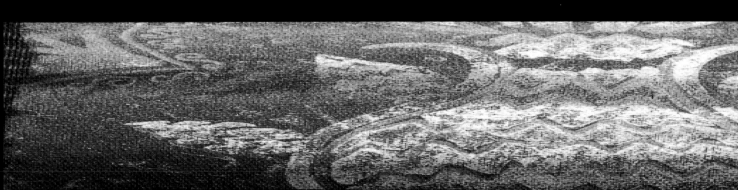

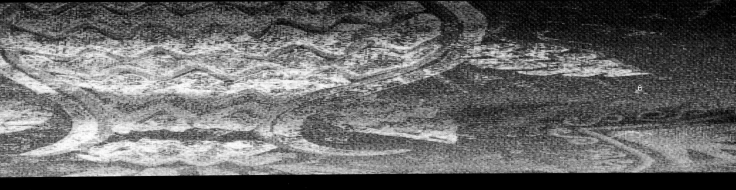

call was extremely timely, as James had just accepted an offer from Holzman to head Elektra's operation on the West Coast. Because of this, James told them that he wasn't in a position to be able to advise them on the contract but did emphasize that, should they decide to go with Elektra, he would personally ensure that they were looked after, unlike the way they had been treated by Columbia. He also told them they should get themselves some independent legal advice before signing the contract.

James' comments were relayed to Ronnie, who suggested they take the contract to her lawyer, Al Schlesinger. Ronnie had expressed an interest in managing the band and, had this arrangement come to fruition, using her lawyer would have proved to be a conflict of interest. Eventually, Robby discussed the situation with his father who recommended that they used his own legal adviser, a Beverly Hills lawyer called Max Fink.

*The Alta Cienega Motel in 1990 - Jim's room was just above the entrance.*
Photo: Rainer Moddemann

**M**ax looked over the contract and confirmed that if they wished to proceed with the deal, he would be happy to negotiate it for them. This left the band with a decision to make - should they sign to Elektra? On the plus side, they respected and admired Jac Holzman and felt secure with Billy James at the helm of the West Coast office. They also began to see the intimacy of a small label as a positive aspect. With so few bands signed, they would have less chance of being forgotten as they had been at Columbia. Also, less bands meant that the staff would be able to apply themselves more directly to promoting the acts efficiently. These points more than compensated for the fact that Elektra wasn't a 'major' record company. In addition, they had no other offers to consider. If Jac Holzman was willing to take a risk, they felt it prudent to do the same. To this effect, they instructed Max to being the negotiations.

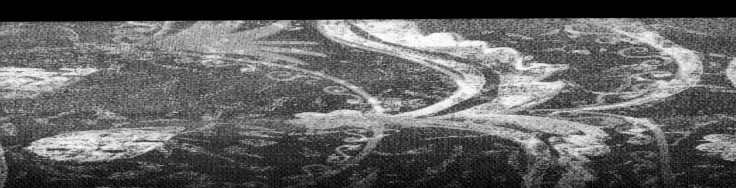

Whilst the negotiations were taking place, Jim's onstage performances were becoming more and more outrageous. Offstage too, he was unusually tense, his behaviour became even more erratic and his drinking and drug taking escalated accordingly. Due to this, two days after they signed with Elektra, The Doors were finally fired from their residency at the Whisky with immediate effect.

By nine-thirty Jim hadn't arrived at the club for the first set, so Robby, Ray and John took to the stage without him and played some blues, with Ray providing the vocals. When they had finished they were cornered by Phil Tanzini who demanded that they find Jim in time for the second set. John and Ray hurried to the Alta-Cienega Motel where they were met by an extremely incoherent Jim who could only manage to utter three words: "Ten thousand mikes." John and Ray couldn't believe their ears but, with Jim providing the evidence in front of them, they knew what he was saying was true. A normal dose of LSD was around 500 micrograms and Jim had taken twenty times this amount. He was totally blitzed. Ray was desperate to get Jim onstage to pacify Tanzini so they helped him dress and threw him the back of the car.

The second set was, not unnaturally, a complete mess but just before they were due to go onstage for the third time, Jim appeared to have come down enough from the acid to take control and stated that he felt like doing their showpiece, 'The End', a simple 'goodbye song'. The others nodded, not knowing what was going to happen but fearing the worst, just thankful that he was still standing.

Jim shuffled on to the stage, his eyes vacant and heavy-lidded. There was a feeling of anticipation in the Whisky that night creating a shiver through everyone present in the club. They were expecting something to happen, never imagining they would witness what was about to occur. Jim began to sing eruditely and quietly and, gradually, everybody became mesmerised by the figure on the stage, with his head thrown back and his eyes closed. Even the waitresses who were, by now, accustomed to Jim's unpredictable antics, stopped and watched. John, Ray and Robby could sense the tension and noticed that some unfamiliar lines were making their debut in the song. He began what is now known as the 'Killer awoke before dawn' sequence. They were not particularly surprised

59

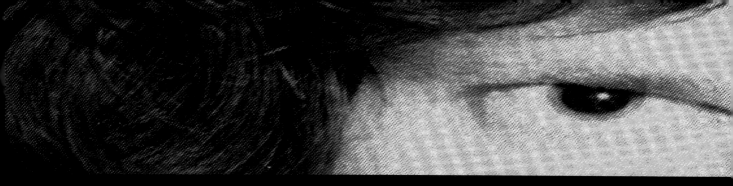

by this, Jim was always doing it and it was up to them to keep the beat steady and go with Jim's flow. Suddenly, Jim opened his eyes and glowered at the audience, hypnotising all who happened upon his gaze and what was to follow would establish Jim Morrison as a legend which couldn't fail to grow.

"Father...Yes, son?  I want to kill you/
Mother...I want to ...
FFFUUUCCKKK YOOOUUU!!!"

Jim screamed the last line as if he was on fire and then continued with the song as if he had done nothing abnormal and Ray, Robby and John, although they were open-mouthed, somehow managed to continue playing without missing a beat. If Jim was going for dramatic impact, he certainly achieved it that night.  The whole audience went crazy, mostly with delight but some with shock.  The set finished with the end of the song and no-one applauded or even spoke.  The band made their way back to their dressing room where they were met by Phil Tanzini who was shaking with rage shouting "You foul mouthed Morrison!  You guys are fired.  Don't you ever come back to this club.  Nobody has a right to say that about their mother.  You don't ever say that about your father.  You're fired!"  Somehow they knew that this time he meant it.

61

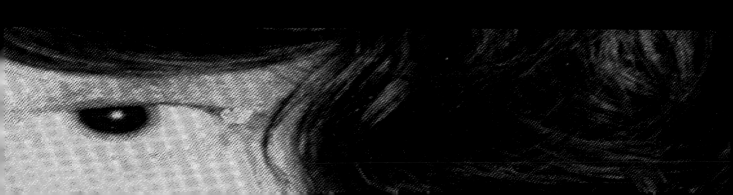

# THE DOORS OPEN WIDE

**T**he Doors went into the studio with producer Paul Rothchild to record their debut album. The sessions were held at Sunset Sound Recording Studios which were located at 6650 West Sunset Boulevard in Los Angeles in September 1966. The whole album took only six days to complete due to the amount of time they had spent working the songs live. Everything was there and ready to be recorded onto tape and Paul was as eager as the band to make a success of it.

*Sunset Sound Studios - 1990*
Photo: Rainer Moddemann.

Ray said later: "Our relationship with Paul was a marriage made in heaven. He was just what we needed. He came down to the Whisky for a couple of nights, and we found him to be a man of like mind, someone who knew his poetry, knew his jazz, rock 'n' roll and folk, and was an excellent producer. He was very strong in the studio, yet knew enough to give us our heads when we needed to go in our own directions. He never really got in the way, never really said 'Well, don't do it this way, do it that way.' Any suggestion he'd have to offer would be along the lines of 'Listen, you guys, what do you think of doing it this way?' Many times his suggestions were correct and so we'd say 'OK, sounds like a great idea - let's do it that way.' Paul was an excellent manipulator in the studio."

Paul's ability to draw the best out of the musicians who had

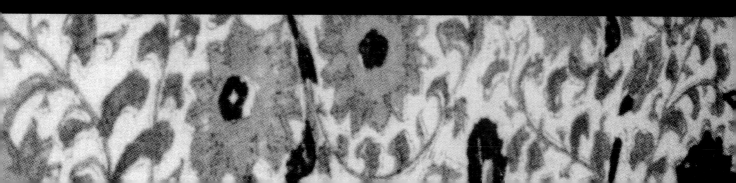

little or, in Robby's case, no studio experience whatsoever was the mark of a fine producer. He explained later: "The common concept of recording studios - which wasn't mine - was that they were hospitals were the music was operated on. I liked to get as far away from that as possible, convert the atmosphere and emotion of the studio into something warmer..let's sit around and play music for a while - not even, let's sit around in the club and play, because that's also a little alien. So, what we did to break the recording cherry of The Doors, so to speak, was to go into the studio with the band feeling that they're going in for a session. I realised that we'd probably blow a day or so, but we went in to cut masters, not to screw around. We went in and cut two tunes, neither of which showed up on the first album; we didn't stop at a perfect take, we stopped at the one we felt had the muse in it. That was the most important thing, for the take to have the feel, even if there were musical errors. When the muse came, that was the take."

**P**aul's ability to capture The Doors' raw sound without clouding it with special effects, thus losing the soul, was only eclipsed by the patience he exhibited when dealing with Jim's erratic behaviour. Although the majority of the vocals were recorded in just two or three takes, Jim decided he could perform more effectively if his already surreal mood was enhanced further by large quantities of alcohol and drugs rendering him incapable to sticking to the arrangements. At times, the other band members wondered if they would ever get the tracks down but Paul seemed to have an empathy with the erratic singer. He explained in Crawdaddy magazine: "At one point Jim said to me during the recording session, and he was tearful, and he shouted in the studio, 'Does anyone understand me?' And I said yes, I do, and right then and there we got into a long discussion and Jim kept saying over and over 'Kill the father, fuck the mother' and essentially it boiled down to this, kill all those things in yourself which are instilled in you and you are not of yourself, they are alien concepts which are not yours, they must die. The psychedelic revolution. Fuck the mother is very basically mother, mother-birth, real, you can touch it, it's nature, it can't lie to you. So what Jim says at the end of the Oedipus section, which is essentially the same thing that the classic says, kill the alien concepts, get back to reality, the end of the alien concepts, the beginning of personal concepts." It was good that Paul understood what Jim was trying to say because the rest of the

BILL GRAHAM PRESENTS IN SAN FRANCISCO

THE TUES. WED. THURS. ONLY YARDBIRDS

FRI. SAT. SUN. ONLY THE DOORS

PLAYS ALL WEEK JAMES COTTON BLUES BAND RICHIE HAVENS JULY 25-30 FILLMORE

B. MACLEAN © BILL GRAHAM 1967 #75

TICKETS

SAN FRANCISCO: City Lights Bookstore; S.F. State College (Hut T-1); The Town Squire (1318 Polk); Kelley Galleries (3673 Sacramento); Wild Colors (1418 Haight); Bally Lo (Union Square); BERKELEY: Discount Records, Shakespeare & Co.; SAN MATEO: Town & Country Records; REDWOOD CITY: Redwood House of Music; PALO ALTO: Dana Morgan Music; SAN RAFAEL: Record King; SAUSALITO: The Tides Bookstore

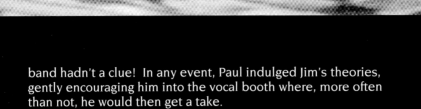

band hadn't a clue! In any event, Paul indulged Jim's theories, gently encouraging him into the vocal booth where, more often than not, he would then get a take.

**R**othchild also described the recording of 'The End': "That half an hour when we recorded 'The End' was one of the most beautiful moments I've ever had in a recording studio. I was totally overwhelmed. Normally, the producer sits there just listening for all the things that are right and anything about to go wrong, but for this take I was completely sucked up into it, absolutely audience. The studio was completely dark except for a candle in Jim's booth and the VU

ASCAP
Nipper Music

Time 2:52

EK-45615-A
Produced by
PAUL A. ROTHCHILD
Engineer.
Bruce Botnick

**LIGHT MY FIRE**
(Words & Music by The Doors)

ELEKTRA RECORDS · 51 WEST 51 STREET · NEW YORK CITY

meters on the mixing board; all the other lights were off, it was a magic moment, and it was almost a shock when the song was over. It was like, yeah, that's the end, that's the statement - it can't go any further. There were about four other people in the control room, and we realised the tapes were still rolling because Bruce, the engineer was completely sucked into it. His head was on the console and he was just absolutely immersed in the take - he became audience too...so the muse did visit the studio that time, and all of us were audience; the machines knew what to do, I guess..."

There was only one original track recorded at this time that had lyrics written by someone other than Jim. This was

entitled 'Light My Fire' and was composed almost entirely by Robby - the first he had ever written. Sophisticated in its simplicity, the song would eventually go on to become the band's signature tune and the anthem of a generation.

In 1981, debating the reason behind the longevity of The Doors' popularity, Paul Williams wrote of 'Light My Fire' in Rolling Stone: "The closest thing I can think of to its instrumental build up is the long version of The Who's 'Won't Get Fooled Again'. Certainly, it was an inspiration for Cream's 'Spoonful', out of which grew a whole generation of British blues-rock raveups. But no one has ever made it feel so Dionysian, yet look so Apollonian, as the Doors did. The place where music and sex come together is explored effectively, thoroughly, joyously; how could such a song fail to be eternally popular with the postpuberty age group."

After the recording sessions were completed, the album took a further five weeks to mix. The band then flew to New York. They were there for two reasons, firstly to attend an official Elektra signing bash, and secondly to play their first gig outside of Los Angeles.

They were booked to play at Ondine's, a small but chic club in Manhattan and, although they were unknown on the East Coast, word of their highly disparate sound and sexy singer soon spread and, by the third night the club was packed with potential groupies. However, it wasn't just the females in the audience who were mesmerised by his onstage insolence. All the Elektra executives turned up to see their new signing and were instantly impressed. Elektra vice president Steve Harris was stunned by the band, or more particularly, Jim and has been quoted as saying: "He (Jim) sauntered over to me from the bar and I thought to myself, if this guy can recite the phone book he's going to sell a million records. He was gorgeous, magnetic. Whenever he was introduced to journalists or record company people and they had their wives with them, he would always try and conquer the wife first. And he usually did."

The band also finalised their business with Elektra, signing their publishing to Jac Holzman's Nipper Music. They discussed, at length, the marketing strategy regarding the album release as well as supervising the editing of what was scheduled to be the first single 'Break On Through'. Holzman,

ever mindful of the strict moral code adhered to by radio programmers, wanted the word 'high' edited out of the single to ensure maximum airplay. After much haggling the band begrudging agreed. Holzman also suggested holding back the release of the album until January, a time when no other Elektra artists were scheduled for release, enabling the company to treat it as a priority. The band also agreed that Jim would be featured prominently in all promotion, which was to include a advertisement for the album on a billboard on Sunset Strip, the first of its kind. They also approved the artwork for the sleeve, designed by Elektra's art director, Bill Harvey, and helped write the press releases and biographies which would accompany the album. All in all, a great deal was achieved in those few weeks in the Big Apple, after which the band headed back to Los Angeles.

O n their return, their life-style began to change. Robby and John rented a house on Lookout Mountain Drive in Laurel Canyon, thus escaping from the clutches of their parents and Jim moved also moved to Laurel Canyon with his long-suffering girlfriend, Pamela Courson.

Jim had been seeing Pam regularly for over a year and they grew close. However, Jim's idea of 'moving in' was clearly far removed from Pam's own. She desperately wanted a secure, stable, 'normal' relationship with her man which was the one thing that Jim was totally incapable of giving her. He loved her but life was too exciting for him to commit himself and living together consisted of Jim appearing at the house once or twice a week, sometimes not at all. They certainly had a lot in common, a love of drugs for one. Mirandi Babitz, a friend of Pam's who lived at the house for a while, said in the Morrison biography by James Riordan and Jerry Prochnicky, 'Break On Through': "They had some really wild times. They both really liked macabre things...spiders and black magic, things like that. They used to scare each other. They'd play chicken. If someone got too freaked out then they would go over to UCLA and get a B12 shot or whatever it was they were giving people to bring them down. It was pretty regular that Pam would get too freaked out. She'd scare him and he'd scare her back too much. He'd do things like turn off all the lights and creep around outside or pretend he'd been stabbed. They were always seeking that kind of thrill. But they did very dangerous things too. Like putting the car on the railroad tracks or driving with their eyes closed down Mulholland at night while on acid.

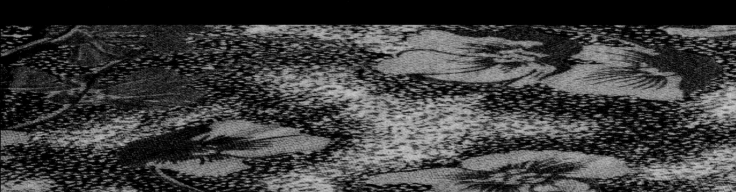

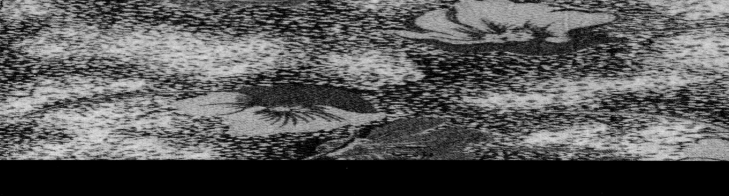

It was a little tense being around them sometimes. We were game for a lot of things, but they were a little bit gamer."

Certainly, Pam was willing to give Jim as good as she got. She was hurt by his constant philandering but responded by being unfaithful herself. Whilst Jim was in New York she had been unable to contact him at his hotel, although she had tried calling him over a period of several days. Pam was many things but stupid wasn't one of them and she knew Jim would be taking full advantage of all New York had to offer. In

revenge, she began an affair with a young actor named Tom Baker and took pleasure in revealing the details in full on Jim's return. However, it was Pam's tolerance of Jim's irresponsibility and his need to take care of her that would keep them gravitating back to each other until the end.

During December, Elektra were gearing up for the release of what was going to be the most stunning debut albums in the

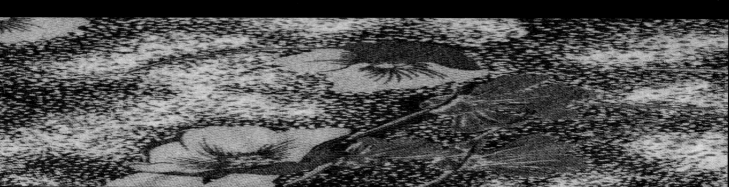

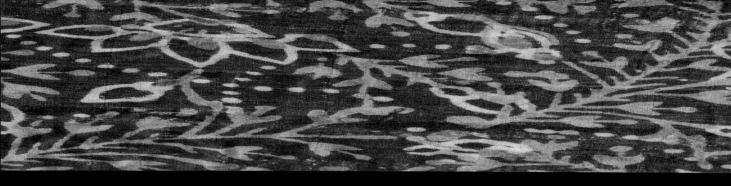

history of rock. The billboard went up on Sunset Strip heralding the album with the words "The Doors Break On Through With An Electrifying Album" as well as a sleeve shot of the album. The press releases were ready and the promotional photographs had been chosen, highlighting Jim's image as a cruel cool,sexual, rock 'n' roll rebel. Elektra's promotional machine began to grind into action and, in the first week of January 1967 the single 'Break On Through' and the album entitled 'The Doors' were both released. The album included the tracks: 'Break On Through', 'Soul Kitchen', 'The Crystal Ship', 'Twentieth-Century Fox', 'Alabama Song', 'Light My Fire', 'Back Door Man', 'I Looked At You', 'End Of The Night', 'Take It As It Comes' and 'The End'.

The critics loved it. They loved The Doors. The intellectual press viewed 'The End' as the tour de force and the album in its entirety as totally different from anything they had heard before, presenting a far darker side to the summer of love than the good vibrations of The Beach Boys, whilst the teen press thought the pretty lead singer was manna from heaven. Ray told British journalist John Tobler later: " The first album was an existential album. It's four incredibly hungry young men, striving and dying to make it, desperately wanting to get a record, a good record, out to the American public and wanting the public to like the record. I think any artist wants the public to like his act, or his record; I think that any artist creates from a driving inner need, but there's this outer need that's very important too, and that's acceptance by some people, somewhere, somehow...someone saying to you, 'I like the work you've created.' That's what being an artist is. So 'The Doors' was that incredible, existential first time - 'Here they are, first time out, fresh, brand new and hungry as hell!'"

Paul Williams wrote in Crawdaddy: "'The Doors' is an album of magnitude. Thanks to the calm surefootedness of the group, the producer, the record company, there are no flaws; The Doors have been delivered to the public full-grown (by current standards) and are still growing (standards change). Gestation may have been long and painful; no one cares. The birth of the group is in this album, and it's as good as anything in rock. The awesome fact about The Doors is that they will improve."

New York magazine's Richard Goldstein wrote: "Their initial album, on Elektra, is a cogent, tense, and powerful excursion. I

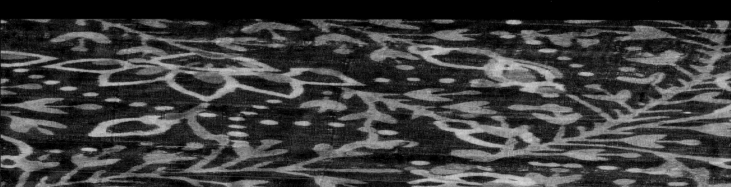

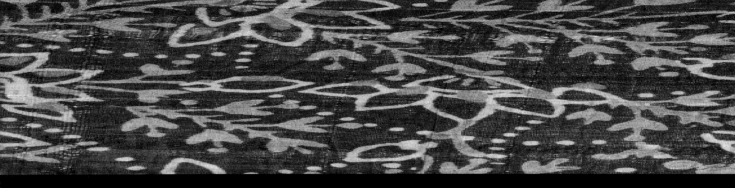

suggest you buy it, slip it on your phonograph, and travel on the vehicle of your choice.  The Doors are slickly, smoothly dissonant.  With the schism between folk and rock long since healed, they can leap from pop to poetry without the fear of violating some mysterious sense of form.  But this freedom to stretch and shatter boundaries makes pretension as much a part of the new scene as mediocrity was the scourge of the old. It takes a special kind of genius to bridge the gaps in form.

"Their music works because its blues roots are always visible. The Doors are never far from the musical humus of America - rural, gut simplicity.

"The Doors are a major event for Los Angeles.  Their emergence indicates that the city of Formica fantasy is building a music without neon, that glows anyway."

The Doors set off to promote the album and their first port of call was a gig at Bill Graham's premier venue, the Fillmore Auditorium in San Francisco.  They were booked to appear third on the bill to the Young Rascals and the Sopwith Camel from whom they stole the show with a spellbinding performance.  They did the same thing to the Grateful Dead  when they returned to the venue three weeks later. Their following was growing so rapidly in San Francisco that in mid-March, they played their first headlining gig at the Avalon Ballroom.  Before this, however, they played a benefit concert for KPFK-FM and worked for a week at a club called Gazzarri's on Sunset Strip.  Francine Grace reviewed one gigs at the club for the Los Angeles Times: "The Doors weld a rock 'n' roll beat with continuous jazz improvisation to produce an intense, highly emotional sound.  They call their music 'primitive and personal' and find it hard to work without audience reaction. Their numbers change constantly at live shows and new ones are written as they perform...Numbers start with the unhurried loud wail of an electric organ, joined by a low, groaning electric guitar and backed up by a steady drum.  The words build with the music into an accelerating crescendo of frenzied sound.

"Trying to avoid the 'hard straight sound' of many rock groups, The Doors aim for 'dramatic impact' in their music.  Gazzarri's crowded dance floor proves that The Doors' lyrical freedom hasn't hurt their strong rock 'n' roll dance tempo."

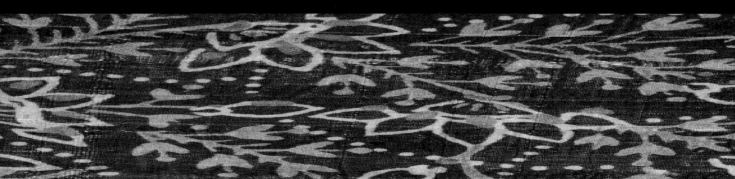

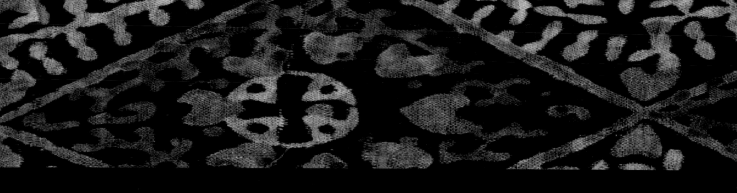

These various appearances helped push 'Break On Through' into the bottom end of the Los Angeles Top Ten but the single failed to break into the national charts. The album, however, was faring much better and entered the Billboard 100 in March after another week at Ondine. Richard Goldstein, this time writing for The Village Voice, was impressed with what he saw: "A typical East Side opening - with this difference. The Doors are a vital new group, with a major album and a sound that grips. Would they make it live?

"The four musicians mounted their instruments. The organist lit a stick of incense. Vocalist and writer Jim Morrison closed his eyes to all that Arnel elegance and The Doors opened up. Morrison twitched and pouted and a cluster of girls gathered to watch every nuance in his lips. Humiliating your audience is an old game in rock 'n' roll, but Morrison pitches spastic love with a raging insolence you can't ignore. His material - almost all original -is literate, concise and terrifying. The Doors have a habit of improvising, so a song about being strange which I heard for the first time at Ondine may be a completely different composition by now. Whatever the words, you will discern a deep streak of violent - sometimes Oedipal - sexuality. And since sex is what hard rock is all about, The Doors are a stunning success.

"You should brave all the go-go gymnastics, bring a select circle of friends for a buffer, and make it up to Onedine to find out what the literature of pop is all about. The Doors are mean; and their skin is green."

Journalist Richard Goldstein was one of the earliest supporters of the band, having caught them playing at Gazzarri's during a visit to the West Coast. He was stunned by what he witnessed and called Jim a "street punk gone to heaven and reincarnated as a choir boy." As one of the most important rock critics in America, Richard heavily influenced the music scene and critical acceptance by the media followed hot on the heels of his rave reviews. The Doors had emerged from the underground to become a top main-stream attraction and they could do no wrong.

The biographies which were circulated to the press proved to cause as much interest as their album. Each band member wrote his own biography so as well as providing personal details such as date of birth and favourite singing groups,

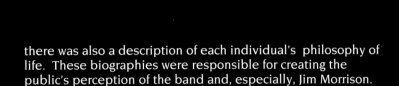

there was also a description of each individual's philosophy of life. These biographies were responsible for creating the public's perception of the band and, especially, Jim Morrison.

Robby wrote: "...In The Doors we have both musicians and poets, and both know of each other's art, so we can effect a synthesis. In the case of Tim Buckley or Dylan you have one man's ideas. Most groups today aren't groups. In a true group all the members create the arrangements among themselves." His ambition, he stated, was to produce.

John's was more succinct. "I've been playing for six years. I don't really have too much to say about all of this....I used to play sessions in Compton and Topanga Canyon. Since last year it's been rock 'n' roll and these creeps." Although John had little to say at the time, in 1990 he wrote his own story of life with The Doors. In the work, entitled 'Riders On The Storm' he had this to say whilst reflecting on these first biographies: "You (Jim) had to say you were especially interested in activity that seemed to have no meaning. Frankly, I thought your brain was full of 'disorder and chaos!' after we signed the contract. It was the beginning of the erosion of my sanity. My ticket to manhood, to the world, was being shredded as I tried to cash it in. You - or what you stood for - fucked with my head. I wanted to believe that 'All You Need Is Love.' You forced me to confront the dark side of the world. I wanted to remain a child, I suppose. You wanted me - all of us - to see the things that haunted you..."

Ray wrote: "I think The Doors is a representative American group. America is a melting pot and so are we. Our influences spring from a myriad of sources which we have amalgamated, blending divergent styles into our own thing. We're like the country itself. America must seem to be a ridiculous hodgepodge to an outsider. It's like The Doors. We come from different areas, different musical areas. We're put together with a lot of sweat, a lot of fighting. All of the things people say about America can be said about The Doors. All of us have the freedom to explore and improvise within a framework. Jim is an improviser with words."

Jim's was altogether more profound: "You could say it's an accident that I was ideally suited for the work I am doing. It's the feeling of a bowstring being pulled back for twenty-two years and suddenly being let go. I am primarily an American,

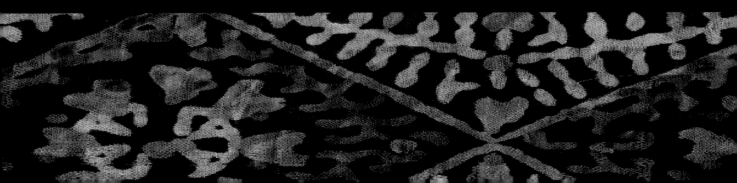

PRESENTED BY
KACY AND
JIM SALZER
DOORS
AUG. 5
SAT. 8 P.M.
LIGHT SHOW BY THE FAMILY CAT
$2.50 IN ADVANCE
$3.00 AT DOOR
LAVENDER HILL MOB
JOINT EFFORT
EARL WARREN SHOWGROUNDS SANTA

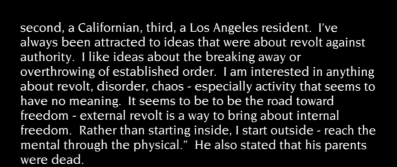

second, a Californian, third, a Los Angeles resident. I've always been attracted to ideas that were about revolt against authority. I like ideas about the breaking away or overthrowing of established order. I am interested in anything about revolt, disorder, chaos - especially activity that seems to have no meaning. It seems to be to be the road toward freedom - external revolt is a way to bring about internal freedom. Rather than starting inside, I start outside - reach the mental through the physical." He also stated that his parents were dead.

The band returned to the studio. Radio stations were giving 'Light My Fire' a great deal of airplay and it was widely regarded that it was an ideal choice as the second single. However, there were problems in that it was nearly seven minutes long and an average single lasted less than three minutes. There were various options and all were carefully considered. It could be released in two parts, a shorter version could be recorded, the original album track could be edited down to the required format or they could release the single unedited, as Dylan had with the six-minute 'Like A Rolling Stone'. Jim was all for the last option but Jac Holzman saw it as commercial suicide, knowing that radio stations would rarely play a single that long.

After much discussion, the band agreed to try to record a shorter version of the song. With this in mind, they and Paul Rothchild went back to the studio. All attempts to re-record the song failed dismally and finally, Paul produced the editing block and cut a large section of the instrumental break. The shortened version was released as a single in April and The Doors continued with their round of promotional gigs. They played at Ciro's, a rock club on the Sunset Strip which had recently spawned The Byrds and a week later played to ten thousand, their first large audience, supporting Jefferson Airplane at a high school stadium in San Fernando Valley. The audience had primarily come to see The Doors and, after they had performed, over a third of the audience left the stadium.

Little by little, Jim was gaining confidence in his stage performance and had began to experiment with his technique. Instead of clinging on to the microphone for dear life with his eyes closed exuding a sense of menacing debilitation, he tried whirling around the stage like a dervish, jumping in the air, writhing on the floor and generally whipping up a storm. The

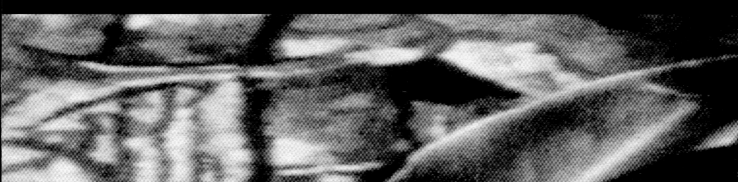

audience loved it and Jim was delighted at their reaction, fascinated by the control he was beginning to exercise over the crowd. His indulgence in stage theatrics grew and along with the writhing and contorting, he would often execute an 'accidental' fall into the audience to wild screams from the girls in the front rows.

'Light My Fire' had entered and was rapidly climbing the national charts and The Doors made their first headlining appearance at the Fillmore in San Francisco, supported by the Jim Kweskin Jug Band. They then flew to New York for a successful three-week residency at The Scene and the atmosphere was described in Hullabaloo: "The Doors were in New York for the third time for some concerts and a three-week gig at Steve Paul's The Scene. It was not quite the same as their two previous trips to New York. Last fall, when they were playing here for the first time, they were virtually unknown except to the innermost circles of hippies and groupies. Early in the spring, when they returned, their album had been released and was a big underground item - big enough to keep it in the national charts around number 100 and big enough to keep the club in which they were playing chock-full of the in-crowd every night.

"But now we were in the midst of a Doors boom. Their album and single were number one on the West Coast, and the week prior to their arrival in New York, both had jumped about thirty points (which is very fantastic) on the national charts. In three weeks they would be Top Ten, album and single, and no new group since The Monkees had seen their first album go Top Ten. We were transporting, in our limousine from Newark, daisies and superstars - and we all knew it.

"Even while they were here, the phenomenon was growing even bigger. Everyone came to see them and I arrived at The Scene one night to find Jim Morrison and Paul Newman talking about the title song for a movie which Newman was planning to produce. And when I called the directors of the Central Park Music Festival to arrange passes for The Doors to the Paul Butterfield concert, I was told to have them enter the theatre one at a time or they would be in danger of being rushed. Which I told them - but they came in together and were rushed and loved it. If they had stayed another week, they would have needed bodyguards. Their exit was well-timed; the day after they left, we had a request to use The Doors in a singing

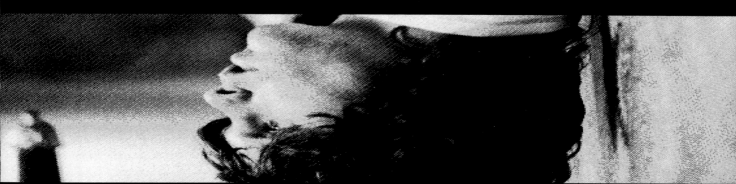

deodorant commercial, and I think everyone was relieved not to have to make a decision about that offer.

"The Doors played their last set at The Scene on a Saturday night. At 3.00am, when all of the paying customers had left, Steve Paul locked us all in and gave a party for his boys, who had been the biggest draw in the history of the club. And on his part, Steve had been a good and groovy employer; I remember John asking Jim why he (Jim) would get to The Scene so well in advance of the time they had to perform, and Jim answering, 'Well, I like to hang around Steve Paul and listen to him rap. He's funny.' Anyhow, there was a case of champagne for the closing night party, and it didn't matter that it wasn't quite chilled because everyone was happy, sloppy and tired and it was a beautiful party. Robby did his imitation of a shrimp, and Jim found something lying on the floor which looked like a balloon but wasn't, so he blew it up and let go, whereupon it landed in Ingrid Superstar's champagne glass, which made Jim laugh, and everyone loved each other without an uptightness. It would be good if everything The Doors ever have to do ends so nicely."

Following the success of their three-week stint at The Scene, The Doors played two other dates, supporting Simon and Garfunkel at Forest Hills in New York and headlining at a high school auditorium in Greenwich, Connecticut. At the Simon and Garfunkel gig, Jim encountered his first hostile audience for a long time. They were there to see the duo and were unimpressed by The Doors' theatrics. Jim gave it his all but they remained unmoved and this upset him a great deal. Jerry Hopkins and Danny Sugerman claimed he told a member of Elektra's staff afterwards: "They opened the curtains and there I was and they laughed. Those fuckers hated me. And I hated them. I wanted to kill them. I never hated anybody so much before. The rest of the show I couldn't get off, I hated them so much."

His anger was short-lived. In July 'Light My Fire' reached number one in the national charts and the album climbed the charts, finally peaking at number two and only being held off the number one slot by The Beatles' 'Sgt. Pepper's Lonely Hearts Club Band.' In any event, 'The Doors' was to spend the next two years in the charts and selling well over a million albums.

The Doors were now big business and, in accordance with popular belief, they decided to surround themselves with a professional team. Up until now, the band themselves had handled their own business and bookings, ably assisted by Robby's father, but the whole job was becoming too much for them. They were not short of offers of management but finally settled on Sal Bonafide and Asher Dann. The pair had recently formed a new partnership from the proceeds of Dann's prospering real estate company and had already taken on two artists for management, an East Coast band called Dion and a female middle-of-the-road singer named Lainie Kazan. Their first task after taking on The Doors was to find them a booking agency and publicist. Todd Schiffman took care of their bookings and quickly negotiated them a higer concert price. Publicity was handled by top public relations firm Rogers, Cowan and Brenner under the personal supervision of Mike Gershman, head of the newly opened rock division. This team complimented the work being done by the staff at Elektra and their lawyer, Max Fink.

With both their album and single riding high in the Billboard charts, The Doors confidently returned to Sunset Sound studios to record their second album. Again produced by Paul Rothchild and engineered by Bruce Botnick, the album was significantly entitled 'Strange Days'. Perhaps not quite as stark and raw as their first album, 'Strange Days' was just as erotic, as death-obsessed and twice as eerie. Because they now had some experience in the studio they had time to experiment with their sound, A session bass player, Doug Lubahn, was drafted in to lay down real bass lines, Jim's vocals were echoed on some tracks, Ray played one song backwards, and electronic special effects were used for the first time. The result was compelling listening. All the tracks were Doors originals with Robby responsible for the lyrics on two of the songs: 'Love Me Two Times' and 'You're Lost Little Girl'.

Whilst the band were still in the studio finishing off the tracks, a single 'People Are Strange' was released and shot immediately into the Billboard Hot Hundred at number 12. A month later the album 'Strange Days' was released. Jim had never liked the cover of the first album and had taken charge of the design for 'Strange Days' and very bizarre it was too. It depicted a photograph of carnival performers - a strong man, acrobats, a juggler and two midgets - and the only reference to the band was on a tiny poster on a wall behind the scene. The

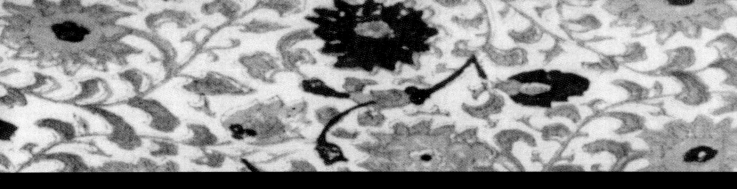

album included the tracks: 'Strange Days', 'You're Lost Little Girl', 'Love Me Two Times', 'Unhappy Girl', 'Horse Latitudes', 'Moonlight Drive', 'People Are Strange', 'My Eyes Have Seen You', 'I Can't See Your Face In My Mind' and 'When The Music's Over'. The album rocketed to the Number 3 position and stayed there for over a year.

Gene Youngblood wrote in the Los Angeles Free Press: "The Doors' new album, 'Strange Days' is a landmark in rock music. It ventures beyond the conventional realm of musical expression: it has become the theatre.

"The Doors' music is the music of outrage. It is not sham. It probes the secrets of truth. It is avant-garde in content if not technique: it speaks of madness that dwells within us all, of the Velvet Underground, of depravity and dreams, but it speaks of them in relatively conventional musical terms. That is its strength and its beauty - a beauty that terrifies.

"The music of The Doors is more surreal than psychedelic, it is more anguish than acid. More than rock, it is ritual - the ritual of psycho-sexual exorcism. The Doors are the warlocks of pop culture. The agonized grunts and screams that fly from Jim Morrison's angelic mouth are indeed as enigmatic as the idea of a butterfly screaming. The Doors are saying there are screams we don't hear, and they're trying to give them shape. Morrison IS an angel; an exterminating angel. He and The Doors are a demonic and beautiful miracle that has risen like a shrieking Phoenix from the burning bush of the new music."

Eric Van Lustbader for Circus magazine felt: "Listening to 'Strange Days' is like watching Fellini's 'Satyricon'. Morrison's words are so cinematic that each song begins to perform pictures in the mind. More than any other American songwriter - lyricist, if you will - he has this quality. Like the film, 'Strange Days' builds its storyline (of people desperately to reach each other through the choking haze of drugs and artificial masks) through the images and characters in a series of vignettes. And the whole becomes more and more visible the deeper one gets into the film and/or the album. Because 'Strange Days' has been set up that way."

Many of the reviews of 'Strange Days' were even more abstract than these two, if that's possible. Richard Goldstein was more down-to-earth, writing in The Village Voice: "The Doors have

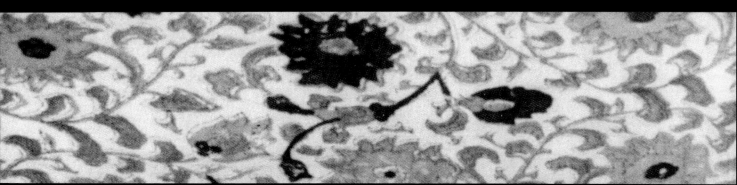

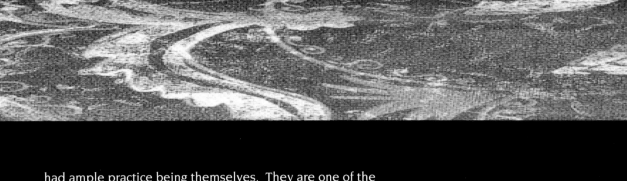

had ample practice being themselves. They are one of the
most oft-appearing groups in pop music and this constant
attention to live effect has produced a crackling confidence in
each other's style which shows on their new album 'Strange
Days' (Elektra). The music is as tight, as controlled, as
satisfying of its own aims as any I have heard in hard rock.
Robby Krieger's guitar slides and slithers around Jim
Morrison's voice like a belly dancer. Ray Manzarek's rock
organ continues to speak in an impressive array of languages
(this album should enlarge the coterie of young musicians now
applying a driving-yet-cool approach). Paul Rothchild's
production is tastefully cut and tapered, and the album's
jacket (let us offer thanks) is not in art nouveau."

The album completed, The Doors embarked on another
tour of America. Jim had considered his image and
bought a tight black leather suit which perfectly
complimented his lithe, muscular body. His dark, wavy hair
was now long but well-shaped, cascading down to his
shoulders and his face had lost all evidence of pudginess with
well-defined cheekbones and large dark eyes. He looked
every inch a superstar.

Jim's new image took to the stage at the Anaheim Convention
Centre  in Southern California and the nine thousand strong
audience went wild, striking matches when the band started
playing 'Light My Fire'. Jim returned the compliment by
throwing lighted cigarettes into the audience. They then
travelled to the other side of the country for a week of dates in
Philadelphia, Boston and New Hampshire before they
returned to Los Angeles to headline at a two thousand
capacity auditorium in Los Angeles called The Cheetah. This
time THEY were supported by the mighty Jefferson Airplane.

Around this time, the press began reporting that Jim's
extraordinary ability to totally capture an audience was a
talent not quite of this world. There were references to Jim's
obsession with shamanism and speculation that Jim was
possessed by a shaman when on stage. Jim, needless to say,
encouraged this theory whole-heartedly. Certainly, his
performances were stunning, blending rock with drama to
create a new theatrical form. Ray was in agreement with the
shaman theory: "The man onstage was an absolute genius, a
human theatricon; from one performance to the next, you
never knew what he was going to be. Sometimes a devil,

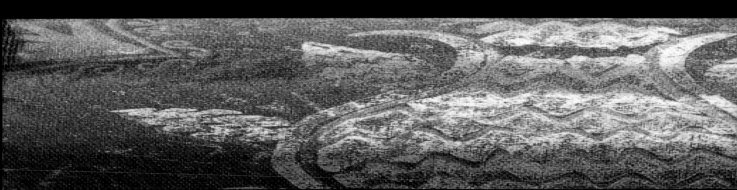

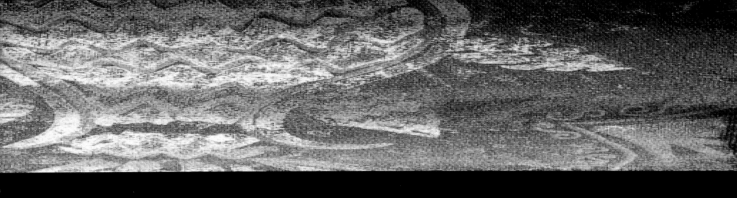

sometimes a saint. Sometimes an angel, sometimes a demon from hell, the Banshee himself. I've never seen a performer like Jim - it was as if it wasn't Jim performing, but a shaman. Traditionally, a shaman was a man of the tribe who would go on a voyage in his mind, who would let his astral body project out into space and, in a sense, heal the tribe and find things that were needed for the safety of the tribe, for the continuance of the species. So, in a modern sense, Jim was exactly the same thing. Jim always said, 'We may never do this again, so let's do it for real, right here and now on this stage, because if we don't do it now, we may never have the opportunity again. The future is uncertain, the end if always near and if we don't do it now...if we don't get in touch with the gods, with out own feelings, our own spirituality, then we've lost this golden opportunity, this moment in reality that will never come again.' Jim was always very aware of the fact that each moment was precious, a jewel, a drop in time, and it's all we had. We had the present - we didn't have the future - and when The Doors stepped on stage, all there was the present. This holy moment; four guys on stage, an audience out there and the energy flowing back and forth between them in what became, in a sense, a communion. My energy had been totally spent, and I felt cleansed of any evil and darkness. We walked out of a concert feeling absolutely in touch with the universe, and that, if any, was the message of Jim Morrison: 'Get in touch with yourself. When you do that, you'll be in touch with God, you become gods.' Jim's message was that every man is a god - all you have to do is realise it."

**W**hilst the audience were receiving this 'communion' there were many who saw Jim's unpredictability not so much as a religious experience but more as a safety hazard. Bill Graham, who would later become the biggest promoter of rock in the world told Bam magazine: "I was in the back of the Fillmore watching The Doors when Jim started swinging the microphone like a lasso, making the swirl larger and larger each time he swung it around. It started with three or four yards of cord, but it kept getting bigger until eventually the swirl went beyond the edge of the stage and over the front of the crowd. I was afraid he was going to hit somebody with the damn thing, so I started to work my way through the crowd, pushing my way to the front. I thought that if Jim saw me he'd stop. Well, when I got about fifteen or twenty feet from the stage, the microphone did eventually hit someone. There were a couple of thousand people there that night, and I

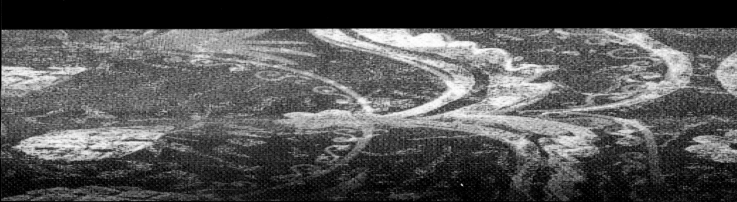

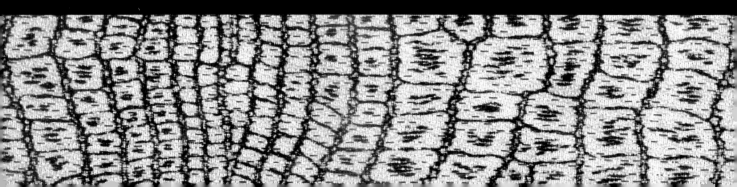

always thought one of the miracles in rock 'n' roll that I went through was that it was my head that it hit. It really conked me pretty hard. So after the set I went upstairs and said to Jim 'Thank God it was me who got hit. We could've had quite a lawsuit over that one.' Jim apologized profusely. He seemed genuinely sorry. A couple of months later when The Doors came back to San Francisco, the group presented me with this big gift box. I opened it up and inside was a construction helmet on which they'd painted 'The Morrison Special.'"

The Doors were, by this time, big business and Elektra and the band's own publicist, Mike Gershman, mounted a media campaign of epic proportions. The media adored Jim with his talk of rebellion, freedom and art. He always provided them with good copy with his revolutionary and menacing, yet erudite quotes and artistic temperament. His beautiful face adorned the covers of magazines as diverse as Time, Vogue, The Village Voice, 16 Magazine and TeenSet. Jim's, whose image was rapidly becoming larger than life, was being hailed as a messiah who would lead the American youth and the Establishment began to worry for the safety of the nation, especially after The Doors put in an appearance on America's finest - The Ed Sullivan Show.

The Doors had been invited on to the show to perform 'Light My Fire'. In their dressing room before the live show went on air, Bob Precht, the show's director and the son-in-law of Ed Sullivan, explained that CBS had a problem with the word 'higher' and requested that they replace it with another line. The band were expecting this request. Elektra had edited the word 'high' on their first album and Bob Dylan had been heavily censored on this very show. They agreed. They also agreed between themselves that they would substitute the word in rehearsal but reinstate it when they were on air live as a way of rebelling against the false moral values imposed by the Establishment. They went on and performed 'People Are Strange' and then launched into 'Light My Fire'.

When Jim sang the line live in front of ten million viewers, emphasising the forbidden word, all hell broke loose in the control room culminating in Bob Precht promising that they would never, ever appear on the show again. The band smiled to themselves, having achieved what they perceived as a 'fait accompli' in their war against convention. However, it was just the beginning.

It was during this time that Jim was at his most prolific as far as interviews were concerned. He was asked about everything from politics to religion and from freedom to sex. He had an articulate and enticing answer to any question put to him. When asked by Lizze James if he saw himself as a saviour who would free the masses he replied: "It's absurd. How can I set free anyone who doesn't have the guts to stand up alone and declare his own freedom? I think it's a lie - people claim they want to be free - everybody insists that freedom is what they want the most, the most sacred and precious thing a man can possess. But that's bullshit! People are terrified to be set free - they hold on to their chains. They try to fight anyone who tries to break those chains. It's their security...How can they expect me or anyone to set them free if they don't really want to be free."

When the same journalist asked Jim to define "freedom" he responded by saying: "There are different kinds of freedom - there's a lot of misunderstanding...The most important kind of freedom is to be what you really are. You trade in your reality for a role. You trade in your senses for an act. You give up your ability to feel, and in exchange, but on a mask. There's can't be any large scale revolution until there's a personal revolution, on an individual level. It's got to happen inside first...You can take away a man's political freedom and you won't hurt him - unless you take away his freedom to feel. That can destroy him."

In an interview with Newsweek, Jim stated: "There are things that you know about and things you don't, the known and the unknown, and in between are the doors - that's us."

He also said: "I think there's a whole region of images and feelings inside us that rarely are given an outlet in daily life. And when they do come out, they can take perverse forms. It's the dark side. Everyone, when he sees it, recognises the same thing in himself. It's a recognition of forces that rarely see the light of day."

November 1967 was an endless round of press receptions and interviews. On one occasion to celebrate the success of 'Light My Fire' at the exclusive Delmonico's restaurant on Park Avenue, all the important editors and radio programmers on the East Coast, as well the likes of as Andy Warhol, had turned out to pay homage to the band. A liberal assortment of groupies were also present and Jim opted to spend the evening getting extremely drunk and throwing ice-cubes at the girls instead of impressing the VIP's with his witty repartee. The mythology which had, by now, begun to surround him, courtesy of the media, cast him as a heavy drinker and he did little to play down the role. He stated in an interview: "I love drinking but I can't see drinking just milk or water or Coca-cola. It just ruins it for me. Getting drunk, you're in complete control up to a point." Unfortunately, on this occasion he had passed that point as he had begun to do with increasing frequency.

An Elektra executive, Danny Fields, could see that Jim was getting out of control and suggested that the bar should be closed before Jim went too far. Jim, however, never appreciated being told what to do by anyone, especially where his drinking was concerned, and reacted strongly by smashing bottles of champagne open by throwing them against a table. Vintage bottles of wine followed and Jim's actions were accompanied by cheers of encouragement from fellow drinkers. The nights' antics were capped off by an uninvited visit to Elektra supremo Jac Holzman's luxury apartment where he hung on the buzzer, ripped up the hallway carpet and threw up in the lobby.

Also in November, a second single 'Love Me Two Times' was released. Taken from the album 'Strange Days' and written by Robby with reference to America's boys going to Vietnam and the band going on the road, it peaked at Number 25 giving The Doors their third successive Top Thirty single. Both their albums had gone Top Five with 'Light My Fire' and 'The Doors' achieving gold status within days of each other. For these achievements to have occurred during a period of only one year was impressive indeed. It was a shame that the events that followed would supersede the band's enviable commercial success.

On December 9th, 1967, the day after Jim's twenty-fourth birthday, The Doors were due to appear in New Haven Connecticut. They had previously made history at a gig at Long Beach in California by playing two shows for which they received fifty percent of the gate, earning $10,000 and holding the record for the most money earnt by a band in one night to that date. They then crossed the country to play Troy in New York on December 8th. Jim had missed his plane and arrived

92

at the gig late and in a particularly black mood. His mood was not lightened by the response of the audience which was one of indifference. This was the one reaction that Jim could not understand nor tolerate and he left the gig depressed and angry. He demanded to travel the 150 miles back to New York City alone and by limousine, refusing to take the plane with the rest of the band.

The next day in New Haven, Jim's mood seemed to have lightened and he spent the time after the soundcheck and before the gig chatting to a pretty student from nearby Southern Connecticut University. The backstage area was buzzing with road crew who were checking the gear and sound system and thirty minutes before The Doors were due onstage, Jim decided to find somewhere quieter to hold his 'conversation' and found a deserted shower room backstage. Within minutes, Jim and the girl were locked in an intimate embrace. For a rock star to indulge in casual sex before a show is not an unusual event but the police on duty were taking their job of clearing the area of unnecessary personnel very seriously due to the feeling of tension amongst the large capacity audience. Jim's impromptu party was interrupted when a policeman who was checking the shower rooms discovered them and demanded they leave the area, not realising he was addressing the star of the show.

The tension in the audience was mounting and the cop was nervous. Jim refused to move despite repeated warnings and eventually put his hand on his own crotch and invited the cop to "Eat it!" This was all too much for the policeman who responded by spraying Jim directly in the eyes with mace.

Jim staggered out of the shower room and into the hallway temporarily blinded, his eyes stinging and streaming with tears, he began screaming, "I've been maced! The fucking pig!" His shouts attracted the attention of The Doors' tour manager, Bill Siddons, who angrily told the officer of his mistake. The cop apologised and helped Bill bathe Jim's eyes with water to get rid of the worst of the mace. Jim emerged from the wash-basin extremely angry with red swollen eyes which were still watering badly. Extraordinarily, the cop still wanted to arrest Jim and it took all Bill Siddons' powers of persuasion to get the police present to agree to allow Jim onstage, only relenting when Siddons pointed out what might happen if the two thousand-strong audience were deprived of

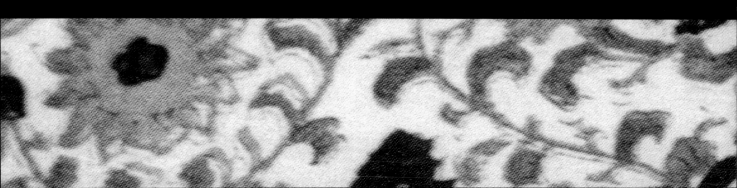

their hero.  Minutes later Jim and The Doors walked onstage to a tumultuous reception and the show began.  John Densmore wrote in his book 'Riders On The Storm': "When Morrison came onstage, I could sense that something confrontational was going to happen.  His eyes were red and he looked mad."

Jim's performance that night was more aggressive than usual.  He writhed and contorted on the floor, threw his microphone stand into the audience and danced his shaman's dance, stirring up the New Haven crowd.  The front of the stage was lined with police facing the crowd, positioned to protect the band should the audience try to rush the stage.  Police also watched, unseen by the audience, from the wings.  The last number of the show was 'Back Door Man' and during the instrumental break in the song Jim began recounting the evenings' events to the crowd, all in perfect time to John's hypnotic rhythm.  He spoke in an exaggerated Southern drawl: "I want to tell you about something that happened a few minutes ago right here in New Haven.  This is New Haven, isn't it?  New Haven, Connecticut, United States of America?"

The audience grew quiet and still as they listened to his story.  After listing the evening's events he said: "And we wanted some privacy and so we went to this shower room.  We weren't doing anything you know.  Just standing there and talking.  And then this little man in a little blue suit and a little blue cap and he said 'Whatcha doin' there?'  Jim was gripping onto the microphone stand hard and raised his voice still further despite the fact that most of the police at the front of the stage had turned around and were staring him in disbelief.  He continued with his rap : "Nothin'.  But he didn't go away, he stood there and then he reached 'round behind him and he bought out this little black can of somethin'.  Looked like shaving cream.  And then he...sprayed it in my eyes.  I was blinded for about thirty minutes..."  All the police were now watching him closely, just waiting for the chance to pounce.  Jim's voice was now screaming: "The whole world hates me!  The whole fucking world hates me!" and with that he crashed back into the chorus of 'Back Door Man' as quickly as he had deviated from it.

After about thirty seconds, the house lights were turned on and police swarmed onto the stage, coming from the sides and from behind the back curtain.  Jim merely thrust the microphone into the face of one of the cops and said: "Say

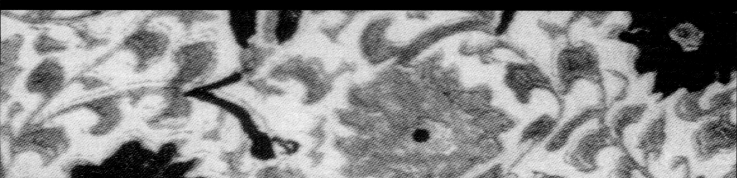

your thing man!" The atmosphere within the auditorium was
becoming hysterical and violent. The crowd couldn't believe
what was happening and began to chant "To the police station!
To the police station! To the police station!". Although there
was obviously a risk that they might incite a riot, the police
dragged Jim bodily off stage and into an awaiting squad car,
placing him under arrest at the same time.

The crowd was now angry and many climbed on to the
stage, where the road crew did their best to protect The
Doors' equipment. Police clashed with fans in the
auditorium and amongst those arrested were two reporters
and a photographer from Life magazine who had recently
returned from Vietnam and who had managed to get shots of
Jim being beaten up in the car park.

Jim spent the rest of the evening in a police cell at the police
station in Court Street, finally being released at 2 am the next
morning on  bail of $1500 which Siddons paid out of the
receipts from the show. He was charged with "breach of the
peace, resisting arrest and indecent and immoral exhibition."
The others arrested were released a few hours later and
backed Jim all the way running features asking questions such
as "How does a truth seeker breach peace?" and Jim emerged
from the unpleasant incident an innocent victim of police
brutality.

Later in December the band members each received a royalty
cheque for $50,000 - their percentage from the sales of 'The
Doors' album. Ray felt he now had real financial security and
decided it was time to make an honest woman of his long-time
girlfriend Dorothy Fujikawa and they were married at the Los
Angeles City Hall. Jim was best man and Pamela their
bridesmaid.

The Doors worked for the remainder of the year. The played
The Shrine, a club in Los Angeles on 22nd and 23rd December,
Winterland in San Francisco on 26th, 27th and 28th December
with Chuck Berry and rounded off 1967 in Denver, Colorado,
ably supported by Allman Joy (later to become the Allman
Brothers). All the dates passed without any further incidents
and as the band saw in the New Year, their album 'Strange
Days' still occupied the Number 3 position in the national
album charts. The Doors were popular, successful and things
couldn't be better but, instead of finding happiness in his

newly acquired fame and fortune, JIm experienced a gnawing doubt which made him question his own worth.

Despite the fact that money was flooding in even faster than their string of hits, Jim was living in a seedy motel a short stroll away from his favourite hangout, the Sunset Strip. One reason for this was that his driving licence had been confiscated due to drunkenness and he found it easier to stagger back to the nearby motel after a nights' heavy drinking. Another reason was that Jim never showed any real interest in material things or putting down roots. This was probably down to his military background when the family never remained in any one place for any length of time. He had got used to travelling light and as long as he had a place to crash after a drunken binge, he didn't worry too much about the ambience.

The motel was often the scene of heated discussions between himself and girlfriend Pamela Courson. Many was the time she would arrive to ask him to come home and find one or more young nubiles in his room and a violent row would ensue. However, despite the frequency of Jim's indiscretion, he could normally sweet-talk her round, often giving her small gifts as tokens of his affection. Pam would calm down until she discovered the present she received was given to Jim by a girl who had frequented his motel room and the row would start again. Their relationship was certainly stormy, but Pam would, more often than not, stand up to Jim and he respected this in her. Of all the girls who passed through Jim's life, Pam was the only one with whom he had more than a temporary affection. There was a true bond between them and he called her his 'cosmic mate', a term he would use for Pam alone.

In early January 1968, The Doors went into Sunset Sound Studios to record their third album. The studio had installed a new sixteen-track desk which was considered state-of-the-art for the time but this new equipment did nothing to inspire the band who were badly lacking new material due to the immense amount of touring and promotion they had undertaken during the previous year. They'd simply had no time to prepare new songs. The initial idea was to try to write the album whilst in the studio, a popular concept which usually proves costly and rarely works.

Jim was under the most pressure to come up with new material and responded by drinking even more heavily than

usual and inviting his drinking buddies into the studio.
Producer Paul Rothchild explained later: "Jim was really not
interested. He wanted to do other things like write. Being
lead singer of The Doors was really not his idea of a good time
now. It became very difficult to get him involved with the
record."

The band decided to devote one side of the album to Jim's
epic recitation, 'Celebration Of The Lizard' a composition not
unlike 'The End' and one that had been recorded on the
band's first demo in 1966. They had one other number, an
anti-Vietnam protest entitled 'The Unknown Soldier', which
was Jim's most political song to date, Paul pushed them hard,
ever mindful of the escalating budget, but, at the same time,
he was a perfectionist and made the musicians re-record until
he had a perfect take. The band felt completely wrung dry,
they had given all they had to give and more. In addition,
they were up against Jim's uncooperative attitude. One night
John felt he could take no more: "The recording became
absurd," John wrote later. " The crowd Jim began hanging out
with made me want to puke. At least Tom Baker, the star of
one of Warhol's films, was talented once...But those other two
creeps, Freddie-the-male-groupie-leech and the blond guy
with the Charles Manson vibes, were the worst. Freddie, who
seemed high all the time, played half-assed piano....I couldn't
see how Ray and Robby could turn the other cheek. I knew
Robby could feel Jim's pain, but he was too shy to do anything.
I knew he liked the success and didn't like confrontations. I
wished Ray would, or could, have stopped the madness. He
was the one who put the group together."

In a fit of frustration, John threw his drumsticks across the
studio, announced his was quitting and stormed out. He
was back for the next day's session but it was apparent that
something would have to be done about Jim's drinking or the
album would never be completed. At Paul's suggestion,
Robby, Ray and John contacted Bobby Neuwirth, Bob Dylan's
ex-minder, in an effort to save Jim from himself. Bobby had a
reputation for being able to out-drink, out-talk and outwit
anybody and was allegedly Dylan's inspiration for 'Like A
Rolling Stone'. He certainly seemed perfect for the post of
baby-sitter. The problem was creating a cover for Neuwirth so
Jim would not be aware that he was being baby-sat.
Eventually, he was engaged under the pretence of making a
documentary on the band but, in reality, his instructions were

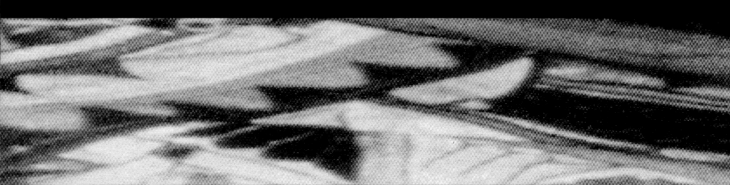

to get as close as he could to Jim. There was little doubt that Jim was fully aware of what was going on from day one but he played along anyway. Jim had already met Bobby in New York and the pair got on well but Bobby soon reported that there was no way on earth that he could stop Jim drinking. The best he could offer was to drink with him and try to keep him out of too much trouble.

On top of all their problems, the band decided that this was the time to change their management, a move they had been discussing for months. Dann and Bonafide had always insisted that Jim would do better by going it alone, as a solo artist. They saw the rest of the band as an expensive indulgence who could be replaced effectively with salaried session musicians and urged Jim to consider their advice. Jim didn't consider it for one moment but did relay the suggestion to the other band members. The Doors approached Elektra for an advance to enable them to buy out their management contract and Jac Holzman readily agreed, having never really rated the pair as managers.

Their replacement was Bill Siddons, The Doors' tour manager. He wrote later: "It was absolutely stupid to hire me. I had no idea what I was doing. They, on the other hand, were controlling their own destiny. They had discovered early in their career that a lot of people had a very different set of motives than theirs."

Also at this time, the band decided to open their own office from which they could manage their affairs more effectively. They moved into an ex-antique shop at 8512 Santa Monica Boulevard which had a large room downstairs in which they could rehearse. There was ample space on the first floor for Bill to have an office of his own as well as work spaces for assistants and secretaries who were hired to lighten Bill's load.

With the dead wood cut out and their new house in order, the band went back to work on the album, the sessions for which were proving ever more troublesome. Jim was late for sessions, often not bothering to turn up at all, leaving the band and Rothchild wondering if they would ever complete the task. By March, two tracks were finally finished including 'The Unknown Soldier' but their initial plan to include 'The Celebration Of The Lizard' had to be scrapped because, try as they might, the song just didn't work. It was disjointed because, according to Jim: "It was pieced together on different occasions rather than having any generative core from which it grew. It doesn't work because it wasn't created spontaneously."

One other potential track of Jim's had also been rejected. Entitled 'Orange County Suite', the song was about Pam but, despite having worked hard on it several times, Robby, Ray and John felt it just wasn't right for the album. As a result, they were still very short of material and, in desperation, they rifled through the few remaining songs from Jim's early Venice rooftop period. The remainder were written and arranged in the studio, without the benefit of being performed live to see if they worked and, as a result, many of the tracks, with the exception of 'Hello' I Love You' seemed to lack energy and direction.

Meanwhile, the public wanted a single and 'The Unknown Soldier' was duly released and accompanied by a promotional film that featured Jim being shot by firing squad whilst the other band members looked on. The anti-war nature of the song and the controversial images of Jim as a martyr in the film prevented the single from getting any real airplay and it barely reached the Top Forty. Jim was disappointed and became increasingly disillusioned by the image that The Doors were now projecting. He retreated into himself - and into a bottle - and turned to writing poetry.

Eventually the album entitled 'Waiting For The Sun' was completed in May and included the tracks: 'Hello, I love You', 'Love Street', 'Not To Touch The Earth', 'Summer's Almost Gone', 'Wintertime Love', 'The Unknown Soldier', 'Spanish Caravan', 'My Wild Love', 'We Could Be So Good Together', 'Yes The River Knows, and 'Five To One'.

Meanwhile, the band had some dates to fulfil and set off on the road again, no doubt delighted to be out of the studio. The problems that manifested themselves in the studio seemed to vanish when Jim was able to take his frustration out onstage. At Bill Graham's newly opened Fillmore East, in New York, The Doors received rave reviews.

Kris Weintraub wrote in Crawdaddy: "Robby and Ray threw notes back and forth across the stage tuning up and John bashed around a little so we wouldn't forget he was there. This went on until everyone was crazy from excitement - then they started the introduction to 'When The Music's Over.' I couldn't believe they'd start with that. How do you follow it? But they did. They went on playing this endless introduction until everyone was leaning out of their seats in anticipation...Then a shadow came out of the wings. A beautiful phantom in a sloppy pea jacket, floppy light brown leather cowboy hat, hair down to here, and these impossibly tight leather pants...There was instant applause and cheering. He stepped to the microphone, grabbed the top with his right hand and the stand with his left fingertips, and looked up so the light hit his face. The world began at that moment....There were a few times when he scared me to death. He grabbed the mike in both hands and screamed and shook until everyone was sure he was being electrocuted. Purely for effect. And even though he tries to hold it back - once in a while he breaks into a smile that is so beautiful you want to hug him."

It was during these shows that the band included a full-length version of 'The Celebration Of The Lizard'. The atmosphere created by this opus was so great that it became apparent why it could never work on vinyl. It was drama at its most intense and, in performing it, Jim was at his best. The gigs finished with the screening of the promotional film for 'The Unknown Soldier' and rock critic Michael Horowitz reported: "When the film played at the Fillmore East, a young audience brimming with anti-war frustration broke into Pandemonium. 'The war is over!' cried teeny-boppers in the aisles. 'The Doors ended the fucking war!' The Doors' little passion play had grabbed the audience. Jimmy and the boys had done it again."

Although onstage Jim was at his best, offstage was another matter altogether. Elektra executive Danny Fields described a memorable night when Jim attended a Jimi Hendrix gig at the Scene in Riodan and Prochnicky's biography 'Break On Through':"Jim was very drunk. Hendrix was jamming and I noticed some commotion up front and there was Jim crawling on the floor toward the stage. He wrapped his arms around Hendrix's knees and started screaming 'I wanna suck your cock,' He was very loud and Hendrix was still attempting to play. But Morrison wouldn't let go. It was a tasteless exhibition of scene stealing - something Morrison was really into. To top it off, Janis Joplin, who had been sitting in the back of the room, suddenly appeared at the edge of the stage with a bottle in one hand and her drink in the other. She stepped in and hit Jim over the head with the bottle - then she poured drink over him. That started the three of them grabbing and rolling all over the floor in a writhing heap of hysteria. Naturally, it ended up with the three of them being carried out. Morrison was the most seriously hurt. His body guards were summoned and he was driven away. I'd heard that earlier in the evening Jim had knocked a tableful of drinks into Janis's lap." Nice story, Danny.

Jim's drinking had now reached epic proportions. Everyone around him knew that he was an alcoholic; that he was incapable of quenching the fire that burned within him no matter how much alcohol he consumed. The rest of the band were worried, they could see only too clearly where Jim's self-destructive streak was going to lead - all the way over to the other side. Whilst they found it hard to witness the demise of their friend and partner, they also felt a deep dislike for this man who had everything but was willing throw away all they had worked for. Their pleas to stop drinking fell on deaf ears. Paul Rothchild told journalist Vic Garbarini: "Stop him? Everybody tried to stop him! You couldn't...strangers would stop him on the street and try to help him. We all tried to stop him. We even hired professionals to stop him. If you'd known Jim for even ten seconds, you'd know one thing: He was unstoppable. He was his own motive force, an astounding human being. There was no stopping him. Not even the woman he loved most could stop him, even for a moment."

107

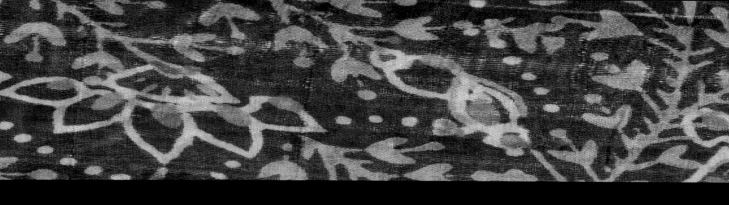

The tour rolled on but Jim's disillusion with stardom and life in general began to show even onstage. He had been getting so drunk that his performances were suffering. He had also started despising his audience and would frequently spit into the crowd to show his contempt. On May 10th, The Doors were playing Chicago. He had felt for some time that he could lead his fans anywhere and chose this date to put the theory to the test. He walked onstage in front of a capacity audience fifteen thousand strong and signalled the band to start with 'The Unknown Soldier' the song which now had become virtually an anthem for anti-war protesters. During the rest of the set he gave the fans everything they wanted - using every stagecraft technique that he knew down to unbuttoning his shirt and throwing it into the audience. He set them alight.

After two encores the band left the stage and Bill Siddons announced that they had left the building. The atmosphere in the auditorium was electric, they crowd had been taken higher than they ever had been before and they wanted more. They began chanting and finally erupted and charged the stage. One teenager decided to practising swan diving from the balcony onto the concrete floor below. The crowd began doing battle with the police who were unsuccessfully trying to hold the stage and kids were kicked and clubbed. The police finally managed to gain control of the situation and, miraculously, nobody was seriously hurt.

Jim denied in an interview that he had deliberately incited a riot: "I just try to give them a good time. They rush on stage because the cops are there and that's a challenge. It's like a game. The kids try to get past the cops and the cops try to stop them...If there were no cops there, would anybody try to get onstage? Think of the free concerts in the parks. No action, no reaction. No stimulus, no response. You see cops with their guns and uniforms and the cop is setting himself up like the toughest man on the block and everyone's curious what would happen if you challenged him. I think it's a good thing, because it gives the kids a chance to test authority. It's never gotten out of control, actually. It's pretty playful really. We have fun, the kids have fun, the cops have fun. It's kind of a weird triangle. Sometimes I'll work people up a little bit, but usually we're out there trying to make good music and that's it. Each time it's different. There are varying degrees of fever in the auditorium waiting for you - this rush of energy potential. There are no rules at a rock concert. Anything is possible.

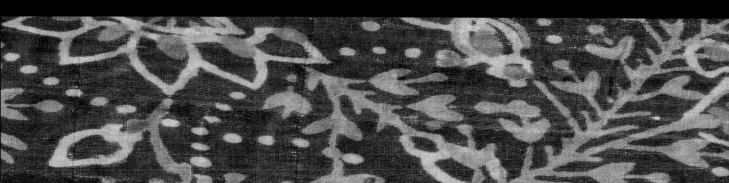

Let's just say I was testing the bounds of reality - I was curious to see what would happen.  Just push the situation as far as it'll go."  Despite this explanation, there were many who found Jim's lack of sensitivity towards his fans just plain reckless and irresponsible.

*"Hello I Love You"*
*- the films*
*master tape.*
Photo: Rainer Moddemann

In early June, amid the rigours of touring, The Doors released a second single from their third album entitled 'Hello, I Love You'.  There was great importance placed on the success of the single due to the comparative commercial failure of 'The Unknown Soldier'.  Nobody need have worried.  The single was an instant hit, storming up the charts to the Number 1 slot and providing the band with their first UK hit although many of the critics felt it was a blatant sellout due to its simple lyrics and trite melody.

The ravages of Jim's steady diet of alcohol were beginning to show.  His eyes were red-rimmed and listless and he had allowed his hair to grow greasy and unkempt.  His face was starting to become bloated, a beer gut was developing and he began to wear his shirts outside his trousers in an effort to conceal it.  It was in this state and shortly after the release of 'Hello, I Love You' that he walked into The Doors' offices in West Hollywood and calmly announced he was quitting the

band. It was apparent to both Bill Siddons and the other band members that this was not a decision that Jim made lightly. He had obviously considered the move carefully and had decided that being lead singer of The Doors was not what he wanted to do anymore. John, Ray and Robby looked at each other in panic and Ray stepped forward to try to talk Jim out of it. He eventually managed to persuade Jim to give it six months when they would all review the situation. Jim agreed.

Also in July, Jose Feliciano released an acoustic version of 'Light My Fire' which immediately shot to the top of the charts. This along with the success the band had enjoyed with 'Hello, I Love You', a lightweight single to many of the diehard fans, ensured that The Doors crossed over into the mainstream pop market. This development was somewhat of a double-edged sword. The cross-over cemented The Doors' commercial success but, by so doing, it alienated the trendy underground who now felt that were far too accessible and had in some ways 'sold out'.

July also saw the release of their third album, 'Waiting For The Sun' and, although it was met with a certain amount of critical disapproval, it was an instant hit, shooting into the Number I position of the national charts with a bullet. Bought mainly by kids more interested in the image projected by Jim than meaningful lyrics, the album sold over five hundred thousand copies on its first day of release.

113

THE DOORS

elektra

are "waiting for the sun" on Ampex stereo tape

4 TRACK 8 TRACK CARTRIDGE

AMPEX STEREO TAPES
AMPEX CORPORATION
2201 Lunt Ave. Elk Grove Village, Illinois 60007

The DOORS' latest album "Waiting For the Sun" featuring their latest hot smash hit "HELLO, I LOVE YOU"

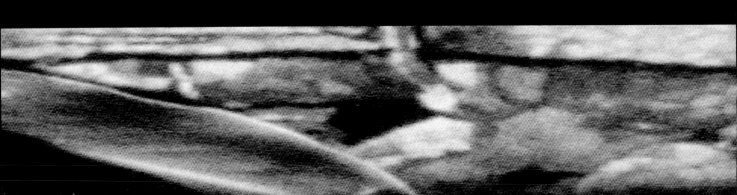

The album itself had an overall feel of fragmentation. It was easy to spot which were the songs from an earlier era and which were the 'fillers'. However, Pete Johnson, rock critic for The Philadelphia Inquirer seemed not to notice and wrote: "The new album from The Doors, 'Waiting From The Sun' is that difficult third LP which seems to thwart a number of contemporary pop groups. The Doors have succeeded. Their first two LPs, 'The Doors' and 'Strange Days', were quite similar both in structure and in mood. Each contained an eleven-minute fantasy number and some shorter songs whose fabric was trimmed from nightmarish visions and sexual images. Both were more grotesque than pretty. Both also were powerful enough to establish The Doors as the hottest group in the United States. 'Waiting For The Sun' contains the fewest snakes, the least ugliness, the lowest number of freaks and monsters, and the smallest amount of self-indulgent mysticism of the trio of Doors' LPs. They have traded terror for beauty and the success of the swap is a tribute to their talent and originality."

Trading "terror for beauty" wasn't quite what the band had in mind when they recorded the album but the weak tracks were more than compensated for by the classic 'Hello, I love You', the inspired 'So Good Together' and the menacing 'Unknown Soldier'. The dramatic 'Five To One' was very much an anti-establishment anthem and thinly disguised drug song which proved to be one of the strongest songs of the album and was very well executed and Robby's flamenco-inspired acoustic guitar on 'Spanish Caravan' emphasised the talent they had acquired for arrangement.

However, the lack of reptiles worried Tim Boxell who wrote in the Minneapolis Daily: "The Doors' latest album, 'Waiting For The Sun' wasn't half what it would have been if the original plan to include Jim Morrison's 'Celebration Of The Lizard' had succeeded." However, reptile lovers weren't totally left out and the text of the poem was reproduced on the inside sleeve of a very poppy cover, designed in bright bubble-gum pink. Jim explained his obsession with reptiles thus: "The lizard and the snake are equated with the subconscious force of evil. There's something deep in human memory that responds strongly to snakes. Even if you've never seen one. A snake seems to embody everything that we fear. 'The Celebration Of The Lizard' is an invitation to dark forces." Jim rapidly realised that this statement was at risk of being misunderstood and

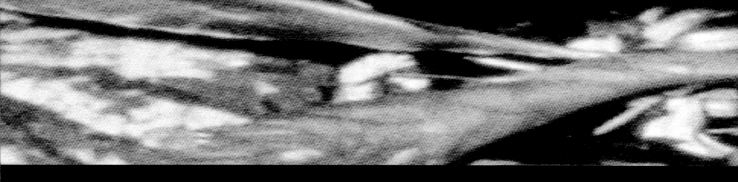

later insisted that "It's all done tongue-in-cheek...it's not to be taken seriously."

**B**ob Shayne, writing for the LA Free Press was extremely disappointed with the album and wrote a scathing review : "This album is unbelievably bad....'Waiting For The Sun' contains three new versions of 'Break On Through', which go by the euphemisms 'Not To Touch The Earth', 'Unknown Soldier' and 'We Could Be So Good Together.'  It contains 'Hello, I Love You', which was better when The Kinks did it as another song...It contains absolutely the worst lyrics I have ever heard

A *billboard* in L.A. - 1990
Photo: Rainer Moddemann

in my life in 'Spanish Caravan'.  The set has none of the vitality, originality, enigmatic quality, believable passion or musicality of the first two Doors LPs.  Worst of all, I hear The Doors actually like this album.  Perhaps they had better do something drastic to get their talents and tastes back into gear. I haven't given up on The Doors.  I anxiously await their fourth album...but the spell isn't working this time."

The success of the album went some way to belittle the opinions of the critics and it made The Doors undoubtedly the biggest band in America and, immediately after its release, they went back on the road to promote it.  This time they were playing to vast audiences in large capacity arenas and sports stadiums.  First stop was the Hollywood Bowl and it seemed

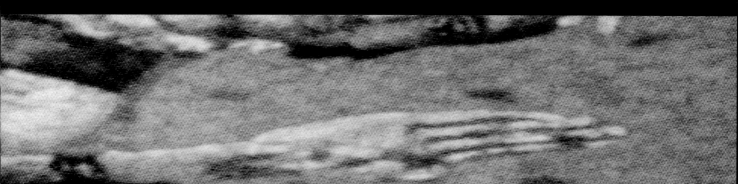

that by upgrading to these vast auditoriums, something of
their drama was lost.  The effect that Jim had on 5,000 serious
fans was stunning but it seemed to be diluted when
performing in front of fifteen thousand screaming teenagers.
Also lost was the spontaneity and improvisation which served
The Doors so well.  Harvey Perr reviewed the Hollywood Bowl
gig for the LA Free Press: "The Doors' concert at the Hollywood
Bowl could have (and should have) been great theatre.  There

*An original Doors*
*promotional lighter*
*for the release of*
*"Live at the*
*Hollywood Bowl"*
Photo: Rainer
Moddemann

was Jim Morrison,
moving with
animal grace,
exuding his own
peculiar
sexuality,
obviously in a
good mood and
ready to give his
audience
everything they
wanted and possibly more...And then the sense of
unpredictability and spontaneity, so important to the success
of such an evening was missing...What The Doors apparently
felt their audience wanted was exactly what they didn't want.  I
think they wanted temperament, the tension that snaps when
an artist has a healthy antagonism toward the natural elements
in the atmosphere.  When the lights didn't go down at one
moment, they didn't want Morrison to stay cool and go on
singing.  At the core, they wanted him to walk off the stage.
And if he didn't come back, they might have screamed for
refunds but they would have understood and they would have
been satisfied...It was a good show and nothing more.  The
mystique had turned mundane.  Perhaps the Bowl itself is to
blame.  It's a forbidding place, forcing us to keep our distance
from whatever is happening on the stage.  Even The Orchestra
could get lost up there.  But at the heart of the matter, the
evening failed not only as Theatre but it failed, as well as a
rock concert."

Undaunted, the band continued around America.  It was
obvious that Jim was finding performing in these venues
a tedious business.  The tension he exuded on stage
wasn't reaching the audience any more and his performance
became increasingly filled with blatantly choreographed
moves.  He felt restricted by the rigid song list and it showed.

117

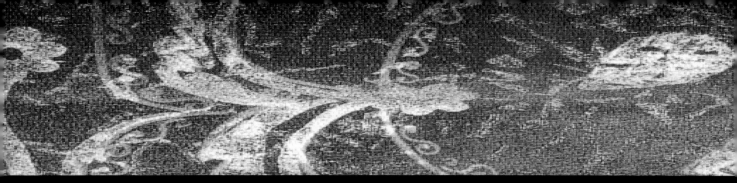

The climax of the tour was to be a massive gig at New York's Singer Bowl on August 2nd where The Doors were to share double billing with The Who. During this latest bout of gigs, The Doors had employed two former UCLA friends of both Ray and Jim, Paul Ferrera and Frank Lisciandro, to produce a full-length documentary of the band. They, in turn, hired 'Babe' Hill as additional cameraman and all three accompanied the band to New York with the intention of filming the gig for inclusion in the hitherto untitled documentary. The arena was located in Flushing Meadows Park in Queens and was left over from the old New York World's fair and the event was a sellout.

The evening began as it meant to go on. The limousine transporting the band to the gig was rushed by hysterical fans as it neared the backstage entrance. Although the car was surrounded, Jim got out and stood in the midst of his mostly female admirers and the film crew followed, capturing his every move. He made his way slowly through the heaving throng to the backstage area where he was met by an army of photographers and members of the press. The ten thousand capacity crowd already in the grounds were tense and ready to explode. They were also chanting Jim's name.

A band called Kangaroo went on stage first. They were a surprise addition to the evening's entertainment and not one that the audience particularly cared for. By the time The Who took to the stage, the crowd were angry. To make matters worse, The Who played a suprisingly bad set. The revolving stage experienced a mechanical fault and the audience were left with a view of the amplifiers and little else. Even Townshend's legendary guitar bashing didn't go according to plan and he had to batter it against the stage several times before it finally exploded. By the time The Who had come off stage the crowd were mad with frustration. They wanted The Doors and they wanted them now. Jim, however, had other ideas.

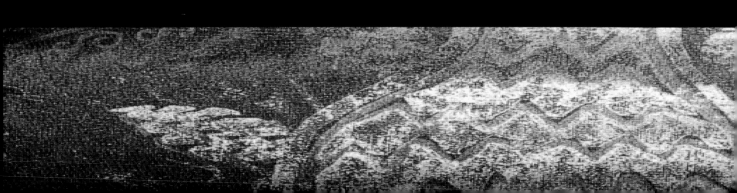

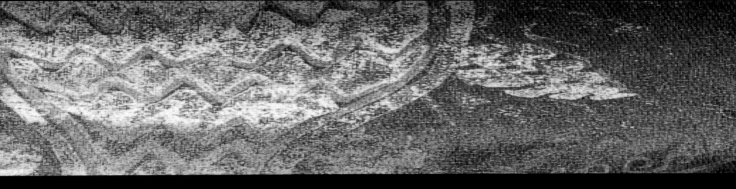

Your ticket
to
THE DOORS ABSOLUTELY LIVE
at
the Felt Forum in New York City
the Aquarius Theater in Los Angeles
the Cobo Arena in Detroit
the Arena in Boston
the Spectrum in Philadelphia
the Civic Center in Pittsburgh

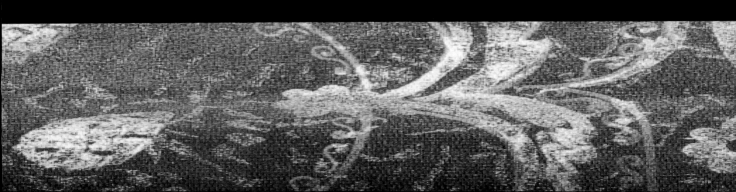

Although he knew the crowd were in a total frenzy, he decided that The Doors should make them wait. An hour passed before Ray, Robby and John sauntered onstage. The police took up their position in front of the stage and the cameramen took up theirs behind it. The lights dimmed and the stage was plunged into darkness. The other three began playing the introduction to 'Back Door Man' while waiting for Jim to come onstage. The crowd roared with anticipation and there was an overwhelming sense of impending violence. Jim took his time.

Eventually Jim walked onstage in the darkness, flanked by heavy duty security. He stood at his microphone, a spotlight flashed on him and the crowd finally exploded. For the next hour, Jim writhed on the floor in simulated pain and ecstasy, jumped in the air and cavorted around the stage. Every time he fell to the floor, the crowd surged forward to get a better view or to simply try and touch him. Every time they moved forwards, the heavy police presence held them back. Jim began his shaman's dance, whipping up the hysterical crowd even further and kids began to climb over each other in a desperate attempt to get closer to the stage. As The Doors wound up their show with 'The End', some of the audience finally broke through the cordon of cops and scrambled onto the stage whilst the remainder clashed with police by throwing hundreds of wooden chairs at them. What followed could only be described as a full-scale riot and The Doors were dragged off the stage to safety by the security staff. By the end of the evening, twenty people had been taken to hospital and two had been arrested.

Next day, the riot in New York made newspaper headlines across the country and The Doors' bad-boy reputation which had been damaged with the release of 'Waiting For The Sun' was suddenly and unequivocally restored.

'Hello, I Love You' had provided The Doors with their first hit in Europe and the band began to prepare for a three week tour, taking in the UK, Holland, Denmark and West Germany.

120

Although they had only had one hit single in the UK, they had quite a healthy underground following due to their promotion by the British rock press and ZigZag magazine in particular. They had gained a reputation as a group with seriously political overtones and Granada Television had requested permission to film their live shows for inclusion in a documentary which was currently in production regarding the political upheavals shaking the USA in 1968. To this effect, they were met at Heathrow Airport not only by hundreds of screaming fans but also by a film unit from Granada.

**M**elody Maker ran advance news of the tour: "Look out England! Jim Morrison is coming to get you! Fresh from being busted by New Haven police for a breach of the peace, giving an indecent and immoral exhibition and resisting arrest, Doors singer Morrison will be in England this autumn for a tour. Exact details are being worked out at the moment.

"Meanwhile, The Doors' new album 'Waiting For The Sun' sold enough copies on its first day to qualify for a golden disk and a single from the album, 'Hello, I Love You' is already at number one in the American chart.

"Like Jagger and the Stones, much of The Doors' image is centred upon twenty-four year-old Morrison, who comes on like a 50s-style rock idol in skin-tight leather pants, but is actually a poet of some stature. Visually he is sufficient to make any writer reach for his stock of adjectives - satanic, fallen angel, dangerous, with curly black hair (recently shortened but still luxuriant by conformist American standards) falling around a painting face like a spoilt Greek statue. His movements have something of Elvis eroticism in them with this difference: his audiences know he isn't kidding. This is no come on. When he sings, 'Come on and light my fire,' his audiences know exactly what he means.

"Sociologists are beginning to think that the sexual revolution of recent years has a wider significance than merely who sleeps with whom. Certainly, in Morrison's completely unambiguous lyrics, it seems to be part of a wider scene where all the comfortable assumptions are challenged. The highbrow critics are comparing a Doors show with the Marat-Sade 'theatre of cruelty,' which it does resemble in a way. But it wouldn't be quite so powerful if it wasn't also just very, very good pop."

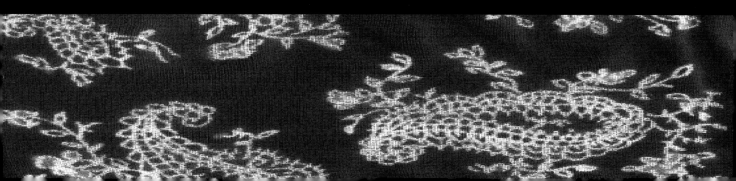

With pre-tour press like this, it was little wonder that all ten thousand tickets for The Doors' four nights at the Roundhouse in London's Chalk Farm were sold out within hours of going on sale and the shows themselves were an unqualified success. Jim's performances were theatrical and dramatic in the extreme and came across well in the intimacy of the Roundhouse. The British audiences were overwhelmed and demanded encores at all the shows and, within four days, The Doors' status in Britain had reached legendary proportions. The Granada crew filmed the band's every move, on and off stage, and the resulting documentary was screened in October entitled 'The Doors Are Open', further enhancing the band's reputation. In one week, The Doors had conquered the British youth. Jim said in an interview with Rave's Mike Grant that the audiences at the Roundhouse "Were one of the best audiences we've ever had. Everyone seems to take it so easy. It's like going back to the roots again and it stimulated us to give a good performance. They were fantastic. That's all I can say. 'Cept that we enjoyed playing at the Roundhouse more than any other date for years."

The Doors proceeded to Copenhagen and Frankfurt, where they were equally well received and it wasn't until they reached Amsterdam that Jim's penchant for excess effected his performance.

In Amsterdam at that time drugs were legal and The Doors and Jefferson Airplane, with whom they shared double billing, spent their first afternoon in the city exploring the famous red-light district which was full of all manner of 'head' shops. It wasn't long before they were surrounded by fans who insisted on making gifts of all manner of drugs, most of which Jim downed on the spot without even bothering to identify exactly what he was taking. This, mixed with a liberal amount of alcohol, both on the plane and through the course of the afternoon started to take effect on Jim during the early evening and, by the time he arrived at the gig, he was well and truly stoned.

Airplane had already taken to the stage and were half way through their set when Jim arrived and, to everybody's dismay, staggered onto the stage and began drunkenly dancing. Airplane's vocalist Marty Balin explained what happened next in Bam magazine: "Jim had his arms over his head and was spinning in circles like a flamenco dancer. I'm singing and he's

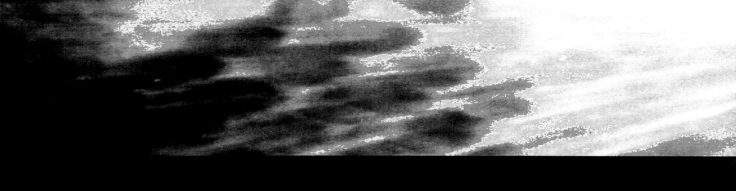

dancing and we were circling each other, wrapping the microphone cord around us. We were tying ourselves up going around and around, and we unravelled at a perfect place in the song. Jim looked at me real funny and then, CRASH! - he dropped to the floor. I finished the song leaning over him. He was totally out. He wasn't moving."

Jim remained unconscious and was rushed to the nearest hospital. Backstage, the three remaining Doors argued about what they should do. Finally, it was agreed that it would be announced that Jim had been taken ill but Robby, John and Ray would go on and play as a trio with Ray providing the vocals. They were so angry with Jim that, rumour has it, they went on and gave the performance of their lives.

Jim was kept in hospital until the following morning, when he woke up feeling fine. However, the mood of the others had not lightened. They were genuinely furious that Jim could have been so stupid and Jim, in turn, was horrified to hear of the outstanding performance they put on without him. He suddenly realised that the band could walk away from him at any time, leaving him more insecure than ever and suffering from a severely bruised ego. However, he was back on form when they played Stockholm a few days later, after which Pam and Jim headed back to London, leaving the rest of the band to fly back to America without him.

Whilst the band were playing other European dates, Pam had stayed in London, renting a luxurious flat in expensive Belgravia. Both she and Jim were fascinated by their first visit to London and avidly explored the city, walking for hours together and buying fashionable clothes in trendy Carnaby Street. Pam had never been happy with Jim's occupation of rock 'n' roll superstar, much preferring him to spend his time writing poems, so she was delighted when they met up with American poet Michael McClure who was in town visiting the exiled movie producer, Elliot Kastner. Jim and Michael got on famously due to Michael's own taste for cold beer and good brandy, and the pair spent many hours locked in deep, drunken conversations.

On one occasion, Michael was at the flat that Jim and Pam were renting and spotted some of Jim's poetry that had been left lying on a table by Pam. Although Jim was initially furious with Pam for leaving them lying around, his anger soon gave way to excitement when Michael told him that he felt the poetry was good enough to be published and wrote down the number of his literary agent. It pleased Jim's battered ego when he realised that this was something he could do that was totally removed from the band and discussed with Michael the benefits of publishing under a pseudonym. Michael agreed and also suggested that Jim should publish his work privately. Needless to say, Jim's first call on his arrival in Los Angeles was to McClure's agent, Mike Hamilburg, who was very enthusiastic about the project and for the first time in a year Jim felt stimulated again.

**W**hilst Jim was in London, another incident had occurred which served to damage relations further between Jim and the rest of the band. An advertising agency had offered The Doors $100,000 for permission to use 'Light My Fire' for a Buick commercial. The agency were on a tight schedule and needed a quick answer to their request. Since Jim couldn't be contacted in London, Bill had to discuss the matter with the other three band members. The song had been written by Robby and, although there was usually a group decision on such matters, on this occasion Bill felt it prudent to allow Robby to decide and they voted for giving Buick the go-ahead. When Jim arrived back a few days later and heard about 'Come on, Buick, light my fire' he went totally berserk, finally contacting Jac Holzman, who still controlled their publishing, to try and block the move. The song was eventually never sold, but Jim felt betrayed that the others would even consider making such a decision without him and the rift that had begun to divide them grew bigger.

Cheri Siddons, wife of Bill, remembered how angry Jim had got in the book 'Feast of Friends': "He was an artist. And I think the angriest he ever was happened when The Doors decided to let Buick use 'Light My Fire'. I just remember this real unhappiness. I think if he ever was going to yell, he would have yelled that day. He didn't yell, but to me it was almost like a light switched off. That was like the last straw somehow. I'm not so sure if he really liked Robby, Ray and John after that. I think he could sense they had different purposes; they were more into the money and the business and would sacrifice some of the art for that. Jim was not willing to sacrifice the art for anything."

At the same time, a problem had developed with the

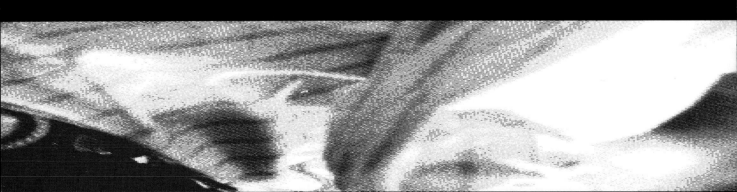

documentary being made by Paul Ferrara and Frank Lisciandro. Although over $30,000 had already been spent, the project was far from finished and it seemed that only Jim thought it worth continuing. Eventually, they decided to drop plans for any further filming and do what they could with the footage which had already been shot. There was a shortfall of around $4000 which was needed to pay for the editing costs. The Doors finally agreed to finance this if both Paul and Frank would handle the editing without salary and make their money by selling the finished film to television. They agreed and went to work, assisted by Jim. The result was a rather shambolic movie portraying The Doors on and off stage called 'The Feast Of Friends' after a line in 'When The Music's Over',

During October, The Doors headed back to the studio to begin rehearsing material for their forthcoming album. They were not going to get 'caught short' as they had been when recording 'Waiting For The Sun'. One day, Bill Siddons visited them there with some disturbing news. The Association of Concert Halls had voted that a rider should accompany all performance contracts issued to The Doors. They had decided that the band were trouble-makers and if the content of their performance was deemed in any way immoral, indecent or illegal the gig would be ended immediately. This posed a problem for the promoters booking the band. Because of the implications of the rider, most of the venues were unenthusiastic about allowing the band to appear and the promoters were having to give personal guarantees that they would accept total liability if the rider was not complied with. Jim, in particular, was upset by what he saw as blatant censorship and it was with some trepidation that they embarked on their next string of dates.

In early November, The Doors played in Milwaukee and Columbus without incident. Jim behaved himself and everybody began to relax. Their relief, however, was premature and during the next eight days Jim plunged the band into a world of violence and riots, the like of which had never been seen before.

On November 7th The Doors were booked to play at the Veterans Coliseum in Phoenix. A vast proportion of the audiences that the band were now attracting were more interested in Jim's unpredictability than The Doors' music and this was particularly so on this occasion. Jim was frustrated at the restrictions being imposed on him and during this show he had decided he would tolerate it no longer. When the band had an equipment problem onstage, Jim filled time by verbally abusing the crowd. He shouted for them to leave their seats and five hundred or so obliged him and rushed the stage, clashing with police in the process.

**N**ext day, the Phoenix Gazette reported: "The show erupted into a war between kids and cops. Lead singer Jim Morrison appeared in shabby clothes and behaved belligerently. The crowd ate up Morrison's antics which included hurling objects from the stage to the audience, cussing and making rude gestures." According to police Captain Bill Foster "Morrison certainly encouraged the problem." and added that if the singer hadn't called for the kids to leave their seats "there would have been no problem like this." There had been well over twenty people arrested for various charges including the use of vulgar language, assault and disturbing the peace.

Similar scenes occurred in Chicago, Cleveland and St. Louis and Jim later reflected on the crowd phenomena in an interview with the Los Angeles Free Press: "The Doors never really had any riots. I did try to create something a few times just because I'd always heard about riots at concerts and I mean I thought we ought to have a riot. Everyone else did. So I tried to stimulate a few little riots, you know, and after a few times I realized it's such a joke. It doesn't lead nowhere. You know what, soon it got to the point where people didn't think it was a successful concert unless everybody jumped up and ran around a bit. I think it would be better to do a concert and just keep all that feeling submerged so that when everybody left they'd take that energy out on the streets and back home with them. Rather than spend it uselessly in a little crowd explosion."

Robby said of the increasing police presence: "It always bothered me to have police hanging around the concerts, waiting to bust us on any word or thing that we did...but we expected it. It was all part of the trip; there were two forces working, one force of change and the other force that wants things to stay the same and not be too far out, and there's always the balance that has to be present there at those situations."

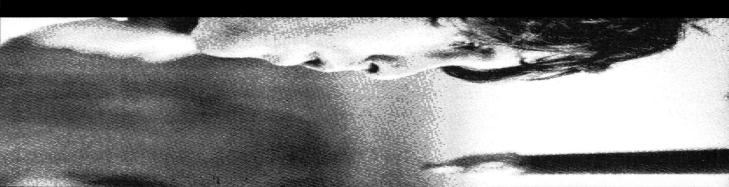

In December, the band began recording their fourth album, stopping only to put in an appearance at the LA Forum in front of an audience of eighteen thousand. The show was opened by a Japanese Koto player whom The Doors' fans found less than rivetting and they booed him accordingly. Jerry Lee Lewis didn't go down much better, insisting on only playing country songs to a rock 'n' roll audience - a move which could only be described as pure folly. Next on was a local rock group called Sweetwater who did the most sensible thing possible by shortening their set in front of the near-rioting crowd and getting offstage as quickly as they could. The crowd wanted The Doors, or more specifically, they wanted Jim to do something outrageous. They had not come to hear music, they had come to see Jim drunk, stoned and belligerent - a clown. They wanted a freak show.

When The Doors finally came onstage, the crowd almost immediately began shouting for 'Light My Fire' and someone threw a handful of lit sparklers onto the stage. Jim walked forward to the edge of the stage and stared solemnly at the crowd who squealed with excitement but they were not going to see the clown that night. Jim was going to make damn sure that he didn't give them what they expected. After a while, he turned and made his way back to his microphone and the band launched into the set. Jim stood stock still throughout 'Touch Me' and 'Wild Child' and then they played 'Light My Fire'. Jim's performance was perfect but there was no jumping, no writhing, no screaming. The audience was here to see the clown and Jim was giving them the poet.

When the song was over, the kids began demanding they played it again and Jim had all he could take. He stared at the audience for a while and then spoke to them, his voice booming through the huge new sound system: "What are you doing here? Why did you come tonight?" The audience went quiet, nobody dared answer. "You want music?" he asked, and then continued "Well, man we can play music all night, but that's not what you really want, is it? You want something else, something more, something greater than you've ever seen before, right?" the crowd's roar of approval was abruptly halted when Jim yelled: "Well, fuck you, we came to play music!" and with that the band launched into a stark beat which accompanied Jim reciting 'Celebration Of The Lizard', all 133 lines of it which took over forty minutes. When it finally ended the band got up and silently walked off the stage. The

audience was stunned. There was no noise, no applause and the fans slowly and quietly left the auditorium feeling cheated.

**M**ichael Lydon of The New York Times, spoke to Jim after the gig: "After the show, Morrison said it had been 'great fun' but the backstage party had a funeral air. And at times that afternoon, he showed he knew their first rush of energy was running out. Success, he said, looking beat in the orange chair, had been nice. 'When we had to carry our own equipment everywhere, we had no time to be creative. Now we can focus our energies more intensely.'
He squirmed a bit. 'The trouble really is now that we don't see each other very much anymore. We're big time, so we go on tours, record and, in our free time, everybody splits off into their own scenes. When we record we have to get all our ideas then, we can't build them night after night like the days in the clubs. In the studio, creation is not so natural. I don't know what will happen. I guess we'll continue like this for a while. Then to get out vitality back, maybe we'll all go to an island by ourselves and start creating again.'"

Elektra released a single from their forthcoming album entitled 'Touch Me.' Written by Robby, it was a surprisingly simple love song featuring a string section, something previously unheard of on a Doors record. The single went straight into the charts finally peaking at Number 3 and staying in the lists for thirteen weeks.

1969 saw The Doors as the singularly biggest American band and, as such, they saw no reason why they should continue to perform in halls with capacities of less than ten thousand and told Bill Graham so when he asked them to return to the Fillmore East in New York for four dates. They wanted to play Madison Square Garden, the most prestigious venue on the East Coast. This move to still bigger venues alienated many of their original fans but The Doors felt that their music should be heard by greater numbers. This theory was probably a mistake as The Doors' music always worked best in a more intimate atmosphere. In the larger venues their drama and theatrics which had so become their trademark, were diluted as Bill Graham pointed out to them in no uncertain and rather acid terms. However, The Doors were the first West Coast band to have even had an opportunity of playing a venue as celebrated as the Garden and they felt it an honour that they couldn't refuse. They left for New York accompanied by a bass

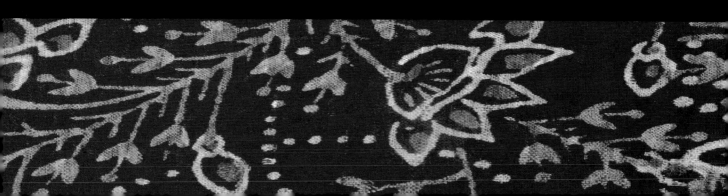

player, a saxophonist and a string section to recreate the sound on their most recent smash hit 'Touch Me'.

The Doors concert at the twenty-thousand capacity Madison Square Garden had sold out over a month in advance and grossed $125,000, making The Doors one of the highest paid acts in the business and when Jim took to the stage on January 24th, he gave the audience a performance that left no one in any doubt why.

He was confident, calm, melodic and even smiling. There was no howling, no writhing and no abuse. Although his physical exertion was kept to a minimum, he struck poses in the crimson lights provided by the sophisticated lighting rig and the crowd went wild with ecstasy. He was in full command and his performance was controlled yet polished. The crowd loved the show but the majority of the critics felt Jim's performance a little too calculated, if not downright jaded. The Village Voice sourly wrote: "Well, the teenies got their show and The Doors and the promoters got lots of money, and money is really all that these monster events, indoor and out, are all about. The Music? Who knows? The sound system in the Garden is abominable, but it mattered a lot more during The Staple Singers' very professional set than when The Doors came on. The Doors originally sounded like one of the freshest, most promising things happening. Now they have released the same album under three different titles and encourage an audience that would be satisfied if they played bubble-gum music as long as up front there was their Jiiimmieeeee."

The Doors' credibility with both the rock press and their original underground audience had waned considerably. The release of the trite 'Touch Me' had done nothing to rectify the situation and the release of a second single from the album, another penned by Robby, entitled: 'Wishful Sinful' strained it even further. The single had no real drive and contained an even heavier string arrangement and only reached Number 44 in the charts, The Doors' worst result to that date. It seemed that the fans were in agreement with the critics and, whilst the rest of the band were beginning to wonder whether the bubble of success had finally burst, Jim was secretly praying that it would. He desperately needed another outlet to satisfy his creative drive or, as he is reported as saying, he would be "good for nothing but nostalgia."

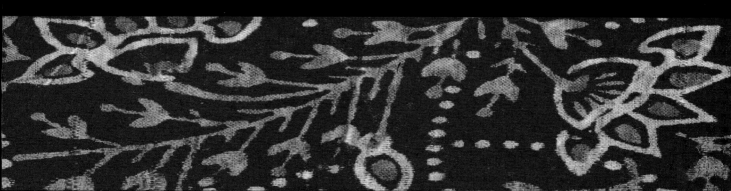

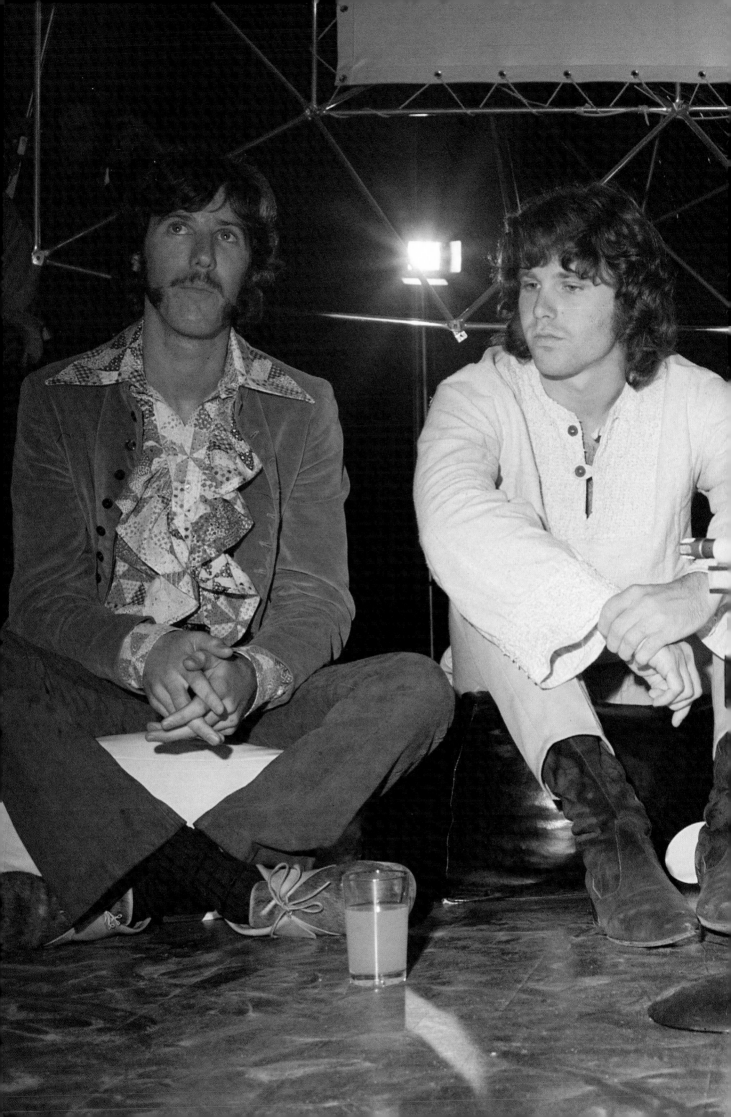

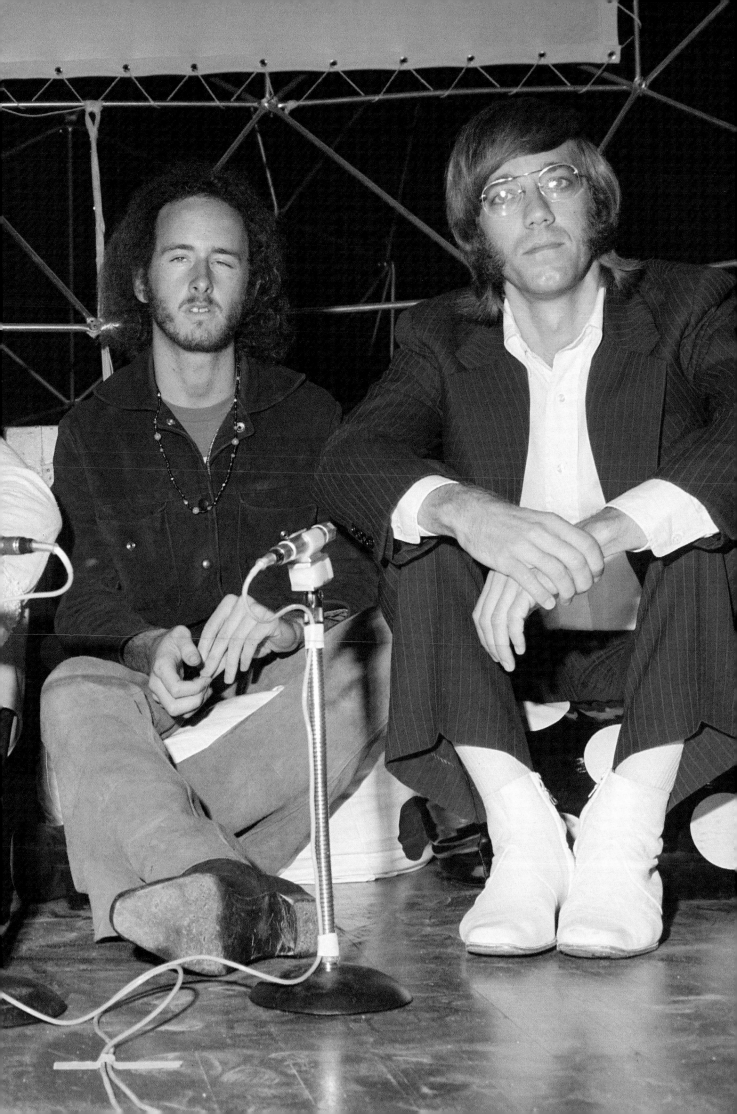

A few months later, everything began coming to a head. The band were now well aware that the sense of inspiration and excitement they had felt back in 1967 was to continue to allude them making it impossible to reaffirm their validity. Jim turned to his poetry which was becoming ever more important to him. Music did not satisfy him any longer and, it seemed, he could not satisfy his fans with it anymore either. The great Doors backlash had begun. The very people who had been quick in spotting and promoting his emerging raw talent two years previously and who were partially responsible for creating the image of the monster which had made him a prisoner of his own device, had turned against him and were busy trying to knock him down. He knew he had to look beyond music to reinstate his ideas and the poetry was his and his alone. Nobody could take it away from him and it provided necessary relief from the boredom and restrictions he felt as Jim Morrison: sex symbol, drunk, rebel, monster.

Something else which Jim felt could help develop his ever diminishing creativity was a troupe of radical performers called the Living Theatre. He had recently read an article which had stated: "they are not really performers but a roving band of Paradise seekers who define Paradise as total liberation, practising hypnology and advocating Paradise now. Their presence and function are in direct opposition to that repressive totalitarian state known as law and order." Jim wanted to find out more and when he heard that they were to perform at the University of Southern California in February 1969, he immediately made reservations for all their shows.

The troupe's techniques were not unlike Jim's own and consisted of dialogue with the audience and getting them to react by shocking them. They would then use the results to comment on political and moral constraints. Jim loved their performances and saw a way that he could extend his own ideas even further.

The show which impressed Jim the most was on Friday, 28th February when The Living Theatre staged 'Paradise Now.' The show started with performers walking through the audience shouting "I'm not allowed to smoke marijuana!", "I'm not allowed to take my clothes off!" and "I'm not allowed to travel without a passport!" This was followed by "I am separated from my fellow man, my boundaries are set arbitrarily by

others!" and "The Gates of Paradise are closed to me!". The barrier between actors and audience began to break down, culminating with everybody hysterically shouting slogans and yelling for Paradise Now. Eventually, as a protest against the culture which "represses love" all the actors and many of the audience removed their clothes until they reached the legal limit when the actors shouted "I am not allowed to take my clothes off! I am outside the Gates of Paradise!"

The confrontative approach was a technique close to Jim's heart and he was fascinated by what he saw. Tom Baker had accompanied Jim to the theatre that night and later wrote about his reaction: "He had a madder than usual look in his eyes, though I knew he was sober. At one point Jim turned to me and said, "Let's start a fire in the balcony or something. Get a riot going."" Jim continued to discuss what he had seen and began to think of ways he could incorporate it into his own show. There was a Doors gig scheduled for the following day at the Dinner Key Auditorium in Miami, perhaps, he enthused, he could start working the techniques into his own show there.

# THE DOORS CLOSE

The concert in Miami the following night was one that nobody would ever forget. The date was the first in what was going to be The Doors first ever real tour. Prior to this, they had always crisscrossed the country, playing a date here and a date there. They had never before slogged continually around the country without a break and this is what they fully intended to do. Because of this, Pam and Jim had made arrangements to have a short vacation in Jamaica after the Miami gig and before the start of the tour proper in eight days time. They had rented a house on the Caribbean island and had even purchased the tickets. Before they set out for the airport to catch the flight to Miami, Pam and Jim had one of their legendary fights. Although they calmed down enough to actually get to the airport, the friction started again and resulted in Pam returning home alone and Jim missing his flight. Jim promptly booked himself on to the next one and drank in the airport bar until it arrived. His drinking continued on the plane and, during a stopover in New Orleans, Jim disembarked from the plane, made for the bar and the plane took off without him. By the time Jim had made arrangements to catch yet another flight and had called the venue in Miami to inform the band he was going to be late, he was well and truly drunk. Jim continued drinking all the way to Miami.

The band were sitting backstage at the gig waiting for Jim. There had been no word since he called from New Orleans to say he was going to be later than expected and they had been due onstage some fifteen minutes earlier. To make matter worse, the promoters had not been on the level and had jammed near to thirteen thousand fans into the auditorium which had been designed to hold a mere

the doors
soft parade
tour

—

BACKSTAGE

# IN THE NAME AND BY THE AUTHORITY OF

## The State of Florida

Claude R. Kirk, Jr. , GOVERNOR OF FLORIDA

ISSUED BY
GOVERNOR
APR 23 1969

To the Executive Authority of the State of California

    Whereas, It appears by the annexed documents, which are hereby certified to be authentic, that James Morrison

stands charged with the crime of Lewd and Lascivious Behavior, Indecent Exposure, Open Profanity, Drunkeness

committed in the State of Florida, and it appearing and I hereby certify that the said James Morrison

(was, were) present in the State of Florida at the time of the commission of said alleged crime, and it appearing that James Morrison

thereafter fled from justice, and (has, have) taken refuge in California

    Therefore I, Claude R. Kirk, Jr., Governor of the State of Florida, have thought proper, and in pursuance of provisions of the Constitution and laws of the United States, to demand the surrender of the said James Morrison as fugitive from justice, and that he be delivered to Lt. Stephen Bertucelli and/or who Sgt. Paul Rosenthal, DS is hereby appointed agent on the part of the State to receive him

    Given Under My Hand, and the Great Seal of the State affixed at the City of Tallahassee, the Capital, this 18th. day of April A. D. 19 sixty-nine and of the Independence of the United States of America the One Hundred and ninety-third Year

seven thousand. There was no air conditioning in the venue and the night was hot and steamy and all those bodies packed in to one small space caused the temperature to rise to a dangerous level. The fans were hot and angry for having to wait for the main attraction, they had not paid seven dollars just to stand around (the promoters had removed the seats in order to make more room) suffocating in this sauna. The atmosphere was tense .

John, Ray and Robby were discussing whether or not to go on without Jim, as they had done in Amsterdam, when the singer finally arrived. Dressed in a black shirt worn outside black leather trousers, he wandered into the dressing room holding a beer bottle. It was obvious to everyone present that he was as drunk as a skunk. Still, they would have to go on. The crowd was getting very rowdy, demanding the band onstage with Miami's hometown boy singing upfront so, without further ado, they headed for the stage and were shocked by what they saw. The whole auditorium was a mass of sweltering bodies jammed so tightly that they were taking their discomfort out on each other in the choking heat. Small fights were breaking out all over as fans pushed and shoved in order to be able to breathe. The other band members walked nervously to their instruments whilst Jim, in his drunken stupor, staggered and tripped, falling onto one of the amplifiers positioned stage right.

Ray signalled to John to begin the intro to 'Break On Through' which they played for over ten minutes while Jim stood on the side of the stage, drinking from a paper cup and chatting to some kids in the audience. Finally, he ambled over to the microphone and began addressing the angry crowd: "I'm not talking about no revolution. And I'm not talking about no demonstration. I'm taking about having a good time. I'm talking about having a good time this summer. Now you all come out to LA. You all get out there." The band began playing 'Back Door Man' and Jim finally began to sing but, after stumbling through only four lines, he stopped and continued talking to the crowd.

"Hey, listen, I'm lonely. I need some love, you all. Come on, I need some good times. I want some love. Love me. I can't take it without no good love. Ain't nobody gonna love my ass? I need ya. There's so many of you out there....how 'bout fifty or sixty of you people come up here and love my ass.

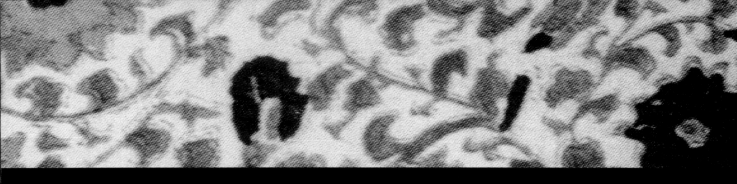

C'mon....Nobody gonna come up here and love me, huh? All right for you baby. That's too bad. I'll get somebody else." Jim paused, giving the rest of the band an opportunity to begin playing 'Five To One' but, instead of singing he just got more belligerent and directed his rage at the audience: "You're all a bunch of fuckin' idiots. You let people tell you what you're gonna do. Let people push you around. You love it, don't ya? Maybe you love gettin' your face shoved in shit...you're all a bunch of slaves." There were gasps of outrage from the stunned crowd as Jim continued with the song.

The band launched into 'Touch Me' and Jim began singing. A few minutes later he began shouting at the audience again: "Hey, wait a minute, wait a minute, this is all fucked up - no wait a minute, wait a minute! You blew it. You blew it." Jim then lapsed into a bout of incoherent mumbling which ended with him screaming: "I'm not gonna take this shit. I'm coming out. I'm coming out!" Jim began to unbuckle the belt on his leather pants shouting: "You didn't come here only for the music did you? You came for something more, didn't you?" You wanta see my cock, don't you? That's what you came for isn't it?" Jim had taken off his shirt and held it down in front of himself, and started dancing around with his shirt covering his groin. Every so often he would pull the shirt away, teasing the crowd.

Ray shouted at one of the road crew, Vince Treanor, to stop him and Vince jumped over John's drum platform and grabbed Jim from behind and stuck his fingers into his belt loops rendering it impossible for Jim to take his trousers down. However, even Vince wasn't entirely sure that Jim hadn't already undone his fly. Jim had obviously meant to remove his trousers as he was sporting a huge pair of boxer shorts which was unusual as Jim rarely wore underwear and it was unknown for him to wear any onstage. Jim finally quit struggling with Vince and the trousers and continued singing.

The tirade of incoherent rambling continued throughout the show as Jim staggered around the stage. He forgot the lyrics, repeated verses and when he did manage to sing a line or two, he was totally out of tune At one point he bent down in front of Robby's crotch and, some later said, simulated fellatio. Whatever he was doing, Robby did a splendid job of ignoring him, concentrating, instead, on playing his guitar. A member

143

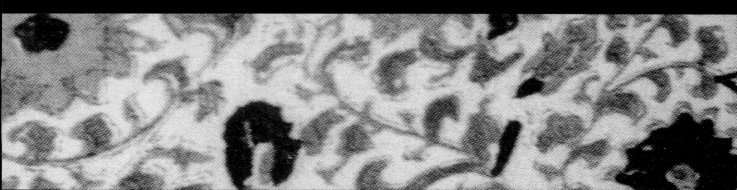

of the audience made his way to the front of the stage and handed Jim a lamb which he carried around on stage for a while. Then Jim grabbed a cop's hat and threw it into the audience a move which the cop in question reciprocated by removing Jim's own and throwing it in the same direction.

All the while, Jim kept encouraging the audience to dance. "I wanna see some dancing, I wanna see some fun," he repeated over and over and continually challenged the crowd to come forward and join him onstage. More than a few fans accepted his invitation and scrambled up to dance with Jim. At this point, the stage began creaking and shaking under the pressure. Finally one of the promoters' security men began throwing the impromptu dancers off the stage as it was clearly in danger of collapsing. As kids were being forcibly removed from the stage, Jim was shouting "We're not leaving here until we get our rocks off!" At that moment, Jim was also grabbed by the security guard and tossed into the audience where he picked himself up and began to lead ten thousand people in a snake dance around the auditorium. Jim appeared briefly in the balcony and then was gone. Minutes later, he strolled into the dressing room, with the sound of cheering still audible from the auditorium. What the concert had lacked musically, it more than compensated for in spectacle. Jim had, once again, given his audience the unexpected.

145

What followed the concert in Miami was somewhat confusing. Whilst the majority of the audience and all those onstage at the time did not witness Jim actually exposing himself - Ray claimed later that it would have been impossible due to the presence of the boxer shorts - it seems that there was a conspiracy afoot and Jim's future would be decided by politicians and police. On the following Sunday, highly worrying press reports began to emerge. The Miami Herald wrote: "Morrison appeared to masturbate in full view of his audience, screamed obscenities, and exposed himself. He also got violent, slugged several Three Image officials, and threw one of them off the stage before he himself was hurled into the crowd. The exhibition went on before the eyes of thirty-one off-duty City of Miami policemen, most of them uniformed. Morrison, as he did in most of his shows, stole the hat of one of the policemen. The officer wandered about onstage during the climax of the show trying to get it back. He was paid for the loss." The journalist who wrote the report then called several local politicians and asked them what they planned to do about the immoral display.

Curiouser and curiouser. Whilst there was no denying that Jim was very drunk indeed and there was certainly no shortage of inflammatory remarks and his behaviour towards the crowd could at best be called abusive, who exactly witnessed this 'exposure'? He undoubtedly meant to take his trousers off which was the reason for the underwear but had been prevented from so doing by Vince Treanor. If he had managed to unzip his fly before Vince's timely intervention and, as the Miami Herald reported, exposed himself, why did the police present not arrest him immediately? Unfortunately, even Jim couldn't shed any light on the matter because he was so drunk he could even remember being in Miami. Robby recounted his version of events in 1978: "We finally went down and started to play, and Jim was in one of his more evil moods that night, I would have to say. He'd just had a fight with his girlfriend that day, which didn't exactly help matters...and what happened was, there was a lot of confusion on stage. We didn't play one of our best sets, I have to admit. I remember starting one of the songs about three times before we finally got into it - but the kids were having a great time, and the cops were having a great time. They were laughing and boogieing around. The allegation is that Jim whipped it out in front of the audience, right? Well, I personally never saw that happen, nor did Ray or John, and out of about the two or three hundred photographs that were taken that night, there's not one shot that shows that happening."

Ray was suitably vague in Creem magazine: "I don't think he ever really did it.....no-one knows for sure. I was five to eight feet away from Jim onstage, and I always have a tendency to put my head down. I'm not concerned with what Jim was doing physically onstage. We didn't have to look at each other - we weren't communicating on that plane...so same thing in Miami. I wasn't really looking. He said to me next day, 'Did I do anything wrong?' And he played along; whether he was putting us on or not, we'll never know, because he looked us right in the eyes and said, 'I don't remember a thing. I had a lot of drinks and I don't even remember getting to Miami.' So who knows?"

The day after the show, Jim and the band travelled to Jamaica as planned, but without Pam. Whilst Jim spent time lazing in the hot Caribbean sun, he was unaware that, in Miami, moves were being made which would ultimately lead to his downfall. With pressure being bought to bear by the press, the Miami

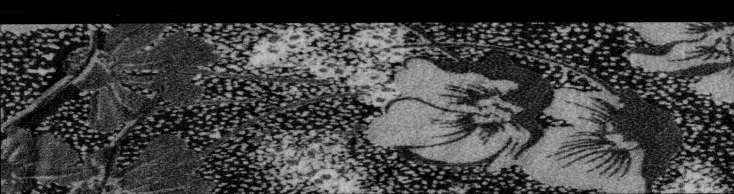

authorities had to be seen to be doing something about the 'incident' which was rapidly being blown out of all proportion. The police stated that when they found a policeman who had witnessed the profanity, they would issue warrants for Jim's arrest. Apparently no such witness could be found as, shortly after making this statement, they began to make pleas in the media for photographs and recordings of the show that might be used in evidence against Jim. The police then covered themselves by stating that to have arrested Jim at the time may have incited a riot.

On Wednesday 5th March a complaint was finally lodged against Jim by Bob Jennings, not surprisingly a clerk in the state attorneys office. It is true to say that the city powers had over-reacted to what could only be described as a chaotic rock concert but now the situation was altogether more serious. The Establishment saw this as their opportunity to get rid of James Douglas Morrison, The Enemy of America, for once and for all and charged him with one felony - lewd and lascivious behaviour - and three misdemeanours - indecent exposure, open profanity and drunkenness for which he could be sentenced to as much as three years in a state penitentiary. They wanted to silence him for good.

The charges became public property within hours and the nation's press had a field day. The morning papers were filled with reports of Jim's wildly exaggerated antics causing public outrage. Some papers even went so far as to suggest that Jim was on the run from the law due to his pre-planned vacation in Jamaica. Even Rolling Stone carried a Western-style 'wanted' poster of him, whilst other papers blasted him for providing the Establishment with the ammunition they needed in their war against rock 'n' roll. Public opinion was running high indeed.

The first Jim heard of the charges was when Bill called him in Jamaica. He was having a lonely time without Pam and decided to return to Los Angeles, not realising the seriousness of the situation. When every city on the forthcoming tour cancelled and radio stations began removing The Doors from their play lists, he realised that it was no laughing matter.

Ray told Musician magazine: "I'm getting some sun, relaxing in the Caribbean, and I get this call. 'Ray, you better get back here, there's big trouble.' Trouble, what do you mean? 'You

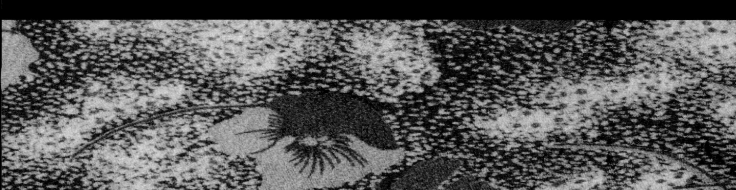

guys are busted.' Busted? I'm sitting on an island in the middle of the Caribbean. How can I be busted? 'Do you know Miami? Well, you're busted.' And the shit hit the fan. It was never the same after that. It was a turning point as far as Jim was concerned. I don't really think it affected his poetic output or his singing, and it didn't affect our actual music. But it did affect us in relationship to public performances. We had a twenty-city tour scheduled after Miami - every city cancelled out. Do not bring those guys into town. We are not going to allow The Doors to perform in a public or municipal facility. So we lost the entire tour."

However sorry the other band members felt for Jim, they all harboured an underlying feeling of resentment. Jim's excesses had brought down their career and had firmly placed them at the centre of a cyclone.

Due to Jim's refusal to go to Miami to answer the charges, in late March the FBI issued a warrant for Jim's arrest, charging him with unlawful flight to avoid prosecution and an agent duly arrived at The Doors' office. Max Fink was immediately consulted and it was on his advice that, on April 4th, Jim turned himself in, He was released on $5000 bail and, shaken by the whole experience, he focused his attention on his poetry and a new film project.

Jim was scared. The Miami incident and the forthcoming trial brought it home to him that he was in deep trouble and could count on few supporters. Certainly, the press, who normally championed his every move, had turned against him and public opinion was not in his favour. He drank to dissipate his anguish and block out his fears but he found little solace in the bottle.

Jim said later of his growing disillusionment leading to the night at Miami: "I think I was just fed up with the image that had been created around me which I sometimes consciously, most of the time unconsciously, co-operated with. It was just too much for me to really stomach and so I just put an end to it in one glorious evening."

Jim told journalist Joyce Haber: "Six guys and girls are naked every night in 'Hair' and nobody calls the cops. My audience expects me to do something freaky. If I'd been in LA or New York, nothing would have happened." Over the next few months, Jim's appearance began to change dramatically. The pronounced boozing caused him to gain a great deal of weight and he cared little for his appearance, letting his beard and hair grow long and rarely bathing. He gave up trying to fit into the leather trousers which were tight even in earlier and thinner days. He now roamed around in baggy pants and shirts, not looking remotely like Jim Morrison the sex-symbol, the image he so desperately wanted to be free of.

He retreated to the house he and Pam rented in the Beachwood Hills area of Hollywood and arranged for two more volumes of poetry to be published. Entitled 'The Lords: Notes On Vision' and 'The New Creatures', one hundred copies of each were initially printed and would later be published in one volume by Simon & Schuster. He also formed his own film production company, HiWay Productions, and he brought in his old friends, Frank Lisciandro, Babe Hill and Paul Ferrara. Using most of the equipment that had been bought when they filmed 'Feast Of Friends', they set about making another movie. This time, the film starred Jim as well as being written, directed and produced by him and death in the desert dominated the plot.

Filming took place in the Californian desert near Palm Springs and the result was a fifty minute cameo shot on 35mm film. A bearded Jim is portrayed wandering in the mountains, swimming in waterfalls whilst bathed by moonlight. He tries to hitchhike to Los Angeles and the story essentially traces his journey. Jim later said of the film: "It's more poetic, more of an exercise for me, kind of a warm up. Essentially there's no plot, no story in the traditional sense...A person played by me comes down out of the mountains and hitchhikes his way through the desert. We don't see it, but we later assume that he stole a car and he drives into the city and it just ends there. He checks into a motel and he goes out to a nightclub or something. It just kind of ends like that...and when the music's over, turn off the lights...It's a very beautiful film."

Whilst Jim was occupying himself with films and verse, the rest of the band were ensconced in the studio attempting to finish off the backing tracks for their fourth album. It had been arranged that when they completed the tracks, Jim would come in and overdub his vocals. In May, the third single from the album was released, entitled 'Tell All The People' it was also penned by Robby. Although the arrangement was clever, it featured a brass section so prominently that the single was not easily identifiable as a Doors track and this, coupled with the ban by radio stations since Miami, ensured that the single only reached Number 57 in the charts.

The album 'The Soft Parade' was released in June to a complete bashing by the critics. It included the tracks: 'Tell All The People', 'Touch Me', 'Shaman's Blues', 'Do It', 'Easy Ride', 'Wild Child', 'Runnin' Blue', 'Wishful Sinful' and 'The Soft Parade.' Only a few months before, The Doors were the most popular group in America but, with the release of 'The Soft Parade' they found themselves at an all time low. The high level of orchestration on the album seemed to hide flaws instead of enhancing The Doors' sound. Certainly, the recording that had begun in November 1968 and which didn't finish until May 1969 was fraught with difficulties, not least the 'Miami incident'. Paul Rothchild recalled : "It was bizarre...it

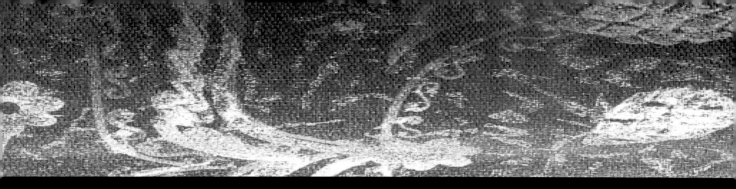

was the hardest I ever worked as a producer. It was nearly impossible to get Jim to sing well and have the band play well on a whole take. It was hell. By this time, they'd run out of all their material and what they came in with was raw, very green stuff. As the talent fades the producer has to become more active."

Jim said later of the album: "It kinda got out of control, and took too long in the making. It spread over nine months. An album should be like a book of stories strung together, some kind of unified feeling and style about it, and that's what 'The Soft Parade' lacks."

The failure of 'The Soft Parade' emphasised the band's financial situation and it was not good news. The album had cost $86,000 to make and due to losing the twenty-five dates after Miami, the band had lost over a million dollars in revenue. Whilst 'Touch Me' had sold well, Jim's legal bills were escalating and, in addition, they were being sued by dozens of promoters for money lost when The Doors were banned from appearing. The Doors desperately needed to earn some fat concert fees but all the major cities were suffering from post-Miami paranoia and most concert promoters wouldn't touch The Doors. There seemed no way out.

The way out was provided by West Coast Promotions, a company run by Rich Linnell, who began to lobby all the hall manager associations. They began to keep what they called a clean file, which was, essentially, a record of The Doors clean shows and good reviews. Most halls didn't want The Doors - they were just too risky - although there were some who were willing to negotiate but demanded some assurances. These 'assurances' were known as the 'fuck clause' since verbal obscenities were what it was designed to guard against. In addition, West Coast Promotions had to post a five thousand dollar bail on each show which was only recoupable if the show was clean and passed without incident. Some promoters

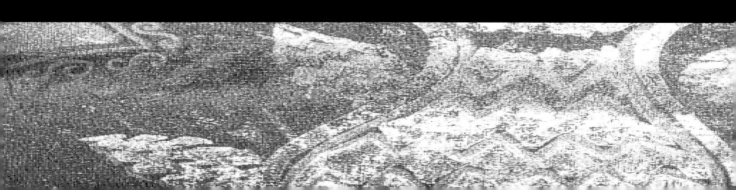

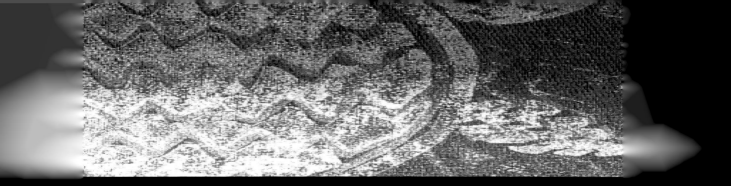

insisted a special clause in the contracts which meant that they
would be fined $1000 each time Jim said the word "fuck" and,
although Jim was totally opposed to the close scrutiny under
which he was to perform, the assurances finally enabled
several shows to be scheduled and, in June, The Doors played

two sell out gigs at the Auditorium Theatre in Chicago.

The gigs were very different from what had gone before.  Jim
was careful not to use obscenities and didn't dress in his usual
uniform of tight leather.  He was relaxed and seemed pleased
about the way the shows were going.  They were altogether
more intimate affairs and maybe he felt that the audience
expectations were lower.  In any event, he gave stunning
performances and each concert was better and more
spontaneous than the one before.  James Spurlock reviewed
one gig for The Chicago Daily News: "Jim Morrison didn't 'do

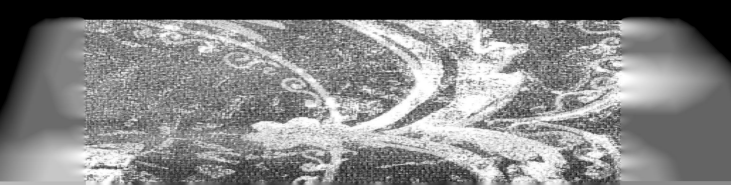

it.' The rock singer of The Doors, whose allegedly obscene performance last March in Miami still has him in legal troubles, came to Chicago for two shows at the Auditorium Theatre Saturday night, and he didn't do it. But he did do a lot of other things. Like, Jim comes out on stage for the first set and, oh wow, he's got a beard. Not one of those tame ones that cries out against the very idea behind a beard, but a woolly wild one. Outasite.

"The first set, Jim gives a little of the image that has been manufactured around him. He's singing about following him down, and you're all set with those images of here stands a broken man. The Doors do two encores, one a planned one of 'Light My Fire' and the other a blues rendition in which Jim sings, 'I'm only twenty-five but I'm an old blues man...' and angry thoughts run through your mind about how he is one all right and they really crucified him.

"For the second set, Morrison, dressed all in brown, swings into action. He even rolls around on the floor. Sandwiched between the jumping around and the screeching, however, is his different side - his funny side. His side remarks have a lot of the audience laughing, instead of sitting on the edges of their seats waiting for him to 'do it.' This set lasts for two hours, and The Doors still end up doing a 'Light My Fire' encore at 2 a.m. after Ray comes to the fore of the stage and says 'It's good to be home.' 'See you guys later', Morrison says, and he walks off the stage."

Life on the road for Jim had also altered. Instead of wild alcoholic binges, he remained relatively sober and spent his time reading, going to the movies or simply sightseeing. If the restrictions imposed on Jim annoyed him, he didn't show it and seemed, for once, content with life, despite the increased police presence at their shows.

In Las Vegas the sheriff arrived at the venue brandishing blank warrants made out for each of the Doors, waiting to fill in the charges if there was even a hint of trouble. There was no need for the warrants, the shows went off like clockwork with Morrison on his best behaviour.

Promoters were still nervous, however, and in Hawaii, two shows were cancelled and one in St. Louis was pulled at the last minute. There was also trouble for some proposed dates in Mexico City. They were originally booked to play the Plaza Monumental, the city's largest bullring to a capacity crowd of forty-eight thousand but the date was cancelled when city officials realised that the date The Doors were due to appear was the anniversary of the 1968 student uprising. It would have been a fit occasion for dissenters to commemorate the revolt by demonstrating and the officials were not willing to take the risk. West Coast Promotions tried to reschedule the show and attempted to book The Doors at the Mexican Arena, the National Auditorium and at Mexico's National University but permission was refused for all three. Eventually, they were offered the Forum, a one thousand-seater supper club owned by a twenty-six year old singer called Javier Castro. The local promoter, Mario Olmos negotiated a deal with Javier and agreed that the band would play four nights at the club for $5000 a night. The tickets were priced at $16 each which only the well-heeled could afford.

The Doors were only informed of these changes at the last minute and were, understandably, furious but, due to the fact that an advertisement had already been posted in the Mexico City newspapers, there was little they could do but go along with the arrangements.

The Doors' could not have wished for a better reception than the one they received in Mexico. They were far more popular than they had thought and the shows were some of the best they ever played. It amused Jim that the audience knew the words to every song, even providing the responses in 'The End'. When the week was up, they were sad to leave the city that embraced them so appreciatively.

With the shows in Hawaii and St. Louis cancelled, The Doors were only left with one firm booking for July - two shows at The Aquarius Theatre in Los Angeles. The tickets for these homecoming events sold out within hours of going on sale and the gigs themselves were to be recorded for inclusion on a live album that Elektra wanted to release by the end of the year.

Jim took to the stage in Los Angeles sporting his heavy beard and wearing a white shirt over loose fitting trousers. Robert Hilburn of the Los Angeles Times was there: "He [Jim] looked less like a sex symbol as he sat almost motionless on a stool at centre stage. Puffing slowly on a cigar while the sound system was being tested, Morrison stroked his new, full beard and stared through tinted glasses into the auditorium darkness....He seemed only remotely interested as the theatre doors opened at a little past 7.30pm and the stream of fans moved inside. Two girls, who were in the first wave, were walking by the front of the stage when they realized the bearded guy above them was indeed Morrison. They finally composed themselves long enough to take a picture. At 8.15 pm, the concert began, Morrison cupped his hands around the microphone, closed his eyes, moved his mouth next to his hands, and began singing 'Back Door Man,' a gutsy song from his first album. The other Doors play simple but solid rock support. Morrison's range as a vocalist is limited but he has a sensual intensity and deliberate phrasing that makes his delivery powerful.

"The reaction was overwhelming at the first show. The audience seemed to sense Morrison was trying something different and it was with him. By ridding himself of all the old symbols, Morrison was trying to demonstrate that he is more than a black leather freak, more than a rock sex symbol, more than a Miami incident. Perhaps more mature and more serious, Morrison is concerned with a higher ambition. He wants to be recognised as an artist.

"Without doubt he was an artist last Monday. If he continues in his new bag, Morrison may prove that, far from being as bad as much of his past publicity would have one believe, he is as good as many of his fans have long felt he is. He took a giant strike in that direction at the Aquarius."

Jim's belligerent, unpredictable and often obscene behaviour was always triggered by alcohol and, like all alcoholics, he was able to keep his addiction under control for periods of time. However, he would always have lapses which, if they coincided with a concert, meant one thing - trouble. It was trouble Jim ran into during a three-day rock festival in Seattle. Besides The Doors, Led Zeppelin, Vanilla Fudge, Ike & Tina Turner, Santana and Chuck Berry were featuring at the event and The Black Panthers provided the security for a forty thousand-strong audience. Jim had been drinking and journalist Ed Jeffords recorded the result: "The tension was high. Only a chicken wire fence separated the stage from 40,000 rock fans, fronted by a phalanx of screaming teeny-boppers who had come out from Seattle for the day just to see Morrison. Black panthers recruited by promoter Boyd

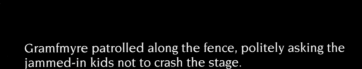

Gramfmyre patrolled along the fence, politely asking the jammed-in kids not to crash the stage.

"'We want Morrison.' 'We want The Doors.' 'We want Morrison.' Empty wine bottles and garbage cans were converted to drums which accommodated the hollow chant. Those of us in the press area felt the animal presence revealed in the primitive rhythm of the chanting audience. For

the first time, we seriously began discussing an escape route in case the crowd should rush the stage...Then came Morrison. Looking old and a little wild he walked to his microphone, lovingly stroked his black moustache, smiled evilly at the fourteen year-old girls behind me, and laughed. 'This is where it's at, now,' he said, still running his hands through his beard.

"When he opened with 'When The Music's Over,' Morrison sounded almost like the singer he used to be. As the song continued, however, so did his crude asides. When he was

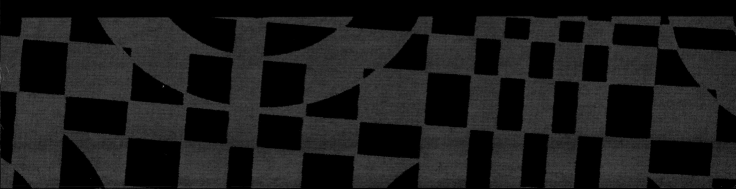

through someone tossed a crumpled cup at him. Morrison gave his unseen assailant the finger. The crowd dug it. The Doors ran through an obligatory five minutes of 'Light My Fire,' a song Morrison told an interviewer earlier this year he wouldn't perform again in public. 'It stinks. We're behind that now,' he had said. His performance of the song, only a ghost of the recorded version, indicated he probably does think it stinks - and that's the way he sang it. More than anything else, Morrison's attitude dominated the stage throughout the show. Puffing on a cigar borrowed from a stagehand, he continued on his uninterrupted ego trip, all the while abusing, insulting and ridiculing his audience.

"It was apparent that this wasn't the Morrison the young chicks had come to see. The tension on the fence behind me relaxed, and we no longer feared the teeny-boppers would try to crash the stage. They didn't want him that bad."

So, having gone some way to dispel the myths and to make people take him more seriously, Jim destroyed all the good work in just one gig and cities began cancelling scheduled concerts again. He was his own worst enemy and he and the other band members knew it. In addition, his legal problems relating to the Miami incident were increasing. The state of Florida was trying to extradite him on the 'fugitive from justice' charge and his background was being thoroughly investigated by the FBI in preparation for the prosecution. It was not a good time for Jim to get out of hand.

On November 9th, Jim finally returned to Miami accompanied by Max Fink. He flew in from LA, was officially arrested and appeared in front of Judge Murray Goodman to enter a plea of not guilty. The case was adjourned and the trial was set for the following year on April 27th. Jim paid the $5000 bail and left Miami for Los Angeles immediately.

Jim spent the next two days trying to relieve the stress of the Miami trip by drinking himself into oblivion. On 11th he impulsively invited Doors publicist Leon Barnard along with Frank Lisciandro and Tom Baker to go with him to see the Rolling Stones play in Phoenix. The whole trip was a big mistake and both Jim and Tom were blind drunk before they even boarded the flight. When they learned the flight would be delayed, they wandered around the plane, annoying the other passengers and flaunting the No Smoking regulations.

0-20 (Rev. 11-3-69)

Tolson
DeLoach
Walters
Mohr
Bishop
Casper
Callahan
Conrad
Felt
Gale
Rosen
Sullivan
Tavel
Soyars
Tele. Room
Holmes
Gandy

Thomas Baker
CAA

291A

DOORS 11/12 HC 1

PHOENIX, ARIZ. (UPI)--JIM MORRISON, LEAD SINGER OF THE DOORS ROCK GROUP, WAS INDICTED WITH A COMPANION WEDNESDAY FOR DISRUPTING AN AIRLINE FLIGHT FROM LOS ANGELES.

MORRISON, 25, AND THOMAS BAKER, 29, WERE CHARHED IN CITY COURT PRIOR TO THEIR INDICTMENT ON THE FEDERAL CHARGES. THEIR BOND ON THE INDICTMENT WAS $2,500 EACH AND ON CITY CHARGES OF DRUNK AND DISORDERLY CONDUCT $66 EACH.

POLICE ARRESTED THEM TUESDAY NIGHT AFTER A CONTINENTAL AIRLINES PLANE LANDED AT SKY HARBOR AIRPORT. THEY WERE ACCUSED OF INTERFERING WITH THE FLIGHT BY ASSAULTING, INTIMIDATING, AND THREATENING FLIGHT ATTENDANTS.

BAKER IDENTIFIED HIMSELF AS A PRODUCER-DIRECTOR. BOTH ARE FROM LOS ANGELES.

MORRISON AND HIS GROUP APPEARED AT THE COLISEUM HERE LAST YEAR AND SINCE HAVE BEEN BANNED FROM FURTHER APPEARANCES ON GROUNDS THEY WERE VULGAR AND OBSCENE.

THEY WILL APPEAR FOR ARRAIGNMENT ON THE FEDERAL CHARGES NEXT WEEK. IF CONVICTED, THEY COULD FACE FINES OF UP TO $10,000 AND SENTENCES OF 20 YEARS.

VR/JY609PPS

MCT-3

164-1021-1

NOT RECORDED
128 NOV. 20 1969

6 - place in case file

56 NOV 28 1969

WASHINGTON CAPITAL NEWS SERVICE

96

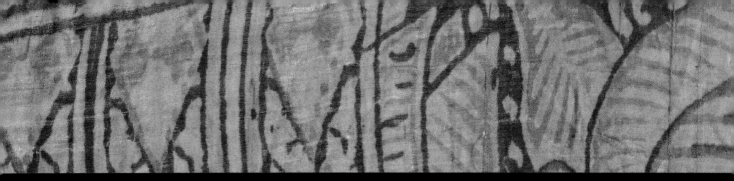

Half an hour later, the plane took off and Tom and Jim's boisterous behaviour became worse. Their noisy and obscene jokes even interfered with the stewardess's instructions for emergency procedures and they were finally reported to the captain after several passengers complained about their foul

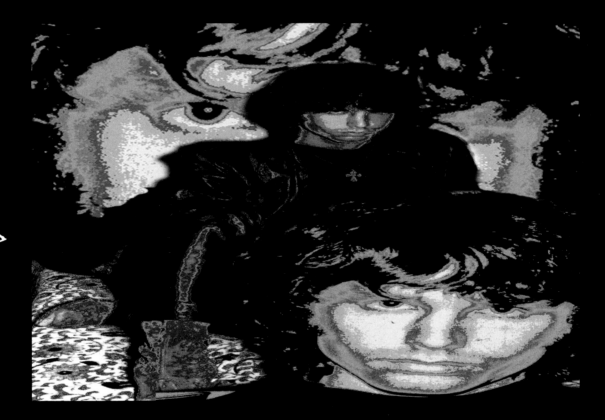

language. Captain Craig Chapman told them that he was prepared to take the plane back to Los Angeles where they would be arrested if they didn't calm down and they were quiet, for a while. Soon Baker began fooling around again, throwing bars of soap around the cabin, one of which landed in Jim's drink. Jim called the stewardess who they then began to harass by tripping her up and throwing empty glasses at her. Baker, in particular became increasingly rowdy and began kicking drinks out of Jim's hand and trying to grope a stewardess called Sherry, managing to reach her thigh. Baker was causing such a commotion that the noise was fully audible

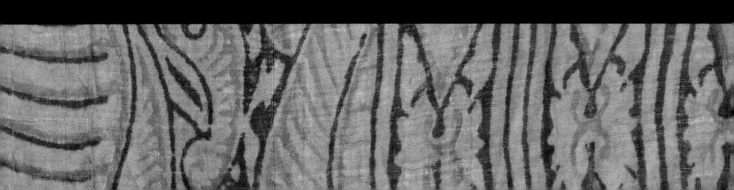

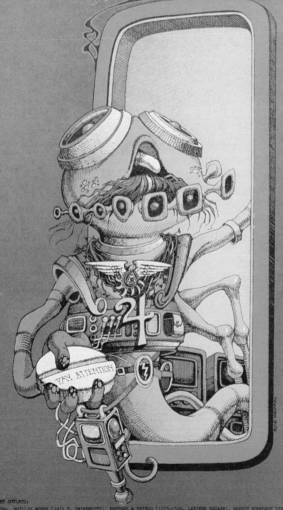

in the cockpit and Captain Chapman decided to radio ahead
to Phoenix and request police intervention.

The plane was met atPhoenix by members of the police
department and the FBI who came on board and
immediately arrested and handcuffed both Jim and Tom.
They were obviously drunk and, in addition, a large knife was
found when the police searched Tom. They were taken off the
plane and into custody  in full view of dozens of
photographers, after which they spent the night and most of
the following day in jail.

Tom and Jim were both charged with being drunk and
disorderly and interfering with the flight of an aircraft, the
latter an offence against the new skyjacking law that could
result in a $10,000 fine and a ten-year jail term. Leon and
Frank had decided to go to the Stones' concert where they
managed to locate Bill Siddons who rushed to the police
headquarters to try and help although he could do little but
contact Max Fink.

Jim and Tom appeared before magistrates the following day,
pleading not guilty to the drunk charge. Bail was set at $66,
they were not released but turned over to the custody of a US
marshal who re-arrested them on the federal charges. They
were charged on three counts of assaulting, intimidating and
threatening a flight attendant, all of them being felonies. Bill
provided the bail of $2,500 for each man and they were told
that, although they could return to California, they could not
leave that state and were instructed to appear before the court
in Phoenix on November 24th for arraignment and bail review.

They failed to appear on the 24th and the judge issued an
order for their appearance on December 1st. This time they
did attend and entered pleas of not guilty to all three charges
and a trial was set for February 17th 1970. Things were getting
worse and worse.

Back home in Los Angeles, things were not really working out
between Pam and Jim. Pam was taking a lot of tranquillisers as
well as indulging a secret heroin addiction and her mood
swings were unpredictable and frequent. Jim was drinking
more than ever, rarely lucid and impossible to talk to. The
result was a lot of violent exchanges which only seemed to
wear them both down instead of clearing the air. The
relationship became increasingly strained.

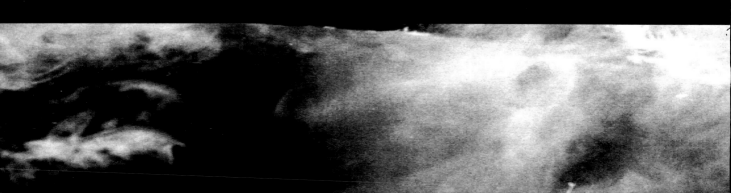

Pam saw rock 'n' roll as the source of all evil and, because of this, hated him being in the band. She constantly demanded that he quit, reasoning that without rock 'n' roll he would be free to concentrate on his poetry and could become more anonymous, and by so doing, avoiding his frequent brushes with the law enforcement agencies. Jim answered these accusations by spending even more time with several women with whom he was having affairs and, when Pam found out as she always did, she took away her pain with a handful of downers or a line or two of smack.

On top of all this, Elektra were pressurising The Doors to come up with some new product. The label were anxious to release a live album in time for Christmas and, as a result, the band had spent September rehearsing the new tracks and by November they were in Sunset Sound recording them. Instead of being a prison for Jim, the studio at this time became a welcome retreat from the pressures of the outside world and he threw himself into the album. There was no shortage of material this time, either, as Jim had been writing prolificly as a means of escape during the last harrowing year and the new songs were vital and strong. Lyrically, the album 'Morrison Hotel' was Jim's best in years and he said later: "Our music has returned to the earlier form, using just four instruments. We felt we'd gone too far in the other direction, ie, orchestration and wanted to get back to the original basic format."

'Morrison Hotel' saw The Doors return to a more crude, raw R&B style. The horns and strings were dispensed with because according to Robby "We listened to 'The Soft Parade' a couple of times and decided that it would probably sound just as good without the brass." Although Jim was usually drunk during the sessions and it often took all night to record his vocal, nobody minded this time, they were on to a winner and they knew it. They were creating something that was going to make the critics sit up and take notice and something through which they could redeem themselves in the eyes of the public. For the fist time in years they felt they were on a roll.

With the dawning of the new decade, the band were still having problems getting the live work which was necessary to promote the forthcoming album. Eventually, two shows were set at the Felt Forum in New York. The crescent-shaped Felt

Forum was a four-thousand capacity, acoustically cheerful venue and it was ideal for The Doors. They had decided against another outing at Madison Square Garden for a number reasons but primarily it was the sheer size and the poor sound which put them off. Again, like the performances in Los Angeles the previous summer, they were to be recorded for inclusion in the planned live album. Jim had lost a fair amount of weight and had shaved his beard and went out to prove that he was still capable of an outstanding performance.

Patricia Kennealy, with whom, it should be noted, Jim was having an affair, wrote in Jazz & Pop: "'Yeahhh, we're really gonna git it on t'night.' Jim Morrison leered encouragingly

from the stage of the Felt Forum. The audience, apparently not too willing to suspend disbelief, merely giggled and emitted a few polite catcalls, but by the time the evening was over, they were thronging to the stage area, arms upstretched, 'Touch Me,' 'Touch Me,' as though the white-shirted Morrison were a piece of the True Cross....Anyone who thinks The Doors are dead should have been tied to the orchestra railing and made to listen to all four shows that the group did; The Doors are rusty, they may even be jaded, but they are not dead. They are just someplace different.

Live Felt Forum New York 17.1.1970

Never Before Released Live Concert

Though Morrison received approximately the same audience reaction he has been receiving for the past few years (ie vocal adoration/vituperation, flung tokens of affection such as bras, panties, rings and lighted cigarettes) one had the impression he would have been equally happy, nay, happier still, had the audience sat quiet and listened to what The Doors were doing."

The Doors were back and going to do the business. They toured confidently for the next month and their concert at Long Beach in Los Angeles was caught by Judith Sims who wrote in the Los Angeles Free Press: "For nearly two hours The Doors played music. When the instrumental breaks came, Morrison turned his back to us, bending close to the drums, shaking maracas. He didn't even ask the audience for a cigarette. He sang, sang very well despite a voice all cracked and husky from four sets in San Francisco...A more relaxed Doors concert I've never seen. There was only one moment of tension, and that was handled briefly and casually. A heckler near the stage kept bugging Morrison, demanding Albert King. 'Yeah, we'd like to hear him too, but he's gone, so you're stuck

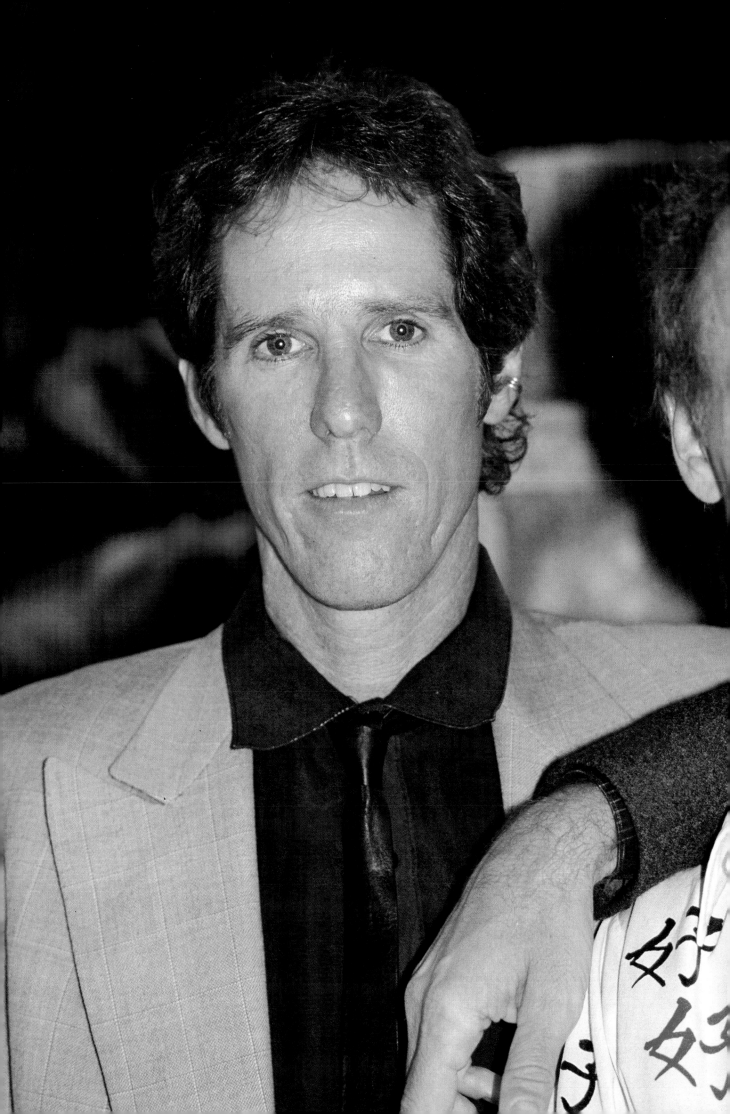

with us.' The heckler didn't shut up. 'You know, sometimes I wish this weren't a democracy,' Morrison mused, 'because if it wasn't, we could take this guy out somewhere and beat the shit out of him.' The audience cheered."

In the wake of these successful concerts which saw Jim giving excellent performances clad in black jeans and shirt, the new album 'Morrison Hotel' was released and included the tracks: 'Road House Blues', 'Waiting For The Sun', 'You Make Me Real', 'Peace Frog', 'Blue Sunday', 'Ship Of Fools', 'Land Ho!', 'The Spy', 'Queen Of The Highway', 'Indian Summer' and 'Maggie M'Gill'. The album was very well received by the press and went straight into the national charts at Number 4. It stayed in the charts a full six months even though no single preceded it. Dave Marsh wrote in Creem magazine: "The Doors have presented us with the most horrifying rock and roll I've ever heard. When they're good, they're simply unbeatable. I know that this is the best record I've listened to...so far."

While Jim should have been happy that 'Morrison Hotel' had provided The Doors with their road back to critical and public acclaim, Jim was far from happy. The trial in Phoenix was looming and he was anxious about potential sentences he could receive. Fines he could deal with, but jail? He wouldn't last two minutes in prison and he knew it. It was a very apprehensive Jim Morrison, dressed in a white shirt and double-breasted jacket with his hair brushed smartly back behind his ears, that attended the court hearing in Phoenix at the end of March.

The trial was a farce. A stewardess who was the chief prosecution witness, continually confused Jim's actions with those of Tom and, whilst the more serious federal charge was dropped, Jim was found guilty of assault. Tom was acquitted of all charges, a strange turn of events seeing as it was Tom who had caused all the trouble. Sentencing was set for two weeks hence by which time, the stewardess decided to change her testimony admitting that she might have made a mistake and the sentencing was deferred for a further fortnight. By April 20th, one week before the deferred sentencing was due, Max Fink was in possession of affidavit by the stewardess admitting she had confused Jim and Tom's identity. A Judgement of Acquittal was issued, the sentencing date vacated and Jim was exonerated - at least for the time being. There were storm clouds on the horizon, however, gaining momentum as they swept across the skies ever closer to Jim Morrison.

There was a small gleam of sunshine in April, lifting Jim's spirits, with the publication by Simon & Schuster of 'The Lords and The New Creatures'. This hardcover edition of his poems had many features he wasn't entirely happy with, the use of Jim Morrison instead of his full name, the well-known 'Young Lion' publicity shot on the front and back covers and reference to his career as a rock star. All of the things he wanted to avoid in order for his poetry to be accepted as a serious work but, nonetheless, he was happy with the result. Michael McClure, who had encouraged Jim to publish his poetry, recalled that when the first copies had arrived by mail, he found Jim in his room, holding a copy of the book, crying. He told McClure: "This is the first time I haven't been fucked." He also sent a telegram to his editor in New York thanking Simon & Schuster for the book. He was pleased that the b[...]d been published, the first thing he had truly a[...]hed on his own. Two days later, however, the stor[...]began to gather bringing an air of brooding men[...]hung over Jim like a dark shroud.

In April 10th The Doors played Boston an[...]ough Jim was drunk he had performed well. The show was running late and, despite pleas from the promoter to stop, they band were enjoying themselves and continued playing. At 2 am the hall manager and decided that enough was enough and pulled the plug on the band. The power was cut off mid-song and the equipment went dead. Unfortunately, Jim's microphone was

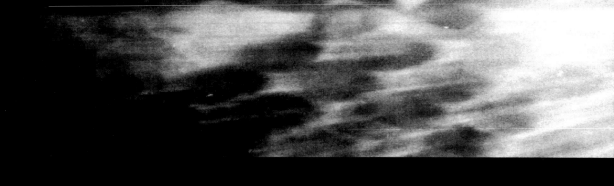

the only piece of electrical equipment on the stage which was still working and he shouted "Those cocksuckers" loudly.

Ray reacted quickly, clamping a hand over Jim's mouth and dragging him off the stage but Jim managed to break Ray's hold and jumped back onto the stage shouting "We should all get together and have some fun, because the assholes are gonna win if you let them!" The following morning the band learnt that a show in Salt Lake City scheduled for that day had been cancelled. The hall manager had been in the audience at Boston and was not impressed.

The band did go on, however, to perform at a huge convention centre in Honolulu and received glowing reviews for a show in Detroit before Jim hit the bottle again before a concert in Seattle and insisted on playing with his microphone until it squealed with feedback which he continued for the majority of the show.

Tour manager Vince Treanor talked to him after the show and told him his antics that evening were way out of line. Jim took no notice, his drinking was well beyond his control now and once again, his appearance began to decline. He regained his bloated appearance, the beard grew back and he spent his time brooding about the impending Miami trial , depressed and preoccupied. He was scared and he had every right to be. The Establishment fully intended to crucify him. He talked to friends of spending the time leading up to the trial, which was set for August, in Paris which was a move everyone encouraged. It was heart-rending to see Jim so low and his friends felt the maybe a change of scene would lighten his mood.

In the event, Jim did make it to France after negotiating a deal with MGM to produce and star in two films. En route, he stopped off in New York to deliver the live album tapes to Elektra for editing and mastering, staying with Jazz & Pop editor Patricia Kennealy whilst he was in the city. Jim was genuinely fond of Patricia, whom he had been seeing when business took him to the East Coast for some time, but even she was stunned when he suddenly announced that they should be married. Patricia was a practising member of a New York coven of witches and suggested that, instead of an ordinary ceremony, they should take part in a Wicca, or witch, wedding. On midsummer night, 1970, in front of the high priestess, Jim and Patricia marked their signatures in blood.

The next day Patricia awoke to find Jim delirious with a temperature of 105 F. He had pneumonia. Whether the ritual the previous night had anything to do with the illness or whether Jim was delirious when he suggested that he and Patricia should be married is not known but it should be said that she spent a week nursing him back to health.

As soon as he was recovered Jim went ahead with his planned trip to Paris, accompanied by Doors' publicist Leon Barnard, giving many people the impression that he didn't take the wedding seriously. However, Patricia Kennealy disagreed in the biography 'Break On Through': "He proposed to me right in the middle of Central Park on a lovely spring afternoon...Anyway it was not a traditional relationship and it was not a traditional wedding, not even legal. But whether people like it or not, it was a real spiritual commitment and I am the only woman with whom he ever went through any form of wedding ceremony. We seemed to like and need the long-distance thing. I don't necessarily think we wanted to be around each other all the time which, frankly, suited me very well. I don't exactly see Jim and me in a cozy domesticity, having to wash his socks or whatever. I'm not the sock-washing type."

On arriving in Paris, Jim and Leon checked into the expensive George V Hotel and spent a week wandering around the city, exploring its artistic charm and visiting numerous sidewalk cafes where he could relax, unwind and forget his troubles for a while. Jim also contacted his old friend from UCLA, Alan Ronay, who was also in Paris at the time and together they did the usual tourist trip, visiting the haunts of Left Bank existentialists and mingling with the performers on the streets of Montmartre.

Jim then moved on to Spain and Morocco for a further two weeks. Just before he was due to fly back to America he had a recurrence of the pneumonia he had suffered in New York and by the time he stepped off the plane in Los Angeles after the long flight he was seriously ill. He went immediately to the apartment he shared with Pam and called Bill Siddons and asked to have the trial postponed. Although Max tried to have the trial delayed whilst Jim recovered, he was refused permission as he had been when he tried to get the trial halted due to constitutional grounds. Miami were going to have their crucifixion whatever state of health Jim was in.

Typically, he soon shook off the illness and, by the time Elektra released the long-awaited live album in July, Jim was back in the best of health. 'Absolutely Live' was a double album of tracks which had been recorded live at various concerts between July 1969 and May 1970 and included six previously unreleased tracks including: 'Who Do You Love',

'Love Hides', 'Build Me A Woman', 'Close To You', 'Universal Mind' and 'The Celebration Of The Lizard.' Jim said of the album: "I think it's a true document of one of our good concerts: not insanely good, but a true portrait of what we usually do on a good night."

'Absolutely Live' was popular with the public if not with the critics and went straight into the charts at Number 8, ironically, the day after Jim left for his long-delayed and dreaded trial in Miami.

From the beginning the trial was a media circus and Judge Murray Goodman who was up for re-election in November knew that the publicity from the Morrison against the Establishment trial could considerably brighten his prospects. This situation worried both Max Fink and Jim's Miami attorney, Robert Josefberg and Max wasted little time informing the press of his fears. He also told them that he planned to request that the jury be taken to see the movie 'Woodstock' and to sit through a performance of 'Hair', enabling them to put Jim's performance in perspective and to show it was perfectly in keeping with the tendencies of the times. This was, essentially, the overall brief with which Max would attempt to defend Jim and, after reading the lengthy document, Jim felt that there was, perhaps, a slim chance that he might walk from the court a free man.

The trial was held at the Metropolitan Dade County Justice Building and The Doors stayed nearby at the Carillion Hotel. On the first day of the trial the proceedings were brief. Judge Goodman had decided that he was too busy to allow the trial to start and put it back a further two days which did nothing for Jim's state of mind. On Wednesday August 12th, the trial officially commenced but the jury were not sworn in until two days later, on Friday 14th. Both Max and Jim were astounded at the choice which the Los Angeles Free Press also observed: "Jurors in Florida, although half in number, are apparently twice as good as elsewhere. They are also twice as old; the youngest juror is forty-two, the rationale apparently being that anyone under the age of forty-two is necessarily prejudiced..."

On the following Monday, the trial began with the formal reading of the charges, the defence's opening address and the first of the witnesses for the prosecution taking the stand. The charges were as follows: "The defendant did lewdly and lasciviously expose his penis in a vulgar or indecent manner

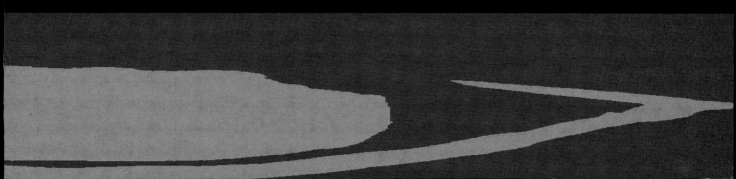

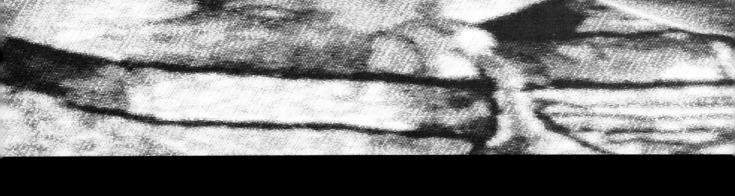

with intent to be observed, did place his hand on his penis and shake it, and further the said defendant did simulate the acts of masturbation upon himself and oral copulation upon another..."

By the end of the third day Max had cross-examined each of the prosecution's witnesses, managing to uncover inconsistencies in all their statements. The stumbling block for Jim came when the sixth witness was called to the stand. Bob Jennings was the clerk in the state attorney's office who had filed the original complaint and there was nothing Max could do to sway Jennings from convincingly proposing the accusation that Jim had exposed himself "for between five and eight seconds."

Thursday should have been a day off but, due to the fact that The Doors were contracted to perform two concerts in California on Friday and Saturday, Judge Goodman agreed to continue the hearing. They should have taken the day off as the results were ruinous to Jim's case. The day started with a single witness who could remember nothing untoward happening at which point around 150 photographs taken the night of the Miami show were introduced as evidence. None of them showed Jim doing anything illegal. Then, out of the blue, the judge ruled that no evidence concerning "community standards" would be deemed permissible, thus undermining Max Fink's whole defence. Max immediately asked for the jury to be removed and began to argue strenuously for half an hour. Judge Goodman could not be swayed and suddenly Jim's fate seemed well and truly sealed.

The following Tuesday, the two California shows completed, Jim and his entourage were back in the Miami courtroom witnessing the prosecution's evidence of four policemen who had all either heard or seen an obscene word or gesture. Max asked them all why Jim wasn't arrested backstage after the show. One witness said they feared the crowd would riot, an answer which Max invalidated by pointing out that there was certainly no "crowd" in the backstage area, only the band and their roadcrew. The prosecution then played a tape of the concert that had been made by someone in the audience. Jim's drunken rambling were clearly audible to all and, taken out of the context of the gig, did indeed sound reasonably obscene.

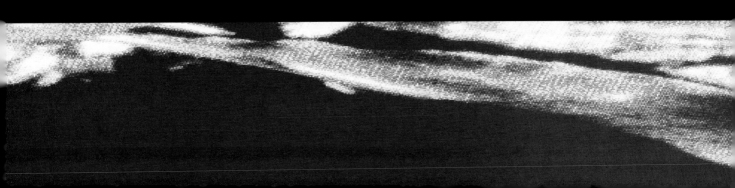

The next night Jim flew to London to join the other Doors
at the second Isle of Wight festival, a three day event
which also featured Jimi Hendrix, The Who, The Moody
Blues, Emerson, Lake and Palmer, Sly and the Family Stone
and Free amongst many others. The Doors were scheduled to
appear between Emerson, Lake and Palmer and The Who. Jim
had never liked appearing outdoors but he took to the stage
in front of an audience of 500,000, exhausted and drained and
his performance that night was lack-lustre. Backstage after the
show, John Densmore was angry that Jim should have turned in
such a mediocre performance in front of the huge festival
crowd and was heard to say that it would be the last time he
would ever play with Jim. Jim later told the press that the Isle
of Wight would be his last live appearance.

Back in Miami the following Wednesday, the prosecution
rested its case. They concluded that Jim had exposed himself
and simulated oral copulation on Robby without any hard
evidence. There were no photographs of the acts and whilst
the tape of the show substantiated the allegations of obscene
language, there was nothing in the crowds' behaviour which
would indicate exposure. Most of the witnesses for the
prosecution were inconsistent in their stories and several
stated that, although they were close to the stage they saw
nothing untoward occur. Because of this, Jim's defence
entered a plea for acquittal on the grounds that the state itself
had raised reasonable doubt. Nobody was surprised when
Judge Goodman denied it. He also said that only seventeen
witnesses would be permitted to testify for the defence and
there were to be no experts amongst them.

The trial continued with Max parading witnesses who
countered the prosecution's claims. They were close to the
front of the stage and saw nothing. They were a mixture of
housewives, doctors and policemen who would of surely been
shocked to witness Jim's alleged exposure. After a lengthy
recess and more defence witness - including The Doors
themselves - the trial ended and the jury withdrew. Two hours
later they returned finding Jim guilty of profanity but acquitting
him of the lewd behaviour and drunkenness charges. They
were undecided on the subject of exposure and Judge
Goodman sequestered them in a Miami hotel and recessed
court until 10am the next morning.

The next day, the jury filed in and announced they had found Jim guilty of exposure and sentencing was set for late October and bail raised from $5000 to $50,000. Jim was stunned and the news of Jimi Hendrix's death when he left the courtroom did nothing to alleviate his black depression.

One month later Jim was back in Miami for the sentencing and, as expected, the maximum sentence was levied - a $500 fine and six months in Dade County Jail. Max rapidly filed an appeal and Jim said: "I was quite relieved that I wasn't taken into the jail and booked. They could have done it easily...The judge's attitude seemed to be that he was trying to prosecute me to the limits of the law. That will be one of our appeals, that I didn't really receive a fair trial because of judicial prejudice. We're going to fight the sentence until it is wiped clean off our records. The appeal motion will first have to go to the circuit court in Florida and if it doesn't pass muster there, it will go to the state court and eventually to the Supreme Court. If they accept it there, it will be a final decision then."

Interestingly, Judge Goodman was busted a year after Jim's trial for taking a bribe in a gambling case. He was acquitted but died shortly afterwards.

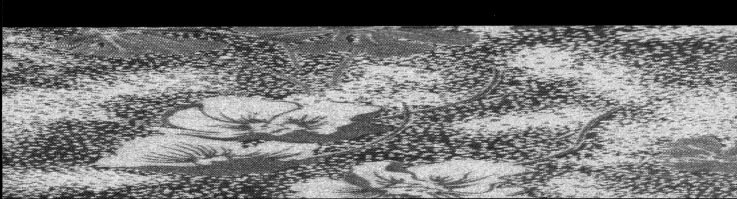

The Miami trial seemed to have a detrimental effect on The Doors' relationship with their record label Elektra. Holzman was unhappy about the whole Miami incident and the way the trial had gone and instructed his staff not to talk about the subject. The company was anxious to release Doors product for the lucrative Christmas market and is was apparent that, due to the trial, the band had not even begun to work on their next album. Since the band had a contractual obligation to provide Elektra with material to release, the company took it upon themselves to put out a compilation album. Entitled '13' it contained most of the popular songs from the first album right through to 'Morrison Hotel' and included the tracks: 'Light My Fire', 'People Are Strange', 'Back Door Man', 'Moonlight Drive', 'The Crystal Ship', 'Land Ho', 'Roadhouse Blues', 'Touch Me', 'Love Me Two Times', 'You're Lost Little Girl', 'Hello, I Love You', 'Wild Child' and ' The Unknown Soldier'.

The band were unhappy about not having the opportunity to get involved with the choice of material but when they saw the artwork for the album they were furious. The cover depicted a considerably younger Jim Morrison that had been blown up much larger than the shot used of the rest of the band. They began rehearsing new material immediately, almost as a way of protesting against the album's release.

The material for the new album came together quite quickly, Jim had been reasonably prolific in the months that preceded the trial and the Paris trip especially resulted in him rediscovering his gift for rich, mysterious imagery. Paul Rothchild dropped by their rehearsal room which was located within The Doors' offices and didn't like what he heard. He didn't like the material, calling 'Riders On The Storm' "cocktail music" and could sense the tension between the individual band members. In addition, Jim had taken to doing a lot of cocaine, so where he would previously have lost consciousness through alcohol, he now drank the same amount but the stimulant effect of the drug kept him awake and over-verbal throughout his belligerent rambling, going on and on until he had driven everybody crazy. To Rothchild, this all seemed a bit too much like hard work and he decided to pass on producing the album, suggesting instead that they should produce themselves.

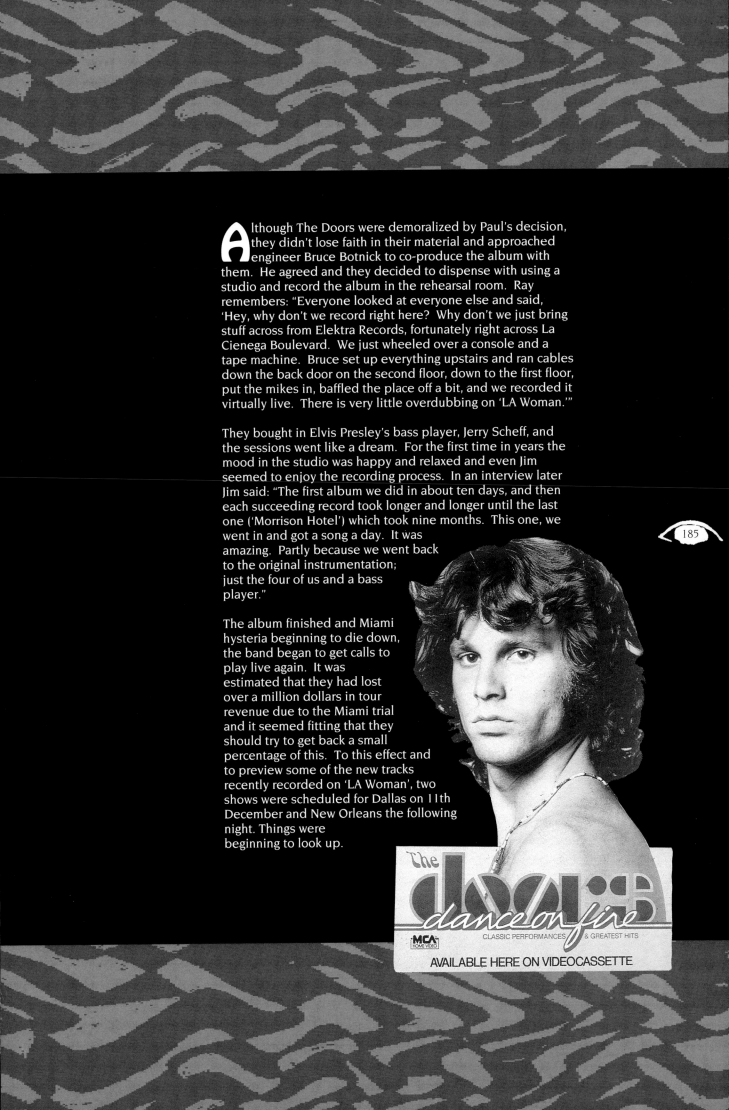

Although The Doors were demoralized by Paul's decision, they didn't lose faith in their material and approached engineer Bruce Botnick to co-produce the album with them. He agreed and they decided to dispense with using a studio and record the album in the rehearsal room. Ray remembers: "Everyone looked at everyone else and said, 'Hey, why don't we record right here? Why don't we just bring stuff across from Elektra Records, fortunately right across La Cienega Boulevard. We just wheeled over a console and a tape machine. Bruce set up everything upstairs and ran cables down the back door on the second floor, down to the first floor, put the mikes in, baffled the place off a bit, and we recorded it virtually live. There is very little overdubbing on 'LA Woman.'"

They bought in Elvis Presley's bass player, Jerry Scheff, and the sessions went like a dream. For the first time in years the mood in the studio was happy and relaxed and even Jim seemed to enjoy the recording process. In an interview later Jim said: "The first album we did in about ten days, and then each succeeding record took longer and longer until the last one ('Morrison Hotel') which took nine months. This one, we went in and got a song a day. It was amazing. Partly because we went back to the original instrumentation; just the four of us and a bass player."

The album finished and Miami hysteria beginning to die down, the band began to get calls to play live again. It was estimated that they had lost over a million dollars in tour revenue due to the Miami trial and it seemed fitting that they should try to get back a small percentage of this. To this effect and to preview some of the new tracks recently recorded on 'LA Woman', two shows were scheduled for Dallas on 11th December and New Orleans the following night. Things were beginning to look up.

185

The album and the shows, however, were not the only things motivating and exciting Jim and, on December 8th, 1970, on his twenty-seventh birthday he entered the Village Recorders in West Los Angeles with his poetry proudly tucked under his arm accompanied by two friends, Alan Ronay and Florentine Pabst. Although he arrived at the studio sober, he didn't stay that way for long and for literally hours Jim read his way through a thick wad of typed sheets, happy to be at work on his beloved poetry.

The Doors arrived in Dallas in good spirits and went on to play two superb sets, proving to both themselves and their public that they could still conjure up the old magic. They previewed 'Riders On The Storm' which was greeted with tumultuous applause and the band really felt they were back on a winning streak again. The feeling, however, was to be shortlived. The next night in New Orleans the magic had gone and the music was finally over. The spirit of the shaman that was so apparent onstage only the night before, finally left Jim. Ray saw it go: "Everyone who was there saw it, man. He lost all his energy about midway through the set. He hung on the microphone and it just slipped away. You could actually see it leave him. He was drained. Jim picked up the microphone stand and repeatedly bashed it into the stage, over and over until there was the sound of wood splintering. He threw the stand into the stunned audience, turned , and plopped down on the drum riser sitting motionless. When I first met him, he was just full of energy, life, power and potency, and intellectual knowledge, and by the time it was over he was drained and exhausted." The dark and brooding storm-clouds were visible once more, hanging over Jim like a shroud, and this time they could not be blown away.

Back in Los Angeles, Jim was finding life easier with Pam. Just before Jim was sentenced in Miami she had decided that enough was enough and fled to France where she embarked on a torrid affair with a French Count. Jim had been lonely without her and, although there had been no shortage of women in his life whilst she was away, he never really felt complete without her - or the inevitable arguments! She really was the only woman he couldn't live with, or without. He was happy then, when she returned to their apartment on Norton Avenue and he returned to her bed, enjoying a rare period of domestic calm.

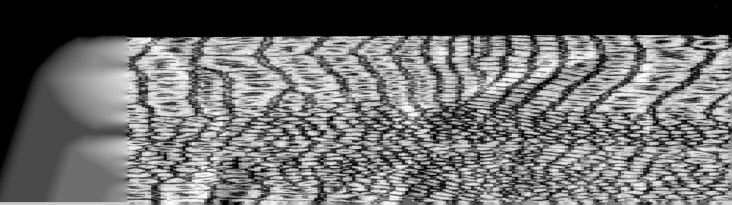

During the winter Jim worked on several of his own projects. The closest to his heart was an album of his poetry which Elektra had agreed to release and for which the company had given him a small advance. There were also discussion about Jim writing and appearing in a movie in Italy and a stage show in which Jim was to play a Vietnam prisoner-of-war. In addition to all this, there was the new offering from The Doors which was being completed in their rehearsal room which would prove to be one of their most powerful and successful albums. Jim seemed relaxed and, for once, reasonably content. However, nobody was surprised when he announced his intention of moving to Paris when the album was finally completed.

Ray explained: "Jim left for Paris right in the middle of the mixing of 'LA Woman' - I think we had maybe two more songs to mix - and he said 'Hey man, everything's going fine here. Why don't you guys finish it up? Pam and I are going to Paris, and we're just gonna hang out for a while, see what happens.' So we said 'OK, talk to you later. Go over there and have a good time, relax, take it easy. Write some poetry.' What Jim wanted to do in leaving for Paris was to immerse himself in an artistic environment, to get away from rock 'n' roll, to get away from all the sensational press that he had. Jim was hounded by a lot of sensational press; a lot of yellow journalism associated with the man and, frankly, he was tired of it. He was tired of being 'The Lizard King'. Jim Morrison was a poet. He was an artist, he didn't want to be the king of orgasmic rock, the king of acid rock, the Lizard King. he felt all those titles that people had put on him were demeaning to what The Doors were trying to do, so in an effort to escape that, and to re-charge his artistic batteries, he went to Paris, the city of art.

He was going to write, maybe look into a few film projects - Agnes Varda had contacted him, as had Jacques Demis and, also back in the States, Steve McQueen had talked to him about doing some films. So Jim was just getting away, taking a breather, a rest...going to become a poet again. And we had finished our commitment to Elektra; we had to deliver seven records over that five or six year period of time. So we had completed our contract, and were free to go to a new record company, continuing making records, not making records, whatever. So, we decided to just take a long hiatus, and there was really no reason for Jim to be there for the mix. He said, 'You guys finish it up, I'm going to Paris.' We said 'OK man, see you later...and I haven't heard from him since..."

**B**efore he left for Paris, Jim granted Bob Chorush of the LA Fress Press an interview and spoke frankly about alcohol and drugs: "I went through a period where I drank a lot. I had a lot of pressures hanging over me that I couldn't cope with. I think also that drinking is a way to cope with living in a crowded environment and also a product of boredom. I know people drink because they're bored. I enjoy drinking. It loosens people up and stimulates conversation sometimes. It's like gambling somehow; you go out for a night of drinking and you don't know where you're going to end up the next day. It could work out good or it could be disastrous. It's like the throw of the dice.

189

"There seem to be a lot of people shooting smack and speed and all that now. Everybody smokes grass - I guess you don't consider that a drug anymore. Three years ago there was a wave of hallucinogenics. I don't think anyone really has the strength to sustain those kicks forever. Then you go into narcotics, of which alcohol is one. Instead of trying to think more, you try to kill thought with alcohol and heroin and downers. These are pain-killers. I think that's what people have gotten into. Alcohol for me, because it's traditional. Also, I hate scoring. I hate the kind of sleazy sexual connotations of scoring from people, so I never do that. That's why I like alcohol; you can go down to any corner store or bar and it's right across the table."

Jim felt it wise that Pam should go to Paris ahead of him and sort out their living arrangements a suggestion to which she readily agreed. A few days before she left, they visited her birthplace in Weed and then drove on to Orange, eight

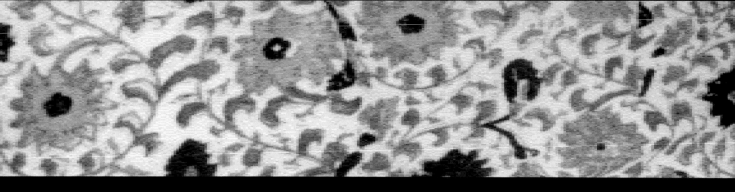

hundred miles north, to say goodbye to her parents. They had made arrangements for her parents to take care of their labrador, Sage, and it was here that they left him. On February 14th Pam left Los Angeles for Paris where she checked into the sumptuous George V Hotel and busied herself looking for an apartment to rent. She was relieved that Jim was finally going to be able concentrate on, what she saw as his true vocation, being a poet, without the distractions that Los Angeles and superstardom provided. Paris expected nothing from Jim Morrison the rock superstar, allowing him space to rechart his life and to salvage a dream.

Jim spent his last day in Los Angeles with his old buddies Babe Hill and Tom Baker, who had recently returned from a spell in London. Babe noticed that Jim was already making positive changes and told Frank Lisciandro in the book 'A Feast Of Friends': "He was very sober. He hadn't been hanging around with me that much. We hadn't been getting drunk together. He seemed like he was trying to divorce himself from everything in a kinda sober, final way...He was concentrating more and more on his poetry and his publishing and that's all he wanted to do was get away from here and get it all behind him. Towards the end he was taking a longer view of things. He knew that whole phenomenon of The Doors was over. He was burnt out, certainly, on concerts, and on records, being in the studio all that stuff."

After walking on the beach in Venice for the last time, Jim, Babe and Tom had lunch at the Santa Monica Pier and then spent the afternoon in a local amusement arcade. The next day Jim left Los Angeles for the last time and boarded a flight for Paris.

In April 1971 the album, 'LA Woman', was released and included the tracks: 'The Changeling', 'Love Her Madly', 'Been Down So Long', 'Cars Hiss By My Window', 'LA Woman', 'L'America', 'Hyacinth House', 'Crawling King Snake', 'The WASP', and 'Riders On The Storm'. The album's release was also accompanied by the release of a single 'Love Her Madly' which quickly shot up the charts giving The Doors their first Top Ten hit in two years. The album was extremely well received by the critics and Rolling Stone called it "The Doors greatest album (including their first) and the best album so far this year..." The album finally reached the Number 5 position and it was with 'LA Woman' roaring up the charts that they finally and officially left Elektra and this move fuelled

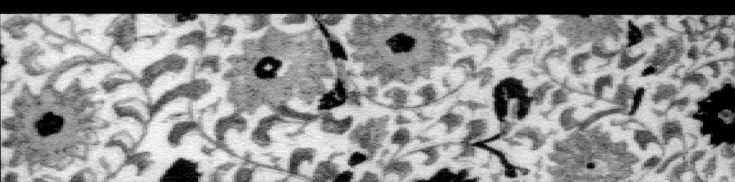

speculation that the band were locked into negotiations with other record companies.

'LA Woman was the most blues-orientated Doors album to date, and Jim's love of the blues was evident by his powerful performance, although he was beset with serious vocal problems at the time. The whole album had a fresh, driving feel to it executed by a mature and confident band. The cover shot featured a clear plastic window with the band's picture impressed on the transparency which came to life when the yellow inner sleeve was inserted. The group shot placed equal emphasis on each member, while Jim had slumped down during the photo-session to make himself look even smaller than the others. He was also sporting a full beard since nobody could persuade him to shave for the shot. The back of the inner sleeve portrayed an unusual and startling illustration of a woman crucified on a telegraph pole - the LA Woman. The album was powerful and stylishly produced and doubters and detractors of The Doors were finally vanquished when it sold like wildfire.

"Home" in Paris, for Jim and Pam was an elegant and spacious apartment at 17 rue Beautreillis in the Marais on the Right Bank, one of the most beautiful sections of the city. On the

third floor, it overlooked the Place Bastille and the open-air food markets and Jim was overjoyed when he first saw it, congratulating Pam on her discerning choice. She had stumbled on the place by chance, meeting a young model, Elizabeth Lariviere, who was planning to spend a few months with her family in the south of France. She offered Pam the lease on her apartment in her absence, which Pam was quick to snap up, paying 3,000 francs a month.

When Jim arrived in Paris, he continued his exploration of the city which he had started some twelve months previously and walked the streets for hours at a time. His attitude seemed to

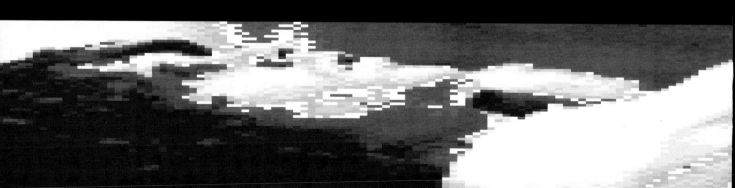

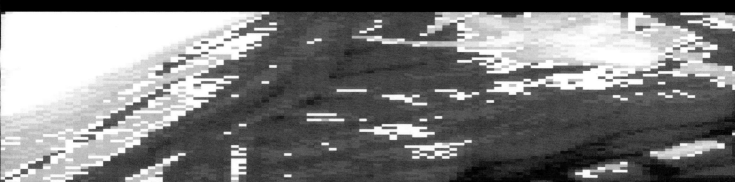

improve and he became excited about the books and poetry he wanted to write and the films he wanted to produce. He shaved off his beard, which served to make him look younger, and even began to shed a little weight. He looked and felt good and was very hopeful and bright about his new life.

Jim was, however, still drinking heavily and the profusion of sidewalk cafes and bars did little to deter him. During this time he developed a bad cough. Whether or not it was a recurrence of the pneumonia is subject to speculation but several witnesses noticed that he was smoking cigarettes very heavily. Pam, ever vigilant of his health (although, by this time, she herself had developed an unhealthy addiction to heroin) suggested that they should take a trip and explore more of Europe and at the end of April, they rented a car and drove through France towards Spain. They arrived in Morocco after two weeks and explored Tangier and Casablanca, recording the marvellous sights with a Super-8 film camera that Jim had bought before they left Paris.

On their return to Paris, some three weeks after they left, their apartment was unavailable for a few nights so they moved to an extravagant haunt of visiting rock stars, the exclusive L'Hotel in St. Germain. The change of location was not for the better and Jim began hanging out in night clubs notorious for the heroin dealing that took place there. One particular club, the Circus, was a firm favourite with Jim and it was here he would indulge in the wild partying that Pam despised so much. He had found himself a whole new set of drinking buddies and chose to spend more time with them than he did with Pam, leading to the inevitable clashes between them. It had only taken Jim a few months to begin living the same life that he was running away from.

This situation became a vicious circle. The more Jim drank the more he blocked the creative process and, as a result this lack of creativity would depress him deeply so he would drink more to alleviate the depression. The downward spiral that had been such a large and destructive part of his life in Los Angeles was beginning again, here in Paris, where even he thought he had found peace. Journalist Herve Muller spent a great deal of time with Jim and observed: "I don't think he was doing anything. I didn't have a lot of do with that side, but while he was in Paris, I don't think he was doing much. He had his notebooks and things with him and he was making notes,

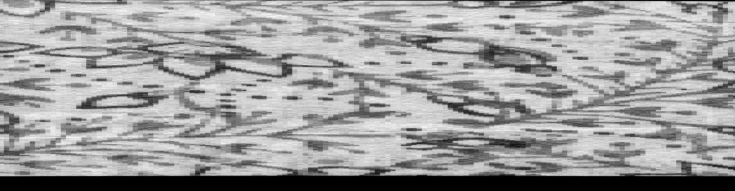

but I didn't see him working. Maybe he did, but..."

At the end of May, Jim and Pam took another trip, this time flying to Corsica. During a scheduled stop at Marseilles, Jim lost his passport, wallet and driving licence and so they flew straight back to Paris where Jim had to pay a visit to the American Embassy in order to acquire duplicates. This accomplished, they flew back to Marseilles and finally on to Corsica where they spent ten days.

Jim was unaware of the success of 'LA Woman' and soon after returning to Paris he called John Densmore to ask how the album was doing. John told him that both the single and the album were selling well and that the press loved them. Jim was surprised and told John "If they like this, wait'll they hear what I got in mind for the next one." This wasn't exactly what John wanted to hear. He had never been Jim's greatest fan, he respected his creative genius but hated his unpredictable and drunken behaviour which he found both annoying and gross. Jim made him nervous and neurotic and he made no secret of the fact that he was relieved when Jim decided to go away for a while.

Since Jim had left for Paris, Ray Robby and John had continued to rehearse new material and, unknown to Jim, had spent some time working, unproductively, with new vocalists. This was merely a precaution, they said later, in case Jim decided not to return or failed to recover his musical inspiration. The notion that Jim might be thinking of returning filled John with horror. He needn't have worried as Jim also put in a call to Bill Siddons and told him that was not ready to return. Indeed, it was Herve Muller's impression that: "He'd left the band, as far as he was concerned, at that point. That doesn't mean he might not have recorded with them again - he wasn't the kind of guy who would think ahead too much."

Shortly after the phone calls, Jim tried to finally sort himself out. He hired a private secretary, a tall, slim, blonde Canadian called Robin Wertle who spoke fluent French. Robin was much-needed if Jim was to conduct any real business in Paris as neither he nor Pam spoke the language. Robin's job included everything from trying to get one of Jim's films screened to looking after the apartment. She typed his letters, made calls on his behalf to America and bought furniture. Robin was involved when Jim decided that he wasn't keen on the cover shot for the paperback version of 'The Lords

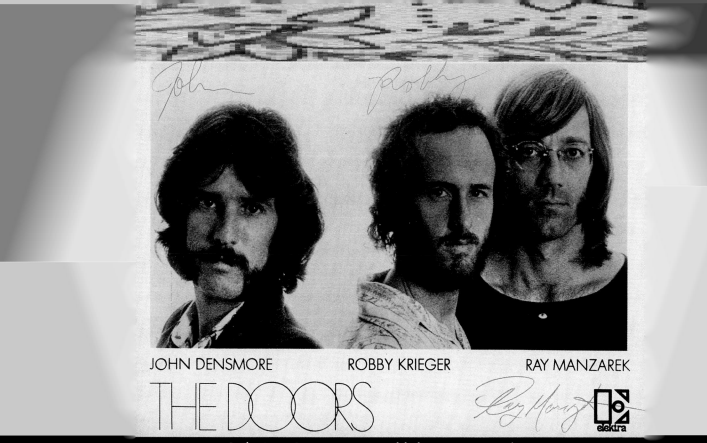

JOHN DENSMORE          ROBBY KRIEGER          RAY MANZAREK

THE DOORS

& The New Creatures'. His publishers, Simon & Schuster were planning on using an early shot of him and Jim sent his contact within the company, Jonathan Dolger, a telegram requesting that perhaps they could use a more recent shot. The telegram was sent on July 2nd.

With Robin looking after business, Jim attempted to do the impossible by quitting drinking. Although he had tried many times before, his sobriety would never last long, but this time he felt compelled to give it his best shot. As the alcohol left his bloodstream, the familiar craving began to knot his stomach which was rapidly followed by a massive depression. His cough got worse, he began to detect blood in his sputum, his chest hurt and he became short of breath when climbing even a small flight of stairs. On top of all this, the craving for the demon drink became too much for him to bear and he went back to the bottle, drinking even more heavily than before but not even alcohol was successful in lifting his tremendous sense of despondency.

Form FS-192
11-19-61

# REPORT OF THE DEATH OF AN AMERICAN CITIZEN

FINAL                                    American Embassy, Paris, France, August 11, 1971
                                                              (Place and date)

Name in full _James Douglas MORRISON_____ Occupation _Singer_____

Native or naturalized _BORN ON December 8, 1943 AT Clearwater,_____ Last known address
                                                                          Florida
in the United States _8216 Norton Avenue, Los Angeles, California_

Date of death _July_____3_____5:00 a.m.____1971__ Age ___27 years_____
              (Month)   (Day)   (Hour) (Minute) (Year)        (As nearly as can be ascertained)

Place of death _17, rue Beautreillis, Paris 4, France_____
               (Number and street) or (Hospital or hotel)        (City)              (Country)

Cause of death _Heart Failure_____
                              (Include authority for statement)

As certified by Dr. Max Vassille, 31, rue du Renard, Paris, France

Disposition of the remains _Interred in Pere Lachaise Cemetery, 16th Division, Paris,_
France on July 7, 1971.

Local law as to disinterring remains _May be disinterred at any time upon the request of_
nearest relative or legal representative of the estate. See Decree Law of December
31, 1941, Journal Officiel, January 26-27, 1942, Page 378.

Disposition of the effects _In the custody of Pamela Courson, friend._____

Person or official responsible for custody of effects and accounting therefor _Rear Admiral George S._
Informed by telegram:                                          Morrison, father.

|  NAME |  ADDRESS | RELATIONSHIP | DATE SENT |
|-------|----------|--------------|-----------|
| N/A   |          |              |           |

Copy of this report sent to:

| NAME | ADDRESS | RELATIONSHIP | DATE SENT |
|------|---------|-------------|-----------|
| Rear Admiral George S. Morrison | Chief Naval Operations | Father | August 11, 1971 |
|  | OPO 3B - Room 4E 552 |  |  |
|  | Pentagon, Washington, D.C. 20350 |  |  |

xTraveling or residing abroad with relatives or friends as follows:

| NAME | ADDRESS | RELATIONSHIP |
|------|---------|-------------|
| Miss Pamela Courson | 17, rue Beautreillis | Friend |
|  | 75 - Paris 4, France |  |

Other known relatives (not given above):

| NAME | ADDRESS | RELATIONSHIP |
|------|---------|-------------|
| Unknown |  |  |

   This information and data concerning an inventory of the effects, accounts, etc., have been placed
under File 234 in the correspondence of this office.
   Remarks: _U.S. passport number L 900083, issued at Los Angeles, California,_
on August 7, 1968 cancelled and returned to father.
Filing date and place of French Death Certificate: July 3, 1971 at the Town Hall
of Paris 4, France._____(Continue on reverse if necessary.)

                                        Mary Ann Meysenburg
[SEAL]                                     (Signature on all copies)
No fee prescribed.             Vice Consul_____of the United States of America.

O 1 Dec 14 51/11 M M

# THE END

On July 1st, Jim was still racked with depression and an air of impending gloom. Although he had been drinking heavily he was trying to write but the words would just not come. He became frustrated and morose and sullenly stared at the blank page in front of him, abnormally quiet. Pam became concerned as she had never seen him so low and tried desperately to cheer him up, as did Alan Ronay who was in Paris and had stopped by to see how Jim was doing. Alan suggested that they all go to see a Robert Mitchum movie 'Pursued' the following evening, perhaps after a meal.

On Friday, July 2nd, Jim left the flat around lunchtime to send the telegram to Jonathan Dolger in New York, requesting that the planned picture from the Joel Brodsky photo-session was replaced by a shot by Edmond Teske. Some time later he met up with Alan Ronay and together they walked in the sunshine back to Jim's apartment, probably stopping at one or two bars in the process. According to Alan, Jim looked tired and unwell and had difficulty in climbing the stairs to the third floor. After Alan left Jim it is difficult to seperate fact from fiction due to the fact that no reliable witness, apart from Pam, saw Jim alive again. The following version of events seems the most likely and is supported by extensive research by photo-journalist Bob Seymore who spent many years researching the facts and finally published them in his book 'The End'.

According to Pam, Jim ate out alone that evening, not wishing to bore his friends with his depression. He returned home and picked up Pam and the two of them went to the late screening of 'Death Valley', leaving the cinema at around 1.00am. Jim's mood had appeared to have lightened a little and they went to bed. Some time later, Pam was woken by Jim who was choking in his sleep. She had difficulty in waking him, finally arousing him by slapping him on the face. Pam was frightened and wanted to call Jim a doctor but he wouldn't allow her to. He told her he wanted to take a bath but, as soon as he climbed in, he called to Pam that he felt sick and wanted to vomit. When he did so, in a bowl that Pam had provided,

197

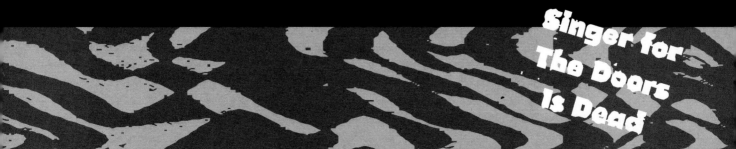

Singer for
The Doors
Is Dead

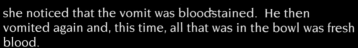
she noticed that the vomit was bloodstained. He then
vomited again and, this time, all that was in the bowl was fresh
blood.

By this time Pam was extremely frightened and again asked
Jim if she should call a doctor. He replied that he was feeling
better and told her to go back to bed and he would join her
when he had finished his bath. Jim's colour had returned
taking the place of the deathly white pallor and, reassured by
this and his attitude, Pam returned to bed as Jim had
suggested and fell asleep. Later she awoke and saw that Jim
still hadn't returned to bed, so she checked the bathroom to
see if he was alright. He wasn't. He was dead. With his hair
matted and wet, he was lying in the bath, his head resting
against the back and he had a peaceful smile on his face.

After finding Jim in the bath, Pam phoned Alan Ronay in a
state of near hysteria. She was crying uncontrollably and
asked him to come over immediately because Jim was
unconscious in the bath. It was around 8.30am. Alan and his
girlfriend, Agnes Varda, rushed to the Morrison apartment and,
after seeing Jim in the bath, Alan called the Fire Brigade, who
received an emergency call at 9.21am. In any event, this is
what Alan said in his statement to the police, although there
seems to be some confusion as to who actually called the Fire
Brigade.

When the Fire Brigade arrived, they pulled Jim from the bath
and tried, in vain, to resuscitate him by external heart
massage. The police were the next to arrive on the scene and
immediately searched the apartment. They also questioned
Pam, Alan and Agnes and then asked them to come down to
the station later to make formal statements. Jim's death was
registered at 2.30pm at the Town Hall by the police and at
6.00pm Dr. Max Vassille arrived to examine the body. The
doctor declared Jim dead from heart failure - probably
provoked by a blood clot from a pulmonary infection, a strange
diagnosis given the symptoms. There was, however, no
autopsy carried out so it is baffling to know how the doctor
came to this conclusion purely on a routine examination.
Another strange occurrence was the speed with which the
funeral directors prepared the body and sealed the coffin.

Some of the answers to these anomalies have been provided
by James Riordan and Jerry Prochnicky in their Morrison
biography 'Break On Through'. They claim that a reliable

source who wished to remain anonymous but who was close to Pam informed them that Jim had taken some of Pam's heroin and overdosed. When others close to Pam were interviewed for the book they also substantiated the claim.

They also investigated why there was no autopsy and discovered that not one but two doctors came to the apartment to examine Jim's body. The first doctor came at the request of Pam and Alan Ronay. This mysterious medic was, by all accounts, prepared to sign the death certificate without asking any questions, so that when the police doctor arrived he was given the certificate, without which he would have had to call for an autopsy. Since the cause of death had already been determined, no further examination needed to take place. Certainly, a heroin overdose would have warranted a cover-up. It would also have been reason enough to keep Jim's body out of a hospital and explains why his coffin remained at the apartment. It also would explain why Jim wasn't flown back to America where questions would undoubtedly have been asked. The theory certainly seems credible enough.

By Monday 5th July the press had been tipped off and there was mounting speculation regarding the truth in the rumour that Jim was dead. The national newspapers in London began calling Clive Selwood at Elektra's London office for verification and he, in turn, called the company's office in Paris but they weren't even aware that Jim had been in France. Both the American Embassy and the Paris police denied that an American named Jim Morrison had died. As a last resort, Clive decided to call Bill Siddons in Los Angeles.

Over the years there had been many reports that Jim had died and, just when Bill began to

199

get worried, Jim would always turn up in the office to disprove the rumours. He wasn't, therefore, terribly alarmed when Clive told him what was transpiring in London. He did, however, decide to call Jim's apartment, expecting Jim himself to answer. Pam picked up the telephone and told Bill that the rumour wasn't true but, when Bill pressed her, she began to cry. Bill was worried enough to catch the next plane to Paris.

By the time he arrived, early the next morning, Jim's body had already been prepared and placed in the coffin which had been sealed. Bill never saw, or asked to see the body. Mourning the loss of his friend, Bill helped in the only way he could, by taking over the funeral arrangements, and both he and Pam agreed that they wanted to avoid making the ceremony a media circus. They decided that Jim should be buried as quickly as possible and that nobody should be informed, thus minimalising any leaks to the press. To this effect, Bill went to the cemetery Pere Lachaise and purchased, with Robin's help, a double grave which was all there was available at such short notice. He wired the money from the states and paid for it there and then in cash in an attempt to keep one step ahead of the media.

On Wednesday, July 7th, at 9.00am Jim was buried in Pere Lachaise with Alan Ronay, Bill Siddons, Pamela Courson, Robin Wertle and Agnes Varda as the only mourners. Jim was in good company as the prestigious Pere Lachaise is the final resting place for numerous celebrities including Balzac, Bizet, Chopin, Moliere, Oscar Wilde and Edith Piaf. It was a simple service with no clergyman present. The five mourners threw their flowers on the grave and said their own quiet goodbyes. Jim was finally at rest and, hopefully, at peace. Bill said later: "We got him buried without publicity and sensationalism which I'm sure is the way Jim would have wanted it. And we buried him where he wanted to be...We'd done it. We'd buried Jim with dignity."

The next day Bill helped Pam go through Jim's few belongings and then he flew back to Los Angeles and, after breaking the news to Jim's family, finally officially announced the news to the public. In a statement to the media which reflected Pam's version of the event, Bill said: "I have just returned from Paris, where I attended the funeral of Jim Morrison. Jim

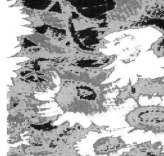

Jim Morrison                1988

was buried in a simple ceremony, with only a few friends present.  The initial news of his death and funeral was kept quiet because those of us who knew him intimately and loved him as a person wanted to avoid all the notoriety and circus-like atmosphere that surrounded the deaths of such other rock personalities as Janis Joplin and Jimi Hendrix.

"I can say that Jim died peacefully of natural causes - he had been in Paris since March with his wife, Pam.  He had seen a doctor in Paris about a respiratory problem and had complained of this problem on Saturday - the day of his death.

"I hope that Jim is remembered not only as a rock singer and poet, but as a warm human being.  He was the most warm, most human, most understanding person I've known.  That

Jim Morrison                1988

wasn't always the Jim Morrison people read about - but it was the Jim Morrison I knew and his close friends will remember..."

201

Jim's death, twenty years on, is still shrouded in mystery but in the weeks immediately after his death, rumours of suicide, murder, death by overdose and no death at all (he was, apparently, seen boarding an aircraft only hours after he 'died') were rife.  Jim was not understood when he was alive, but his death was altogether more baffling.  Mike John summed up the situation when he wrote in the Baltimore Morning Sun: "Morrison even caused trouble after his death.  I spent a few hours working on something for the obit, just finished, when I received a cable from Paris.  It read: 'Unable to confirm Morrison death and am wary of it.  Seems there was no hospital, a death certificate but no doctor's signature on it; he was buried before the news of his death was released; the cemetery was said to be a national monument and it was unlikely that an American rock 'n' roll singer would be buried there; and finally, the official word came from his manager, not from the police, embassy officials, or anyone in authority'.  It took a few more hours to satisfy the newspaper for which I write that he was indeed under the ground.  His father, Rear Admiral George Morrison, said he believed it was true and had

Morrison death rumour exaggerated

RUMOURS that Doors singer Jim Morrison had died of a heart attack over the weekend spread around London this week.

According to our Paris correspondent, who was in touch with a close friend of Morrison, the stories are true and Morrison, who is in Paris, will remain until September.

Elektra Records [...] was the third Morrison rumour in the past month.

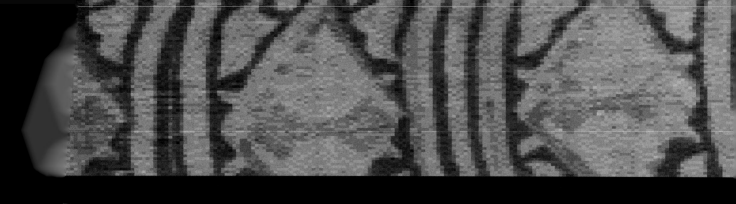

checked with the naval attache in Paris who confirmed it. Where could he be? Following the track of the great and not-so-great poets and novelists from bar to bar in Paris? No, he's gone, it seems, not like Hemingway or even like Jimi Hendrix, but like anyone else. Death and goodbye, that's it."46

A few days after Bill issued his statement, Jac Holzman said in a statement to the press: "Jim Morrison was an artist of stellar magnitude who was able to retain a bemused and detached perspective on his aura, his art and his stardom. His exciting qualities as a performer and writer are universally known to the fascinated public for who Jim was always news.

"Jim admired those people who stretched their lives to the fullest, who lived out on the edge of experience. He possessed special insights into people, their lives and into the dark corners of human existence.

"But beyond his public image, he was a friend to many, and those of us at Elektra who worked with him and The Doors so closely over the past five years will remember him as one of the kindest and most thoughtful people we have known. He is already missed."

A month after this statement was made, Elektra released the single 'Riders On The Storm' which was one of The Doors biggest-ever selling singles.

In Jim's will he named Pam coexecutor of his estate, along with attorney Max Fink. Pam was to inherit everything but she received nothing for two years due to a dispute over the legal fees Max had charged for his work on both the Phoenix and Miami trials. He had submitted a bill for $75,000 which Pam thought extortionate and she sought legal retribution. After a succession of four lawyers attempted to have the bill lowered to no avail, she finally conceded defeat and agreed to pay. When Pam's will settled she received

DÉCÈS

LE TROIS JUILLET MIL NEUF CENT SOIXANTE ET ONZE, QUATRE HEURES, EST DÉCÉDÉ 17 RUE BEAUTREILLIS, JAMES DOUGLAS MORRISON, NÉ A FLORIDA (ETATS UNIS D'AMÉRIQUE) LE 8 DÉCEMBRE 1943, ÉCRIVAIN, DOMICILIÉ A LOS-ANGELES (ETATS UNIS D'AMÉRIQUE) 82-16, NORTON, AVENUE LOS ANGELES, FILIATION INCONNUE DU DÉCLARANT. CÉLIBATAIRE. DRESSÉ LE 3 JUILLET 1971, 14 HEURES 30 SUR LA DÉCLARATION DE MICHEL GAGNEPAIN, 34 ANS, EMPLOYÉ 8 RUE DU CLOÎTRE NOTRE DAME, QUI LECTURE FAITE ET INVITÉ A LIRE L'ACTE A SIGNÉ AVEC NOUS ANNIE JACQUELINE FRANÇOISE TARIN ÉPOUSE MORENO FONCTIONNAIRE DE LA MAIRIE DU IVe ARRONDISSEMENT DE PARIS, OFFICIER DE L'ETAT-CIVIL PARDÉLÉGATION DU MAIRE AM./

**"One of the finest, clearest spirits of our times."**

$150,000 in cash in addition to Jim's sizable investments in land and oil.  According to rumour, the first things she bought with the money were a new car and a mink coat.

**N**o amount of money, however, could compensate Pam for her loss.  She returned to Los Angeles soon after Jim's funeral, manic with grief and would spend hours at Paul Rothchild's house just talking about him.  She sank into a dark depression and attempted to escape from the awful reality of life without Jim by taking more and more heroin.  She refused to believe that Jim was dead and frightened concerned friends by claiming that Jim's spirit had returned in their dog, Sage.  Over the next few years, her state of mind worsened and she attempted suicide several times, eventually joining her beloved Jim by overdosing on heroin three years after his own demise.  The secrets surrounding Jim's mysterious death in Paris were buried along with Pam and , two decades later, despite numerous investigations and exhaustive research, there is no conclusive evidence to indicate what really happened on the night of July 3rd.  Whatever happened it was a tragic end for such a talent.

When the news of Jim's death reached Ray, John and Robby they were terribly shocked.  Although they had come to expect the unexpected from Jim, his death was something they had not envisaged - not in a bathtub in Paris anyway.  John Densmore remembered: "When we received the news from Paris about Jim, we were shock beyond belief.  We just thought, 'What now?'  We sat around and we jammed a bit, and finally we decided to keep on making music.  The vibes between the three of us had been so good that we felt that we just had to continue.  Jim was a friend, somebody we'd lived with and made music with for so long, but eventually we realised that we had the rest of our lives to live, so after we'd gotten over it, we started to think about what we'd do.  None of us really wanted to go play with anyone else, so after five years of being together and getting tighter we decided to start the whole thing again."

After months of speculation about their future, The Doors announced in a press conference that they would continue as a trio. Initially the were going to change the name, how could it be The Doors without Jim Morrison?  After much thought, they decided to keep the name, which they were entitled to do.  Ray Manzarek told journalist John Tobler: "We thought of calling ourselves 'And The Doors' because it had started out as

203

# Jim Morrison: Riding Out The Final Storm

Lead singer of Doors was found dead in bathtub of his apartment in Paris. He had been living there as a writer for last several months. Police listed cause of death as a heart attack.

COUNTY OF LOS ANGELES     **CASE REPORT**     THOMAS T. NOGUCHI, M.D. CHIEF MEDICAL EXAMINER CORONER

## 3

CONTINUATION SHEET

Case No. 7H 05648
Case Name PAMELA SUSAN MORRISON

Date 4·26·74

INFORMATION SOURCE; INV. KAMIDOI LAPD THIS ¿ JOHN MANDELL.

THE DECEDENT, JOHN MANDELL AND CLIFTON DUNN LIVED IN AN APT. AT 105 N. SYCAMORE.

YESTERDAY EVENING DECEDENT AND JOHN MANDELL WENT TO SEVERAL STORES SHOPPING AND RETURNED HOME AT APPROX. 2130 HRS. (4·25). SHE TALKED OVER THE PHONE TO HER PARENTS FOR MORE THAN A ½ HR. MANDELL AND DUNN LEFT THE APT. TO MAKE A PHONE CALL AT A STREET PHONE. WHEN THEY RETURNED APPROX. 1 HR. LATER THEY OBSERVED DECEDENT LYING ON THE COUCH.

THE 2 MEN PREPARED DINNER AND THEN MANDELL ATTEMPTED TO AWAKEN DECEDENT TO EAT. AT 2350 HRS. HAVING NEGATIVE RESULTS THEY CALLED POLICE. POLICE CALLED RA. UNIT. RA#61 DOA 24.00 HRS. DECEDENT ASKED MANDELL TO GET SOME HEROIN FOR SHE AND HER GIRL FRIEND BUT HE DECLINED. GIRL FRIEND WAS AT THE APT WHEN MANDELL ¿ DUNN RETURNED HOME BUT SOON LEFT.

A SYRINGE WAS FOUND BUT NO SPOON OR BALLOON FOUND. A FRESH NEEDLE PUNCTURE WAS OBSERVED (L) ANTE CUBITAL FOSSA. — DECEDENT HAD A HX OF OCCASSIONAL HEROIN USE. DECEDENTS HUSBAND EXPIRED 4 YRS AGO PARIS FRANCE, O.D. HEROIN

G.H. Greene
INVESTIGATOR

4·26·74
DATE

WHITE - FILE
YELLOW - TOXICOLOGY
PINK - INVESTIGATION

The Doors and then, after a few years, it was Jim Morrison and
The Doors...but we kept The Doors because that's who we
were; there were four of us - now there were three of us."
Without further ado, they re-signed with Elektra and began
work on their first album without Morrison. Called,
appropriately 'Other Voices', the album was released in
October 1971 and, although it made Number 31 in the US
album charts, it seemed that the public bought it out of
curiosity rather than on its own merit. Although the songs were
competent enough, it lacked the genius of Morrison and
immediately made it apparent that he WAS more than just
another singer.

Another album was released in 1972 entitled 'Wired Scenes
Inside The Gold Mine'. A double-album set, it included two
songs that were previously only available as B-sides of singles.
'Who Scared You' was the B-side of 'Wishful Sinful' and the
Manzarek sung '(You Need Meat) Don't Go No Further' which
had previously appeared on the flip-side of 'Love Her Madly'.
The album only made Number 55 in the American charts, but it
showed that the remaining Doors were slowly coming to terms
with Jim's untimely death and went some way towards keeping
his memory alive.

Later in 1972, a further album, 'Full Circle' was released and
illustrated how important Jim had actually been within the
band. Without him, The Doors lacked meaning and purpose
and this album seemed empty, confused and shallow. The
Doors after Morrison proved to be somewhat of an anti-climax
and the motivation petered out in the mid-Seventies when
they retreated individually into blues/jazz groups, session
work and unacclaimed solo albums.

When Pam died, Jim's estate went to her parents, Mr and
Mrs Columbus Courson. It was at this time that Jim's
own family contacted the Coursons and they agreed to
split the remaining inheritance with them. Pamela had,

**JIM MORRISON
Stone Immaculate**

**A GRAVEYARD POEM**

however, entrusted her father with something far more important than money. She had instructed him that, should anything happen to her she wanted Jim's words brought to the attention of the world. Therefore, in 1978, an album of Jim's poetry was finally released. Having unearthed the recordings Jim made of 'An American Prayer', the three band members provided an electronic jazz backing for it. Credited to "Jim Morrison with Music by The Doors", Paul Rothchild voiced the opinions of a universe when he said in Bam magazine: "I think anything that was done during Jim's lifetime that might have offended him would disappear into total insignificance compared to what I'm positive would have been his reaction to 'An American Prayer'. That album is a rape of Jim Morrison. When I hear the original tape, I hear something compelling. The poetry is chilling. To me, what was done on 'An American Prayer' is the same as taking a Picasso and cutting it into postage-stamp size pieces to spread across a supermarket wall."

Ray defended the album by saying: "We're bringing people Jim Morrison, the poet. That was always a sore point with him that people never appreciated him as a poet. Now that he's been gone so long and you can forget what a good performer he was, you can begin to realise that he was probably one of the major poets of his time...This is the Jim Morrison we always knew. He was a very warm person. The guy onstage was another person. He could be terrible. The guy we worked with and travelled with though could be a whole lot of fun."

In 1980, a remarkable thing happened. Warner Books released a biography of Jim Morrison entitled: 'No One Here Gets Out Alive', co-authored by Jerry Hopkins and Danny Sugerman. A regular contributor to Rolling Stone, Hopkins had already written an acclaimed biography on Elvis Presley and had painstakingly researched Jim's life for five years. The manuscript for the book, however, was turned down by every major publisher in America and seemed doomed never to see the light of day. When Danny Sugerman, who as a teenager worked for The Doors and was mightily impressed by Jim, suggested he add some personal insight of his own, the manuscript was finally given a home by Warner. The book was a very readable account of Jim's life, containing previously unpublished facts regarding his childhood and teenage years and shot to the top of the best-seller lists and stayed there for six weeks, quickly selling several million copies. Edited by Ray Manzarek, the book was not so readily accepted by those involved within the music industry who felt that, in places, it tended to mix fact with fiction. The book also

addressed the mysterious circumstances under which Jim died and went some way to suggest that he may have faked his own death, although Sugerman denied that this was their intention in later interviews. Jac Holzman went so far as to say: "The book was nothing but a repackaging job - not serious. It was too monumental and tended to sensationalise aspects of Jim's character best ignored. The death rumours? Not only sick but unbelievable. Danny Sugerman - how can I phrase this tactfully - wasn't as tight with Jim as you'd think from the book...I doubt if anyone knew Jim that well."

Whether or not this book served to romanticise or exploit Jim's life, and death, mattered little to the public who lapped it up. It was frighteningly accurate and provided pacey, interesting reading portraying Jim as a dark-tempered, visionary poet who was also a heroic example of the wisdom that can be found by living a life of relentless excess. Whilst Holzman condemned the book, Elektra were amongst the first to cash in on its success by releasing compilations of Doors back catalogue when it became apparent that it had caused a resurgence of interest in the band, or more specifically, in Morrison himself. Almost entirely due to this book, The Doors began to enjoy a renewed popularity that, twenty years later, shows no signs of waning - a popularity that might have proved far more elusive had Morrison survived.

Thereafter followed a live album and more compilations The Doors back catalogue was, by now, selling well in excess of a million copies every year. Books were written on the subject, exploring every detail of Jim's life and investigations were launched into the circumstances surrounding his death. Opinions were exchanged, TV documentaries were made and presented as tributes and Jim's perfectly sculptured features adorned magazine covers world-wide.

In 1991, even Hollywood began to sit up and take notice of this growing phenomena. Oliver Stone, producer of 'Wall Street' and 'El Salvador' had a box-office smash with his award winning portrayal of Jim's life ensuring that The Doors, once again, rode a storm of contention and obsession, twenty-four years after their first coming.

Jim Morrison has refused to die.

# Will and Testament

of

### JAMES D. MORRISON

I, JAMES D. MORRISON, being of sound and disposing mind, memory and understanding, and after consideration for all persons, the objects of my bounty, and with full knowledge of the nature and extent of my assets, do hereby make, publish and declare this my Last Will and Testament, as follows:

FIRST: I declare that I am a resident of Los Angeles County, California; that I am unmarried and have no children.

SECOND: I direct the payment of all debts and expenses of last illness.

THIRD: I do hereby devise and bequeath each and every thing of value of which I may die possessed, including real property, personal property and mixed properties to PAMELA S. COURSON of Los Angeles County.

In the event the said PAMELA S. COURSON should predecease me, or fail to survive for a period of three months following the date of my death, then and in such event, the devise and bequest to her shall fail and the same is devised and bequeathed instead to my brother, ANDREW MORRISON of Monterey, California, and to my sister, ANNE R. MORRISON of Coronado Beach, California, to share and share alike; provided, however, further that in the event either of them should predecease me, then and in such event, the devise and bequest shall go to the other.

FOURTH: I do hereby appoint PAMELA S. COURSON and MAX FINK, jointly, Executors, or Executor and Executrix, as the case may be, of my estate, giving to said persons, and each of them, full power of appointment of substitution in their place and stead by their Last Will and Testament, or otherwise.

In the event said PAMELA S. COURSON shall survive me and be living at the time of her appointment, then in such event, bond is hereby waived.

I subscribe my name to this Will this 12 day of February, 1969, at Beverly Hills, California.

JAMES D. MORRISON

NOTICE: Please attach COPY OF WILL to this petition. (If will is holographic, a Typewritten Copy is required. — Sec. 201 Probate Policy Memorandum)

LAW OFFICES OF MAX FINK
Attorney— for Petitioner

(SPACE FOR FILE STAMP)

9777 Wilshire Blvd., Suite 700
Address
Beverly Hills, California 90212
273-6760  --  272-9181
Telephone

**FILED**

JUL 13 1971

WILLIAM G. SHARP, County Clerk

BY DON J. BROWN, DEPUTY

County Clerk:

You are requested to publish notice of

hearing in   Los Angeles Daily Journal
(Name of Paper)

Signed   Charles R. Eshleman
Attorney for Petitioner

DATE OF HEARING

July 29 - 9 A

## SUPERIOR COURT OF THE STATE OF CALIFORNIA
## FOR THE COUNTY OF LOS ANGELES

ESTATE OF

JAMES D. MORRISON

Deceased

No. P 573952

PETITION FOR PROBATE
OF WILL
AND FOR LETTERS TESTAMENTARY

To the Superior Court of the County of Los Angeles, State of California:

The petition of   MAX FINK

of the County of   Los Angeles  , State of California, respectfully states:

1. That   JAMES D. MORRISON   died on

or about   July 3, 1971  , 19    , at   Paris, France

2. That said deceased at the time of his death was a resident of the County of

Los Angeles  , State of   California  , and left property in the County of

Los Angeles  , State of California.

3. That the character and estimated value of the property of said estate, and the probable annual income therefrom, so far as known to your petitioner, are as follows:

Royalties from musical compositions, intangible oil interests,

Value over $75,000.00;  annual income estimated; $50,000.00

4. That said deceased left a Will dated ............... February 12, ................................, 19 69,

which your petitioner.... alleges... to be the last Will of said deceased, and which is presented here-

with; that a copy of said Will is annexed to this petition, marked exhibit "A."

5. That at the time said Will was executed, to-wit, on the said ...February 12,...., 19 69,

the testat..or...... was over the age of eighteen years, to-wit, of the age of ........ 24 ................ years,

or thereabouts, and was of sound and disposing mind, and not acting under duress, menace, fraud

or undue influence, and was in every respect, competent, by last Will, to dispose of all his ...............

estate.

6.*That said Will is in writing signed by the said testat.or......... and attested by two subscrib-

ing witnesses. Your petitioner....alleges..that said testat..or.......... acknowledged the Will in the pres-

ence of said witnesses, present at the same time, and that said witnesses signed the said Will at the

request of said testat..or........ and in the presence of testat...or......., and your petitioner ..., further

alleges. that said witnesses, at the time of attesting the execution of said Will, were competent.
(*If an holograph will, so state and strike out paragraph 6)

........................................................................................................................................

7. That .... MAX FINK and PAMELA COURSON MORRISON (Pamela S. Courson in Will)

named in said Will as execut..ors.... thereof, consent xxtexkxxx to act as such execut..ors................,

........................................................................................................................................

8. That the names, ages and residences of the devisees and legatees named in the said Will of

deceased are as follows:

| | | over | |
|---|---|---|---|
| Pamela Courson | widow | 21 | 8512 Santa Monica Blvd., Los Angeles |
| Name Morrison | Relationship | Age | Residence (Street, City and State) Calif. 90069 |
| Andrew Morrison | brother | over 21 | 418 Pomona Ave., Coronado, California |
| Anne Graham | sister | over 21 | 418 Pomona Ave., Coronado, California |

9. That according to petitioner's best knowledge, information and belief, the answers given to
the following questions are true and correct:

A. Did the deceased leave surviving (1) a spouse? yes (2) any children? no (3) any
child of a deceased child? no (4) parent or parents? yes

B. Has there been omitted from the list of heirs set forth below any surviving child or any
issue of any deceased child? no

C. (To be answered if deceased left neither issue nor parent) Has there been omitted from

10. That the names, ages and residences of the heirs at law of said deceased, so far as known

to your petitioner...., are as follows:

| Name | Relationship | Age | Residence (Street, City and State) |
|---|---|---|---|
| Pamela Courson Morrison | widow | over 21 | 8512 Santa Monica Blvd., Los Angeles, California 90069 |
| Andrew Morrison | brother | over 21 | 418 Pomona Ave., Coronado, California |
| Anne Graham | sister | over 21 | 418 Pomona Ave., Coronado, California |
| George S. Morrison | father | over 21 | 1327 South Glebe Rd., Arlington, Va. |
| Clara Morrison | mother | over 21 | 1327 South Glebe Rd., Arlington, Va. |

Wherefore, your petitioner.... prays. that the said Will may be admitted to probate, and that

Letters ........ Testamentary ........
(Insert: "Testamentary." If for executor named in will, otherwise "of administration-with-the-will-annexed.")

be issued to your petitioner...., and that for that purpose a time be appointed for proving said Will

and that due notice thereof be given according to law, and that all necessary and proper orders may

be made in the premises.

Dated ........ July 12 ........, 19 71

*Max Fink*

Max Fink

State of California, County of Los Angeles

I, the undersigned, state. That I am the petitioner in the foregoing proceedings; that I have read the same and know the contents thereof, and the same is true of my own knowledge, except as to matters which are therein stated upon information or belief, and as to those matters that I believe the same to be true.**

**The signature, if executed outside the State of California, must be acknowledged before some person legally entitled to administer an oath or affirmation. (Judicial Council Rules of Court do not permit the attachment of jurats and riders.)

Dated ........ July 12 ........, 19 71

I certify (or declare) under the penalty of perjury that the foregoing is true and correct.

*Max Fink*

Max Fink
(Signature of declarant)

......................................
(Signature of Affiant)

Subscribed and sworn to before me

......................................, 19........

......................................
Notary Public in and for the County of Los Angeles,
State of California.

On the date written above, JAMES D. MORRISON, declared to us, the under-signed, that the foregoing document, consisting of two pages, including the page signed by us as witnesses, was his Last Will and Testament, and requested us to act as witnesses to it. He then signed this Last Will and Testament and initialed each page of it in our presence, all of us being present at the same time. We now, at his request, in his presence, and in the presence of each other, subscribe our names as witnesses.

_____ residing at _7668 Woodrow Wilson_
_Los Angeles, Calif_

_Sheila Schweit_ residing at _11655 Mayfield Ave_
_L.A., Calif 90049_

_____ residing at _Beverly Hills,_
_California_

DÉCES

LE TROIS JUILLET MIL NEUF CENT SOIXANTE ET ONZE, CINQ HEURES, EST DÉCÉDÉ, 17 RUE BEAUTREILLIS, JAMES DOUGLAS MORRISON, NÉ À FLORIDA(ETATS UNIS D'AMÉRIQUE) LE 8 DÉCEMBRE 1943, ÉCRIVAIN, DOMICILIÉ À LOS ANGELES(ETATS UNIS D'AMÉRIQUE) 82-:6, NORTON, AVENUE LOS ANGELES, FILIATION INCONNUE DU DÉCLARANT, CÉLIBATAIRE. DRESSÉ LE 3 JUILLET 1971, 14 HEURES 30 SUR LA DÉCLARATION DE MICHEL GAGNEPAIN, 34 ANS, EMPLOYÉ 8 RUE DU CLOÎTRE NOTRE DAME, QUI LECTURE FAITE ET INVITÉ À LIRE L'ACTE A SIGNÉ AVEC NOUS ANNIE JACQUELINE FRANÇOISE TARIN ÉPOUSE MORENO FONCTIONNAIRE DE LA MAIRIE DU IV° ARRONDISSEMENT DE PARIS, OFFICIER DE L'ETAT-CIVIL PARDÉLÉGATION DU MAIRE AM.

213

BY RAINER MODDEMANN
EDITOR OF THE DOORS QUARTERLY MAGAZINE

'Mesmerising', I thought, when I first saw The Doors on German television during a usually boring show called 4-3-2-1 Hot And Sweet. There was this strange man on keyboards wearing ridiculous white boots and shaking his head like he was chasing away a wasp. The drummer sat in the middle of a big square in Frankfurt with a wide grin on his face. The guitarist's hair got blown in the wind and the cable connected to his guitar led directly into the singer's microphone. The singer, dressed in black leather, threw his head backwards and screamed out his song - intense, wild, unbound and loud. Suddenly, I glimpsed something in the music which I had never seen before. This was far-out, probably too far-out for a fourteen year-old kid but what I witnessed that day was enough to make me start collecting articles and photographs of the group. Unfortunately, I was too young to attend their 1968 concert in Frankfurt which, fortunately, was preserved forever on a bootleg.

Soon after that first encounter I bought my first two Doors singles, 'Light My Fire' and 'Hello, I love You'. The first single sported a beautiful cover, with a photo of The Doors surrounded by flames. 'Light My Fire' was a shortened version of their album track, which was suitable for the charts, but without the beautiful solos in the middle, to which we would dance at wild teenage parties.

**E**ven today, over twenty-five years later, I am still wondering what got me into The Doors. Was it the hard time I spent translating the lyrics into German when it soon became apparent that the songs should never be translated into another language? Certainly not! Was it Morrison's voice - the warm, gentle timbre in his voice that made me feel so lonely when I listened to 'I Can't See Your Face In My Mind'? Probably! Was it his looks? This angel-like face with the beautiful cheek-bones that made him look like Alexander The Great. They called him Rock-Rasputin, didn't they? Those deep, dark eyes, even more powerful when he was on acid or booze. Sure, why not! A great many people, especially girls, were turned on to The Doors because of the way Morrison looked in 1968 and were later surprised that this classic face had an even more classic voice and, above that, a brain which produced some of the most powerful lyrics in rock music and some of the most important poetry of modern literature.

Was it the music of The Doors? A swirling classical organ with a solid, mushy bass; a flamenco-orientated electric guitar with blues influences; a jazzy but powerful drum. All of which was perfect to support, if not drive, the vocals to their dramatic intensity. Absolutely!

This all came together for me in this one magic moment when I saw them on the telly way back in 1968. A pretty usual way to get into The Doors, even nowadays. They are omnipresent on video, on TV and they even made their way onto the big screen with the release of a film by Oliver Stone. In my opinion, this was not a film about The Doors or Jim Morrison, but a bad one on Aerosmith! (thanks, Ray, for that quote). I often wonder what this film did to Jim's memory or how it compared to what The Doors intended to be in the Sixties. For me, there's just one positive thing about the movie - it made people wonder how the REAL Doors were way back then. This resulted in a huge resurgence of interest in the band and people started buying the original albums, CDs, videos and the mass of books that were published after the movie's release, and many discovered that Jim Morrison was not the jerk that the movie portrayed and that the three other Doors were certainly not puppets. What a film this could have been! And what a film it turned out to be! Jim Morrison became the star of a Hollywood soap opera and, although a few images in the film were reasonably interesting, it is little else but a flagrant rip-off produced by the myth-making machinery.

I remember the day when I heard about Jim's death. 'Riders On The Storm' had just come out as a single and, after they played it on the radio, the announcer said softly "We have just received the news that Jim Morrison is not amongst us anymore. He died in Paris of a heart attack..." I felt a sudden chill and knew then that my whole world had collapsed. My idol had died and I knew that there would never be another like him. How could he leave the other Doors, his friends and his fans behind with 'Riders On The Storm', the last song he ever recorded, with its whispering second vocal track behind all that storm and thunder? How could he leave us here with just a handful of albums and one book of poetry, 'The Lords And The New Creatures'?

I felt bad for Ray, John and Robby at that time. I knew they would have to struggle hard to survive after a quarter of their precious Doors-diamond had split off. They did another two albums which had a couple of good songs and a lot of trash on them and then they disappeared. They put The Doors to bed but I felt confident that they would awaken again one day. Even Doors-spokesman Ray Manzarek vanished in the haze after one excellent album, 'The Golden Scarab', and an appalling one, yes, that one with the long title (from a Morrison quote) 'The Whole Thing Started With Rock'N' Roll Now It's Out Of Control'. The Doors' world had crashed down with Jim's death.

I first visited Jim's grave in 1973 on a beautiful sunny morning in June. I don't expect new Morrison fans can imagine how peaceful and quiet it was there at that time. I was overwhelmed with my feelings and kneeled down beside the grave for over two hours just talking quietly to him and shivered as if it was Jim's soul responding to what I had said. A hallucination? I am very sure that there was someone whispering something in response. The rider on the storm never showed up, but metaphysically, took a place in my heart on that day and I knew he would never loosen his grip. Since then, I've been to his grave probably more than 100 times but I've never had that feeling again, unfortunately.

In 1978 I had my first chance to meet the remaining Doors in person. They were on a promotional tour of Europe to support the release of 'An American Prayer', the gorgeous poetry album, their movie for the ears. It was the perfect album with which to smoke some mother nature and take a trip through Jim Morrison's consciousness. I talked to all three Doors after their press conference in Hamburg and we shared a couple of bottles of sweet German wine whilst they explained why they had released the album.

The next time I saw them was at The Pere Lachaise in Paris on the 10th anniversary of Jim's death in 1981. A biography, 'No One Here Gets Out Alive' (Frank Lisciandro later renamed it as 'Nothing Here But Lots Of Lies') had just been published and eager fans took all of its content for granted. Some began to live like Jim, including the booze and the drugs and, for the very first time, there were more than 150 people around this tiny plot, asking The Doors for autographs, screaming and disturbing the peace of this beautiful cemetery. In fact, the scenario at Jim's grave was to become even more chaotic in the following years. Ray Manzarek seemed to enjoy the attention but John and Robby tried to stay away from the crowd, although all of them patiently answered the fans' questions. It was here that I had a long talk with Ray, who finally put his hand on my shoulder and said in a sonorous voice: "Hey, you know all the stories, you should start a fan club!"

I kept thinking about what Ray had said for the next two years and I eventually decided to run the Doors Fan Club along with a fanzine called The Doors Quarterly. In the meantime, I was busy collecting Doors material. I got a couple of original Morrison autographs, his privately published book of poetry, 'An American Prayer', thousands of unpublished photos and hundreds of Doors records from all over the world - all of this at a time when Doors' memorabilia was still very cheap and easy to obtain. Tapes began to circulate amongst collectors, most them live and a few of them

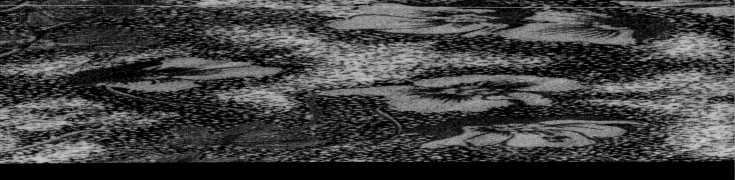

unpublished studio material. Bootleg records began to appear on the market and, as a hard-core fan, I was eager to get all the stuff ever published, not to mention all the various documents which were still very rare at that time. After seven years, between 1971 and 1978, when nothing really happened, there was a big Doors boom, which exploded because of the Hopkins/Sugerman book. Jerry later complained to me how much of his original manuscript had been changed and rearranged by Danny, who used to call himself the number one Doors fan and had become their manager.

I soon realised that I was pretty lost without a direct connection to the band, but it was hard to contact them. Writing to their official address turned out to be unsuccessful - you get back a very casual printed letter if you are lucky, or, in many cases, no reply at all. Writing to their record company was even more of a lost cause - they didn't even bother to answer. So I just put out a few more Quarterlys, which were Xeroxed at that time - very hand made - but compiled with a lot of enthusiasm and love for the band and mailed them directly to Sugerman's house.

This time I received a response from him. He said he loved the magazine and also added that his own attempt to produce a fanzine like this failed some years ago. I also made contact with Robby Krieger who was looking for some deleted German books which I located for him by searching various flea-markets.

At that time, I started to build a kind of Doors archive because I was tired of having to spend hours searching through big boxes for certain articles and photos. Everything was put in small labelled boxes and, more importantly, my vast Doors record collection was indexed and each photo was tagged with the relevant information regarding the photographer and origin. This was a tremendous help for my future work.

Of course, through the magazine, I got in contact with many fans and soon discovered that a "lot of strange people follow The Doors" (a remark made by former Doors promoter Rich Linnell). Oh yes, there were many beautiful people with whom I became good friends, but there were also a lot of creeps who had little else in mind than to steal parts of my collection or copy my tapes without my knowledge or permission in the middle of the night. No wonder that I became very distrustful whenever someone new showed an interest in my collection. Of course, I swopped a lot of items, especially rare tapes, with various collectors and soon began to notice bootlegs circulating which had been taken from my collection without my knowledge. People are strange, definitely!

The Doors Quarterly became a reliable source for Doors fans from all over the world to get to know what the band was doing. People started sending me news and old articles for my collection and also for publication in the magazine. They began to ask me questions regarding the colour of Jim's eyes and hair. Yes, the little girls understood! Above all, The Doors themselves called on me for help. I tracked down a German photographer who accompanied the group on their German and Danish tour in 1968. The Doors' management bought most of the negatives. I was also lucky to find a lost video of the group which was filmed in 1968 in Frankfurt, West Germany, on a tiny square named Roemer. A few people failed to find this one because they were asking for a videotape. After looking at some of the old photos, I had the right idea to ask for a 16mm film and, all of a sudden, there it was in colour - The Doors performing 'Hello, I Love You' in front of some beautiful 17th century German architecture (as featured in their official home video 'The Doors In Europe' and 'The Soft Parade'). From my private collection of videos they used 'Light My Fire' and 'Five To One' for the beginning and the end of 'The Doors In Europe'.

I received an invitation from Sugerman to go to Los Angeles for a meeting with him and The Doors which, of course, I enjoyed tremendously. It gave me the chance to get closer to the guys and

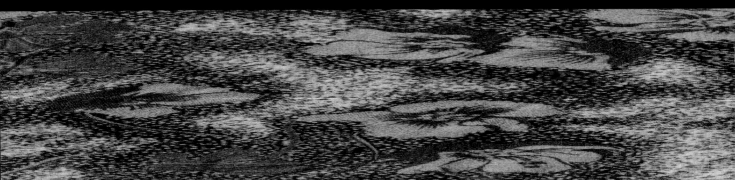

conduct my own in-depth interviews. Robby was particularly helpful in providing information on The Doors' recording sessions and hitherto unseen photos. We spent many lovely afternoons at his home in LA, talking and jamming. During subsequent visits our relationship grew closer and his public relations manager finally asked me to accompany him on his European 'Night Of The Guitar' tour to handle his press. Robby liked my work and gave me his platinum award for 'The Soft Parade' album as a thank you. A great honour, Rob!

I also met John on a couple of occasions and he invited me to watch one of his performances as 'The King Of Jazz'. Ray finally let me come over to his house for an interview and he and his lovely wife, Dorothy, were a tremendous help for the project I was working on at the time, my own Doors book.

I started writing the book in October 1990 and finished it in mid-May 1991, spending twelve hours a day in front of the computer. A great deal of additional research needed to be done, so I returned to Los Angeles where I visited fans and friends of Jim Morrison including Frank Lisciandro, who gave me an intimate insight into the private Jim that he knew. I also researched the death of Pamela Courson and finally found her forgotten grave in a cemetery in Santa Ana near Disneyland. I also put together a Doors gig-guide, using all possible sources including numerous posters, handbills, tickets and flyers. Finally, I decided to write a Doors tourist guide for Los Angeles and Paris (on later visits I watched a lot of people walking around with Xeroxes of my guides) to let Morrison/Doors fans know where to go when they visit these two capitals. Other people like John Tobler, Jerry Hopkins and Patricia Kennealy-Morrison also contributed to my project, along with numerous fans, especially my fellow Doors collector from Germany, Uli Michaelis. Uli assisted me in compliling a complete Doors discography for my book which finally was published in Germany on that fateful 3rd July in 1991 when over 2000 people went crazy in front of the Pere Lachaise cemetery gates. Whilst they were waiting to get in, they got as drunk as hell and clashed with the French police. The whole episode climaxed at midnight when the mob set the gates alight, ramming them with a wrecked car. "Jim would've liked that," Morrison copycat Dave Brock announced the same night during a show with his Doors cover band 'Wild Child'. Are you sure?

217

Talking about cover bands - of course there is a public demand for them. I watched a lot of groups playing Doors music, some were not that bad, like Wild Child or The Australian Doors Show, but none of them comes closer to what The Doors did in the Sixties than a group from New York called 'The Soft Parade'. Their lead singer, Joe Russo, is not only a big Doors fan, but also a very talented performer and, above all, he is very concerned about representing Jim's heart and soul on stage. Needless to say, Joe looks exactly as Jim did in 1968 and his group perfectly images a Doors concert of that time. You can keep your eyes wide open watching them perform and even I forgot it was 1992 and not 1968.

I became friendly with Patricia Kennealy-Morrison and discovered that she, without doubt, is still Jim Morrison's most honest friend and admirer. We helped each other with our respective books (I always begged her to write her memoirs after she allowed me to publish a full-length interview in the Quarterly and in my own book) and I still think that her relationship with Jim meant more to him than people realise.

So, what does devoting my life to this band really mean to me? After all these years I still get a kick out of new Doors tapes e.g. when a new copy of the famous 'Rock Is Dead' session appeared some years ago with a mind-blowing version of a song called 'Queen Of The Magazines'

I still freeze when I listen to 'Someday Soon', Jim's apocalyptic, unreleased horror-vision about death. I can't wait for new Doors concerts to be released by bootleggers - The Doors' record

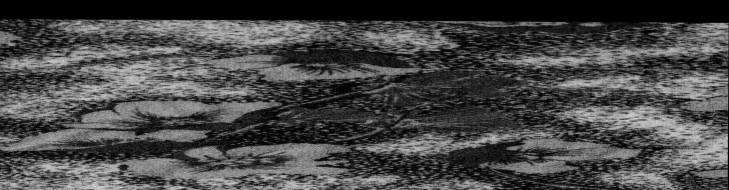

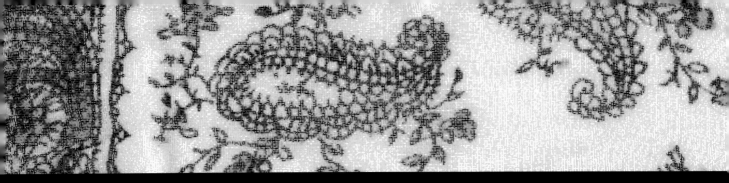

company never treated us fans like adults (when is compilation album number 25 coming out?). I still listen to all The Doors albums with the same intensity as I did 25 years ago. I love each new photograph of Jim and The Doors. I still wait anxiously for even more to be released from The Doors own, or other undiscovered, archives. Of course, I also try to avoid all those terrible T-shirts, posters, buttons and other tasteless rip-offs of Jim Morrison's memory. I know that The Doors did things in the past which are just as important today, and we can be sure that Jim's ideas will be as timeless in 25 years from now as they were in the Sixties. Even then, I'll still be collecting their records from all over the world which portray all the ups and downs this band experienced. Morrison is dead but he seems to be more popular now than in the past. He quit this planet but thanks to his poetry and to the music of The Doors (and the organised 'Doors' boom' which seems to happen every five years or so) he will survive.

For information about the Doors Quarterly Magazine and The Doors Fan Club please send an International Response Coupon to:

The Doors Quarterly
4150 Krefeld 12
West Germany

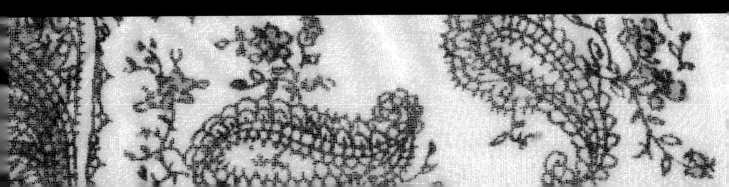

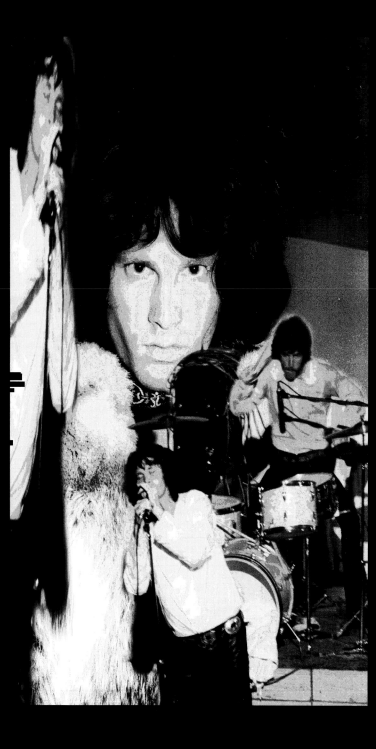

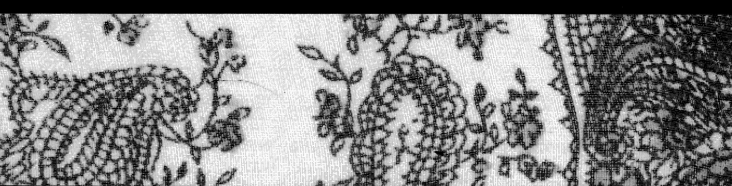

# DISCOGRAPHY

## SINGLES

Break On Through / End Of The Night
ELEKTRA EKSN 45009
Released: February 1967

Alabama Song / Take It As It Comes
ELEKTRA EKSN 45012
Released: May 1967

Light My Fire / The Crystal Ship
ELEKTRA EKSN 45014
Released: July 1967

People Are Strange / Unhappy Girl
ELEKTRA EKSN 45017
Released: September 1967

Love Me Two Times / Moonlight Drive
ELEKTRA EKSN 45022
Released: December 1967

The Unknown Soldier / We Could Be So Good Together
ELEKTRA EKSN 45030
Released: June 1968

Hello I Love You / Love Street
ELEKTRA EKSN 45037
Released: August 1968

Touch Me / Wild Child
ELEKTRA EKSN 45050
Released: January 1969

Wishful Sinful / Who Scared You?
ELEKTRA EKSN 45059
Released: May 1969

Tell All The People / Easy Ride
ELEKTRA EKSN 45065
Released: August 1969

Runnin' Blue / Do It
ELEKTRA EKSN 45675
Released: March 1970

You Make Me Real / Roadhouse Blues
ELEKTRA EKSN 45685
Released: April 1970

You Make Me Real / The Spy
ELEKTRA 2101 004
Released: April 1970

Roadhouse Blues / Blue Sunday
ELEKTRA 2101 008
Released: July 1970

Love Her Madly / You Need Meat
ELEKTRA EK 45726
Released: May 1971

Light My Fire / The Crystal Ship
ELEKTRA K 12001
Reissued: March 1971

The Unknown Soldier / We Could Be So Good Together
ELEKTRA K 12004
Reissued: July 1971

Light My Fire / Love Me Two Times
ELEKTRA 45051
Reissued: August 1971

Touch Me / Hello I Love You
ELEKTRA 45052
Reissued: August 1971

Riders On The Storm / Changeling
ELEKTRA K 12021
Released: August 1971

Tightrope Ride / Variety Is The Spice Of Life
ELEKTRA K 12036
Released: November 1971

Riders On The Storm / Love Her Madly
ELEKTRA 45059
Reissued: February 1972

Ships With Sails / In The Eye Of The Sun
ELEKTRA K 12048
Released: May 1972

Get Up And Dance / Treetrunk
ELEKTRA K 12059
Released: August 1972

Riders On The Storm / LA Woman
ELEKTRA K 12203
Reissued: February 1976

Hello I Love You / Love Me Two Times
ELEKTRA K 12215
Released: May 1976

Light My Fire / The Unknown Soldier
ELEKTRA K 12227
Released: September 1976

Love Her Madly / Touch Me
ELEKTRA K 12228
Released: September 1976

Love Me Two Times / Hello I Love You
ELEKTRA K 12215

Ghost Song / Roadhouse Blues
ELEKTRA SAM 94
Doublepack single
Released: January 1979

Riders On The Storm / Changeling
ELEKTRA K 12021
Included on the album 'Classic Hits Of The Seventies'
Released: June 1981

Riders On The Storm / Light My Fire
WEA OG 9520
Included on the album 'Old Gold'
Released: September 1985

## ALBUMS

THE DOORS
ELEKTRA EKL 74007 MONO
THE DOORS
ELEKTRA EKS 74007 STEREO
Released: January 1967
Reissued: November 1971
ELEKTRA K 42012

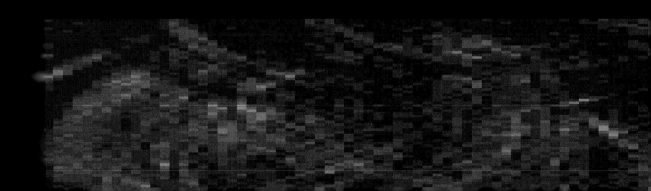

Break On Through / Soul Kitchen / The Crystal Ship / Twentieth
Century Fox / Alabama Song / Light My Fire / Back Door Man 11 /
Looked At You / End Of The Night / Take It As It Comes / The End

STRANGE DAYS
ELEKTRA EKL 74014 MONO
STRANGE DAYS
ELEKTRA EKS 74014 STEREO
Released: December 1967
Reissued: November 1971
ELEKTRA K 42016
CD - ELEKTRA K 2422016
Released: January 1986

Strange Days / You're Lost Little Girl / Love Me Two Times /
Unhappy Girl / Horse Latitudes / Moonlight Drive / People Are
Strange / My Eyes Have Seen You /I Can't See Your Face In My Mind
/ When The Music's Over

WAITING FOR THE SUN
ELEKTRA EKL 74024 MONO

WAITING FOR THE SUN
ELEKTRA EKS 74024 STEREO
Released: September 1968
Reissued: November 1971
ELEKTRA K 42041
CD - ELEKTRA K 242041

Hello I Love You/ Love Street / Not To Touch The Earth / Summer's
Almost Gone / Wintertime Love / The Unknown Soldier / Spanish
Caravan / My Wild Love / We Could Be So Good Together / Yes The
River Knows / Five To One

THE SOFT PARADE
ELEKTRA EKS 75007
Released: September 1969
Reissued: November 1971
ELEKTRA EKS 75005

Tell All The People / Touch Me / Shaman's Blues / Do It / Easy Ride /
Wild Child / Runnin' Blue / Wishful Sinful / The Soft Parade

MORRISON HOTEL
ELEKTRA EKS 75007
Released: April 1970
Reissued November 1971
ELEKTRA K 42080
CD - ELEKTRA K 242080
Released: April 1986

Roadhouse Blues / Waiting For The Sun / You Make Me Real / Peace
Frog / Blue Sunday / Ship Of Fools / Land Ho! / The Spy / Queen Of
The Highway / Indian Summer / Maggie M'Gill

ABSOLUTELY LIVE
ELEKTRA 2665 002
Released: September 1970
Double album
Reissued: November 1971
CD - ELEKTRA K 262005
Released: March 1987

Who Do You Love / Medley: Alabama Song - Back Door Man - Love
Hides - Five To One / Build Me A Woman / When The Music's Over /
Close To You / Universal Mind / Break On Through #2/ The
Celebration Of The Lizard / Soul Kitchen

3
ELEKTRA EKS 74079
Released: March 1971

Light My Fire / People Are Strange / Back Door Man / Moonlight
Drive / The Crystal Ship / Roadhouse Blues / Touch Me / Love Me
Two Times / You're Lost Little Girl / Hello I Love You / Wild Child /
The Unknown Soldier

LA WOMAN
ELEKTRA K 42090
Released July 1971
Reissued on CD: ELEKTRA K 242090 - 1984

The Changeling / Love Her Madly / Been Down So Long / Cars Hiss
By My Window / LA Woman / L'America / Hyacinth House / Crawling
King Snake / The WASP (Texas Radio And The Big Beat) / Riders On
The Storm

OTHER VOICES
ELEKTRA K 42104
Released November 1971

In The Eye Of The Sun / Variety Is The Spice Of Life / Ships With Sails
/ Tightrope Ride / Down On The Farm / I'm Horny I'm Stoned /
Wandering Musician / Hang On To Your Life

WEIRD SCENES INSIDE THE GOLDMINE
ELEKTRA K 62009
Released: March 1972
Double album

Break On Through / Strange Days / Shaman's Blues / Love Street /
Peace Frog / Blue Sunday / The WASP (Texas Radio And The Big
Beat) / End Of The Night / Love Her Madly / Spanish Caravan / Ship
Of Fools / The Spy / The End / Take It As It Comes / Runnin' Blue / LA
Woman / Five To One / Who Scared You / You Need Meat / Riders On
The Storm / Maggie M'Gill / Horse Latitudes / When The Music's
Over

FULL CIRCLE
ELEKTRA K 421 16
Released: September 1972

Get Up And Dance / Four Billion Souls / Verdilac / Hardwood Floor /
Good Rockin' / The Mosquito / The Piano Bird / It Slipped My Mind /
The Peking King And The New York Queen

THE BEST OF THE DOORS
ELEKTRA K 42143
Released: October 1973

Who Do You Love / Soul Kitchen / Hello I Love You / People Are
Strange / Riders On The Storm / Touch Me / Love Her Madly / Love
Me Two Times / Take It As It Comes / Moonlight Drive / Light My Fire

AN AMERICAN PRAYER
ELEKTRA K 52254
Released: November 1978

Awake: Ghost Song / Dawn's Highway / Newborn Awakening To
Come Of Age: Black Polished Chrome / Latino Chrome / Angels And
Sailors / Stoned Immaculate / The Poet's Dreams: The Movie /
Curses, Invocations World On Fire: American Night / Roadhouse
Blues (live) / Lament / The Hitchhiker / An American Prayer

GREATEST HITS
ELEKTRA K 52254
Released: October 1980

Hello I Love You / Light My Fire / People Are Strange / Love Me Two
Times / Riders On The Storm / Break On Through / Roadhouse Blues
/ Not To Touch The Earth / Touch Me / LA Woman

ALIVE SHE CRIED
ELEKTRA 96-0269-1

Released: November 1983
CD - ELEKTRA 060269 -2
Released: July 1984

Gloria / Light My Fire / You Make Me Real / Texas Radio And The Big Beat / Love Me Two Times / Little Red Rooster / Moonlight Drive / Horse Latitudes

CLASSICS
ELEKTRA EKT 9
Released: June 1985

Strange Days / Love Her Madly / Waiting For The Sun / My Eyes Have Seen You / Wild Child / The Crystal Ship / Five To One / Roadhouse Blues (live) / Land Ho! /I Can't See Your Face In My Mind / Peace Frog / The WASP (Texas Radio And The Big Beat) / The Unknown Soldier

THE BEST OF THE DOORS
ELEKTRA EKT 21
Released: November 1985
Double album
CD - ELEKTRA 960345-2

Break On Through / Light My Fire / The Crystal Ship / People Are Strange / Strange Days / Love Me Two Times / Five To One / Waiting For The Sun / Spanish Caravan / When The Music's Over / Hello I Love You / Roadhouse Blues / LA Woman / Riders On The Storm / Touch Me / Love Her Madly / The Unknown Soldier / The End

LIVE AT THE HOLLYWOOD BOWL
ELEKTRA EKT 40
Released: June 1987
CD - ELEKTRA 960741-2

Wake Up / Light My Fire / The Unknown Soldier / A Little Game / The Hill Dwellers / Spanish Caravan

THE DOORS
Music from the original motion picture
ELEKTRA EKT 85
Released March 1991

Riders On The Storm / Love Street / Break On Through / The End / Light My Fire / Ghost Song / Roadhouse Blues / Stoned Immaculate / The Severed Garden Adagio / LA Woman

IN CONCERT
ELEKTRA EKT 88
Released May 1991
Triple album

Who Do You Love / Alabama Song / Back Door Man / Love Hides / Five To One / Build Me A Woman / When The Music's Over / Universal Mind / Petition The Lord With Prayer / Dead Cats, Dead Rats / Break On Through # 2/ The Celebration Of The Lizard: Lions In The Streets - Wake Up - A Little Game - The Hill Dwellers - Not To Touch The Earth - Names Of The Kingdom - The Palace Of Exile / Soul Kitchen / Roadhouse Blues / Gloria / Light My Fire / You Make Me Real / Texas Radio And The Big Beat / Love Me Two Times / Little Red Rooster / Moonlight Drive / Horse Latitudes / Close To You / Unknown Soldier / The End

## Bootleg LP's

A GREAT SET • 3 LP-Box The Night on Fire/First Flash of Eden/Rock Is Dead • Tangie Town Records BRD 1986

ZERO PRODUCTIONS • Imaginary Records USA 1990

APOCALYPSE NOW • Tuna Records Australia 1980

A CELEBRATION • Light My Fire/Roadhouse Blues/Texas Radio And The Big Beat/Love Me Two Times/Touch Me/The End • DOOCE BRD 1986

A CLOSED DOOR IS OPENED • Oh Carol/Hello I Love You/Rock Me Baby/Who Scared You/Money/The Unknown Soldier/Horse Latitudes-Moonlight Drive/Hitler/Texas Radio And The Big Beat/Ghost Song/The End/Graveyard Poem • Eli Records BRD 1981

ARCHIVES • Double-LP Sunburn Records USA 1982

AUDITION DEMOS • Instant Analysis USA 1990

BLUES FOR A SHAMAN • Double-LP My Eyes Have Seen You/Soul Kitchen/I can't See Your Face In My Mind/Summer's Almost Gone/Money/Who Do You Love/Moonlight Drive/Alabama Song/People Are Strange/I'm A King Bee/Gloria/Break On Through/Summertime/Back Door Man/The End • Rockland Records Italy 1985

BREAK ON THROUGH TO THE OTHER SIDE • Do It Records BRD 1989

BRING OUT YOUR DEAD (Strange Gods Are Coming) • Double-King Roadhouse Blues/Break On Through/Ship Of Fools/Crawling King Snake/Alabama Song/Back Door Man-Five To One/Build Me A Woman/Peace Frog/The End/The Celebration Of The Lizard • Tangie Town Records BRD 1986

CELEBRATION • Light My Fire/Touch Me/When The Music's Over/The End/Moonlight Drive/Light My Fire • Swingin' Pig Records Italy 1989

CELEBRATION • Double-LP Intro/Moonlight Drive/Hello I Love You/Summer's Almost Gone/My Eyes Have Seen You/End Of The Night/Go Insane/The Crystal Ship/Alabama Song-Back Door Man/Five To One/Intro/Roadhouse Blues/Ship Of Fools/Universal Mind/Money/Louie Louie/Heartbreak Hotel/Fever/Summertime/Easy Ride/St James Infirmary/Light My Fire/Get Off My Life/Crawling King Snake/I Can't See Your Face In My Mind/The End/Changeling/L.A. Woman • Eli Records Britain 1982

CELEBRATION II - All Rights To This Material • Double-LP Intro/Moonlight Drive/Hello I Love You/Summer's Almost Gone/My Eyes Have Seen You/End Of The Night/People Are Strange/Mack The Knife-Alabama Song/You're Lost Little Girl/Love Me Two 20 Times/When The Music's Over/Wild Child/Money/Back Door Man-Maggie M'Gill-Roadhouse Blues/Rock Me Baby/Oh Carol/Holy Sha Poem/Orange County Suite/The End Copenhagen 68 • 12 Track Records Italy 1988

COPULATIONS • When The Music's Over/Break On Through/Back Door Man/The Crystal Ship/Wake Up/Light My Fire/The End

CRITIQUE • Tell All The People/Alabama Song/Back Door Man/Wishful Sinful/Build Me A Woman/The Soft Parade/Five To One/Jim Morrison 24 Interview/Light My Fire/The Unknown Soldier • Deja Vu Records USA 1980

DEFINITELY CLOSED • Better Days Records Down The Lights • Double-LP TAKRL USA 1988

FAST TIMES AT DANBURY HIGH • Intro/Back Door Man/People Are Strange/The Crystal Ship/Wake Up-Light My Fire/The End/We Came Down/See A Rider/The End

FIRST FLASH OF EDEN • Back Door Man/Break On Through/When The Music's Over/Ship Of Fools/Light My Fire/The End/Crossroads/Lament Of The Indian/The End • Tangie Town Records BRD 1982

FUCK THE MOTHER, KILL THE FATHER • Xero Productions USA 1983

GET FAT AND DIE • Mod USA 1983

IF IT AIN'T ONE THING IT'S ANOTHER • Triple_LP Roadhouse Blues/Ship Of Fools/Break On Through/Universal Mind/Alabama Song/Back Door Man/Five To One/Moonlight Drive/Who Do You Love/Money/Light My Fire/When The Music's Over/The End/Love Her Madly/Back Door Man/Ship Of Fools/Changeling/L.A. Woman/When The Music's Over • Raring Records USA 1982

LIGHT MY FIRE • Double-LP Shooting The Bull Records - USA 1986

LIGHT MY FIRE • Duchesse Luxemburg 1988

IN CONCERT • Double-LP - Back Door Man/Crawling King Snake/Wake Up/The Unknown Soldier/Twentieth Century Fox/My Eyes Have Seen You/Get Off My Life/Five To One/Love Me Two Times/Mack The Knife-Alabama Song/Back Door Man/Who Do You Love/Miami Raps/Light My Fire/Wild Child/Touch Me/The End/Jim Morrison-Interview • Gold Records USA 1980 In The Beginning You Try A Lot Of Doors • Whole In Your Head Music Italy 1987

ISLE OF WIGHT '70 • USA 1989

LEATHER PANTS IN DENMARK • 10" LP (25cm LP) Alabama Song/Back Door Man/Texas Radio And The Big Beat/Love Me Two Times/The Unknown Soldier/When The Music's Over • Tangie Town Records BRD 1984

MR MOJO RISIN'

LIMITLESS AND FREE • Rock Is Dead/The Crystal Ship/Holy Sha Poem/Alabama Song/Back Door Man/Build Me A Woman/Get Off My Life/Ship Of Fools Israel 1987

LITTLE GAMES • Double-LP Shogun USA 1987

LIVE IN STOCKHOLM 1968 • 3 LP-Box Swinging' Pig Records Italy 1989

LIZARD KING PLAYS LONDON • Wizardo USA 1974

MOONLIGHT DRIVE - The Scream Of The Butterfly • People Are Strange/Alabama Song/The Crystal Ship/Unhappy Girl/Moonlight Drive/Summer's Almost Gone/Twentieth Century Fox/Back Door Man/My Eyes Have Seen You/Soul Kitchen/Get Off My Life/Crawling King Snake • Takrl USA 1973

FEAST OF FRIENDS DOUBLE-LP (Soundtrack)/Interview/Light My Fire/The End/Wild Child/Touch Me/Critique/Interview with all four Doors • Towne Records USA 1980

NO LIMITS NO LAWS • Shadow/Play Records BRD 1982

NO LIMITS NO LAWS • Italy 1987

NO ONE HERE GETS OUT ALIVE - The Doors Story • 4 LP-Box Quick-Q Records USA 1980

OPEN THE DOORS • Five To One/Mack The Knife/Alabama Song/Back Door Man/You're Lost Little Girl/Love Me Two Times/Wild Child/Money/Roadhouse Blues/Universal Mind • USA 1988 Orange County Suite • Rock Is Dead/Poetry Session/Orange County Suite • Document Records Italy 1988

PERE LACHAISE • USA 1984

POEMS, LYRICS AND STORIES By James Douglas Morrison • Old Works Revcords Italy 1987

RAY MANZAREK AND HIS FABULOUS DOORS • Sqeeze Records USA 1990

RESURRECTION • Double-LP The Doors Are Open-Soundtrack/Wake Up-Light My Fire/Five To One/Love Me Two Times/Mack The Knife/Alabama Song/Back Door Man/Moonlight Drive/Light My Fire/Who do You Love/Miami-Raps • Paris Records USA 1980

ROADHOUSE BLUES • Double-LP Shogun USA 1987

ROCK IS DEAD • In The Wake Of The Lizard/Ghost Poem/A Feast Beneath The Moon/The Death Bird/Bird Of Prey/Dawn's Highway/Underwater Fall/The Hitchhiker/Words In Frozen Woods/Winter Photography/Whiskey. Mystics And Men/All Hail The American Night/Far Arden/Shirley/The American Night/Holy Sha Poem/Hitler/To Come Of Age/Black Polished Chrome/Siren's Song/Stories From The L.A. Plague/Earth, Air, Fire, Water/Angles And Sailors/Stoned Immaculate/The Carnival Has Just Begun/Graveyard Poem/Rock Is Dead • Tangie Town Records BRD 1982

RUN FREE • Moonlight Drive/Hellow I Love You/Summer's Almost Gone/My Eyes Have Seen You/End Of The Night/Go Insane/People Are Strange/Break On Through/Back Door Man/Maggie M'Gill/Roadhouse Blues/The Crystal Ship/Light My Fire • Clean Sound Records Italy 1984

SINGING THE BLUES • Gloria/Summertime/I'm King Bee/Money/Who Do You Love/Me And The Devil Blues/ Sittin' Round Thinkin'/Rock Me Baby/Close To You/The End • Tangie Town Records BRD 1985

SINGING THE BLUES VOL 2 • When The Music's Over #1/Light My Fire/Break On Through/Manish Boy/Money/Good Rockin'/When The Music's Over #2 • Tangie Town Records BRD 1986

SKY HIGH • Skydog USA 1972

SOMEDAY SOON • Little Red Rooster/Improvisation/The End/Crossroads/Roadhouse Blues/Improvisation/Who Do You Love/The Spy/Miami Raps/Someday Soon/Treetrunk/Wintertime Love/We Could Be So Good Together/The Unknown Soldier/Love Me Two Times/Light My Fire/Soul Train/Geraldine/Henrietta/Just For You/Big Bucket 'T'/Rampage • Do It Records BRD 1989 Something's Rockin' In Denmark • Alabama Song/Back Door Man/Texas Radio And The Big Beat/Love Me Two Times/When The Music's Over/The Unknown Soldier/Light My Fire/Break On Through • Instant Analysis USA 1987

STOCKHOLM 68 • Five To One/Mack The Knife/Alabama Song/Back Door Man/You're Lost Little Girl/Love Me Two Times/When The Music's Over/Wild Child/Money/Light My Fire TAP Productiosn BRD 1983

STONED IMMACULATE • USA 1984

THE BATTLE • IFPI Records BRD 1989

THE BEAUTIFUL DIE YOUNG • Double-LP MIW Records BRD 1985

THE COMPLETE STOCKHOLM TAPES • 3 LP-Box Five To One/Love Street/Love Me 64. Two Times/When The Music's Over/Wake Up-Light My Fire/The Unknown Soldier/Five To One/Mack The Knife/Alabama Song/Back Door Man/You're Lost Little Girl/Love Me Two Times/When The Music's Over/Wild Child/Money/Light My Fire/The End

THE DOORS • Roadhouse Blues/Texas Radio And The Big Beat/Love Me Two Times/Touch Me/Horse Latitudes/Moonlight Drive/The End/Light My Fire • Frog Records Italy 1987

THE DOORS • Light My Fire/Little Red Rooster/The Unknown

# DISCOGRAPHY

Soldier/Moonlight Drive/Horse Latitudes/Spanish Caravan/You Make Me Real • Sakkaris Records Greece 1989

THE END • USA 1983

THE LIVE DOORS • USA March 1967

THE LIZARD KING • Break On Through/When The Music's Over/Five To One/Light My Fire/The End • Round Records 1973

THE RIOT SHOW • When The Music's Over/Alabama Song/Back Door Man/Five To One/The Unknown Soldier/Moonlight Drive/Horse Latitudes/The End/Moonlight Drive/Light My Fire • World Production of Compact Music Italy 1988

THE MATRIX TAPES • 3 LP-Box My Eyes Have Seen You/Soul Kitchen/I Can't See Your Face In My Mind/People Are Strange/When The Music's Over/Money/Who Do You Love/Moonlight Drive/Summer's Almost Gone/I'm A King Be/Gloria/Break On Through/Summertime/Back Door Man/Alabama Song/Light My Fire/The End/Get Off My Life/Close To You/Crawling King Snake/The Crystal Ship/Twentieth Century Fox/Unhappy Girl/Me And The Devil Blues/Sittin' Here Thinkin'/Rock Me Baby • Swingin' Pig Records Italy 1990

THE NIGHT ON FIRE • Break On Through/Alabama Song/Back Door Man/When The Music's Over/Texas Radio And The Big Beat/Hellow I Love You/Light My Fire/The Unknown Soldier • Tangie Town Records, BRD 1981

THE RETURN OF THE LIZARD KING • Record Man USA 1981 CD

THREE HOURS FOR MAGIC • 3 LP-Box Italy 1986

UNDER WRAPS VOL. 1-4 • Starlight Records USA 1989

WEIRD SCENES INSIDE THE HOLLYWOOD BOWL • Oedipus USA 1988

WEIRD SONGS: A CLOSED DOOR IS OPENED • Great Britain/BRD 1981

WEIRD TRIANGLE • Black Gold Records Britain 1980

## Bootleg-Singles and EPs

WHISKEY, MYSTICS AND MEN • Double-LP Pharting Pharao Records USA 1987

WICKED BLUES • TAKRL USA 1988

WILD CHILD/TOUCH ME/FREDERICK/LIGHT MY FIRE/DIALOGUE • Lizard Records Australian 1980

PEOPLE ARE STRANGE/ROADHOUSE BLUES • Tangie Town Records 1984

ROCK ME/BREAK ON THROUGH/HITLER/GRAVEYARD POEM • Great Britain 1992

ALABAMA SONG/BACK DOOR MAN • Italy 1989

ROADHOUSE BLUES/BREAK ON THROUGH/BACK DOOR MAN/FIVE TO ONE • DEP USA 1984

BUILD ME A WOMAN/LIGHT MY FIRE/POEMS • Italy 1988

THE LOUNGE WIZZARD BACK DOOR MAN/FIVE TO ONE • Document Records Italy 1988

A SLICE OF SWINGIN' PIG VOL. 1 • You're Lost Little Girl • Swingin' Pig Records Italy 1988

## Compact Discs

ARCHIVES • Italy 1990

AUTUMN LIFE LIVING LEGEND • Italy 1988

BUILD ME A WOMAN • Great Dane Records Italy 1989

CELEBRATION • Swingin' Pig Records Italy 1989

CRAWLING KING SNAKES • Back Trax Italy 1988

EUROPE SEPTEMBER 1968 • Double-CD Cocodile Luxemburg 1988

FOUR CLOSED DOORS • World Productions of Compact Music Italy 1988

LIGHT MY FIRE • Duchesse Italy 1989

LIVE AT THE MADISON • Square Garden

LIVE AT THE MATRIX • Black Panther Japan 1989

LIVE IN LOS ANGELES • Starlife Italy 1990

LIVE IN STOCKHOLM VOL. 1 AND VOL. 2 • Black Panther Japan 1989

LIVE IN STOCKHOLM 1968 • Double-CD Swingin' Pig Records Italy 1988

NEW YORK BLUES • Roadhouse Blues/Peace Frog/Alabama Song/Back Door Man/Five To One/The Celebration Of The Lizard/Soul Kitchen/Build Me A Woman/When The Music's Over • Document Records Italy 1989

ORANGE COUNTY SUITE • Document Records Italy 1989

POEMS, LYRICS AND STORIES By James Douglas Morrison • Men At Work Italy 1990

RED WALLS BLUE DOORS • World Productions Of Compact Music Italy 1988

THE BEAUTIFUL DIE YOUNG • Living Legend Italy 1989

THE DOORS SUPER STARS BEST COLLECTION • Japan 1991

THE DOORS • Starlife Italy 1990

THE STOCKHOLM TAPES • Document Recors Italy 1988

WELCOME TO THE SOFT PARADE • World Productions Of Compact Music Italy 1989

WHEN THE MUSIC'S OVER • Great Dane Records Italy 1991

THE DOORS LIVE 1968 - 1969 • Ricordi International Italy 1991

THE DOORS OF HEAVEN • Starlife Italy 1990

THE LIVE DOORS - USA MARCH 1967 • Bulldog Records Italy 1991

THE LIZARD KING • Vulture Records Italy 1990

THE MATRIX TAPES • Swingin' Pig Records Italy 1990

THE NIGHT ON FIRE • Living Legend Italy 1988

THE RIOT SHOW • World Productions Of Compact Music Italy 1988

ISCOGRAPHY